Conventional Wisdom and American Elections

Conventional Wisdom and American Elections

Exploding Myths, Exploring Misconceptions

Third Edition

Jody C Baumgartner and Peter L. Francia

ROWMAN & LITTLEFIELD
Lanham • Boulder • New York • London

Published by Rowman & Littlefield
A wholly owned subsidiary of The Rowman & Littlefield Publishing Group, Inc.
4501 Forbes Boulevard, Suite 200, Lanham, Maryland 20706
www.rowman.com

Unit A, Whitacre Mews, 26-34 Stannary Street, London SE11 4AB

British Library Cataloguing in Publication Information Available

Library of Congress Cataloging-in-Publication Data

Baumgartner, Jody C, 1958–
Conventional wisdom and American elections : exploding myths, exploring
misconceptions / Jody C Baumgartner and Peter L. Francia. — Third edition.
    pages cm
Includes bibliographical references and index.
ISBN 978-1-4422-5487-9 (cloth : alk. paper) — ISBN 978-1-4422-5489-3 (pbk. : alk.
paper) — ISBN 978-1-4422-5488-6 (electronic) 1. Elections—United States. 2. Politics,
Practical—United States. 3. United States—Politics and government. I. Francia, Peter L.
II. Title.
JK1976.B34 2015
324.70973—dc23   2015026619

♾™ The paper used in this publication meets the minimum requirements of American
National Standard for Information Sciences—Permanence of Paper for Printed Library
Materials, ANSI/NISO Z39.48-1992.

Printed in the United States of America

Contents

List of Illustrations

BOXES

FIGURES

TABLES

Introduction

This is the third edition of *Conventional Wisdom and American Elections*. In previous editions, we attempted to deconstruct several of the myths and misconceptions surrounding campaigns and elections in the United States. We believe this is necessary because elections, especially presidential elections, generate a seemingly limitless supply of theories, opinions, and predictions from journalists, scholars, and political pundits. The ideas put forth by these observers make their way into popular accounts about elections. Unfortunately, many oversimplify complex subjects or overhype the latest political fads. With ever-increasing venues for people to exchange political ideas, it is thus inevitable that some exaggerated assertions and misinformation become part of the conventional wisdom about American elections. Our objective is therefore to try and set the record straight on several of these subjects.

For example, it is now commonplace for commentators to emphasize the negative tactics and practices of the campaigns of presidential candidates. In 2012, some commentators suggested that the presidential campaign was the "nastiest" ever, with the campaigns of both President Barack Obama and challenger Mitt Romney going to "new extremes" of negativity. But these claims are not new. In fact, they seem to be repeated every four years.

Such claims reflect a misunderstanding about the pervasive role that negative campaign tactics have always played in U.S. elections. For instance, critics of Thomas Jefferson stated that his election in 1800 would bring about legal prostitution and the burning of the Bible. Opponents of Andrew Jackson charged that he was a murderer and that his wife was a bigamist. Perhaps most scurrilous of all, Jackson's opponents even accused his dead mother of being a prostitute.

This and many other falsehoods about American elections persist in the minds of citizens. Based on our experience as college educators, we have identified twelve widely held myths and misconceptions about elections in the United States. Changes between editions of the book are based on the fact that during each presidential election cycle new myths or misconceptions seem to emerge.

The conclusions that we draw throughout the book are based on the most current political science research.[1] In some instances, the literature is clear in debunking popular myths about American elections. On other issues, research findings are more mixed. In either case, we clarify the issues such that readers can discern between those in which scholars have largely resolved and those in which honest debate remains.

PLAN OF THE BOOK

The basis of any election campaign is to understand who voters are and what they want. The first section of the book is devoted to exploring three misunderstandings that have arisen in recent years about the voting public. In Chapter 1, we look at two groups of voters who are often portrayed as being quite similar, namely, so-called independent and swing voters. These two groups receive a disproportionate amount of attention from the media throughout the campaign. This is true in spite of the fact that there is little consensus as to how to define either group, there are far fewer of either than is widely believed, and relatively few of them actually vote. Further, as the chapter makes clear, most people who do vote cast their votes in a partisan fashion most of the time. In the end, independent and swing voters rarely decide election outcomes.

Chapter 2 explores in more detail the claim that the campaign of 2012 signaled the triumph of "big" data. In the aftermath of the presidential election, many pundits credited Barack Obama's victory with his campaign's collection, integration, and use of large amounts of data. Yet accolades afforded to the data-crunching gurus of the Obama campaign were largely exaggerated. As the chapter will show, the use of "big" voter files with consumer data for microtargeting offers only limited utility in predicting voting behavior, and certainly did not play a decisive role in Obama's victory in 2012. Instead, as the chapter makes clear, the best predictor of whether a person will vote, or how they will vote, is rarely based on the consumer data that fills today's most detailed "big" data files.

In the third chapter, we expose the myth that voter turnout in the United States is steadily declining, pointing to the fact that the way most people measure voter turnout is faulty. Although turnout has declined somewhat in recent decades, the decline is not nearly as precipitous as some would have us believe. The chapter also examines the various factors that influence voter turnout and the subject of youth voter turnout. Finally, the chapter examines the evidence surrounding voter identification laws and voter fraud.

Section two of the book shifts attention from voters to various aspects of campaigns themselves. Citing the declining popularity and growing dislike that voters express toward the Democratic and Republican Parties, pundits frequently trumpet the notion that a viable third party is on its way and will soon advance itself into a position where it can seriously compete with the two major parties. Third-party success, however, almost never materializes, and in the rare cases when it does, proves to be short lived. Chapter 4 reviews how the electoral system itself explains why the rise of a third party in the United States is unlikely to materialize in any significant and sustained way.

In the previous edition of this book, we included a chapter on the various misconceptions surrounding campaign finance reform. Since that time, the Supreme Court issued its controversial decision in *Citizens United v. FEC* (2010). This ruling has created real confusion about campaign finance law, which warrants correction. President Obama, for instance, famously chastised the Court in his 2010 State of the Union Address, claiming—erroneously—that the Citizens United ruling "reversed a century of law." While *Citizens United* did not reverse a century of law, it did have significant consequences. Chapter 5 clarifies the state of campaign finance law in the aftermath of this controversial ruling.

Chapter 6 deals with the "veepstakes," a guessing game about who presidential candidates will choose as their running mates. The veepstakes pervades media coverage of the campaign, but unfortunately, much of this coverage is less than completely informed about what presidential candidates look for in a running mate. The chapter goes beyond issues of "balancing" the ticket and examines other factors that have emerged in the past several decades as being important in vice presidential selection.

In Chapter 7, we explore the belief that presidential campaigns have become nastier in modern times. In addition to discussing what negative campaigning really is, we survey several of the truly vicious campaigns throughout our nation's history. Chapter 8 turns the spotlight on the popular idea that news organizations present a biased view of political reality. In fact, while there is a bias in the news, it is not based in partisanship, but rather the product of commercial considerations, or the need to make a profit. The chapter first reviews the emergence of the journalistic norm of objectivity and research on partisan bias in the news. In the end, we expose a number of commercial biases in the coverage of presidential campaigns.

A frequently repeated claim during almost every presidential campaign is that presidential debates can be "game changers." Yet as decades of evidence from the Gallup Poll and other sources reveal, debates have a minimal effect on voters. While a strong debate performance certainly can yield favorable media coverage for a candidate, presidential debates tend to reinforce voters' preexisting beliefs rather than change their attitudes toward and evaluations of the candidates. We examine the claims surrounding, and the reality of, presidential debates in Chapter 9.

Many Americans hold misconceptions about public opinion polls. While some think that polling data paint a precise and error-free representation of American political opinion during presidential campaigns, others see polls as a form of modern-day voodoo. Both views miss the reality. Chapter 10 reviews the basics of public polling methodology and discusses potential problems with, and misuses of, polls.

The third section of the book is devoted to understanding the course and outcomes of modern campaigns. Chapter 11 asks the provocative question of whether or not congressional elections, especially those to the House of Representatives, are truly democratic. The chapter begins by establishing the fact that congressional elections are becoming increasingly less competitive and then provides insight into the various advantages incumbents have in congressional elections.

In the final chapter, we examine the ubiquitous claims following presidential elections that the winning candidate and his political party have won a "mandate from the people." As we discuss, the public's general lack of policy knowledge complicates these "mandate" claims. In this chapter, we review how difficult and rare it is for a winning presidential candidate to have earned a true policy mandate, as well as the consequences that often follow for presidents who claim a mandate when none truly exists.

ACKNOWLEDGEMENTS

In the course of writing and preparing this book, we benefited from a great deal of assistance. Preparation of the first edition was helped greatly by the careful work of our graduate assistant, Michael Shaw. In addition, Nathan Bigelow of Austin College and Renan Levine of the University of Toronto both read the first edition, and their suggestions helped improve the overall clarity and quality of this book.

Our colleagues in the political science department at East Carolina University (ECU) have also been quite helpful throughout our tenure here. In addition to support we received from colleagues, Adam Caldwell and Kelvin Stallings, two of our students at ECU, helped with proofreading and research. We also owe a debt of gratitude to our editor at Rowman & Littlefield, Jon Sisk, for his helpful suggestions and assistance with this project.

Finally, none of this would be possible—or worthwhile—without the love, support, and patience of our wives, Kali Chrysovergis-Francia and Lei Baumgartner.

NOTE

1. There are, of course, a plethora of books that cover campaigns and elections in the United States. Focusing only on presidential elections, there is a fairly long tradition of journalistic accounts of specific elections that date back to Theodore White's *The Making of the President, 1960* (Cutchogue, NY: Buccaneer Books, 1961). This tradition relies on the journalist (or a team of journalists) who are on the inside of the campaign traveling with the candidate. White's books present a detailed chronology of the campaign, relating many interesting anecdotes about the candidate, his family, entourage, etc. While others have made contributions using this approach (e.g., Timothy Crouse, *The Boys on the Bus* [Toronto, Canada: Random House, 1973]), White was the pioneer, and continued the tradition for several election cycles.

More recently, various writers for *Newsweek* magazine have followed a similar approach (e.g., Jack W. Germond and Jules Witcover, *Blue Smoke and Mirrors: How Reagan Won & Carter Lost the Election of 1980* [New York, Penguin Group, 1981]; Thomas M. Defrank, Mark Miller, Peter Louis Goldman, and Andrew Murr, *Quest for the Presidency, 1992* [College Station, TX: Texas A&M University Press, 1994]; Evan Thomas, Eleanor Clift, and the Staff of *Newsweek*, *Election 2004: How Bush Won And What You Can Expect In The Future* [New York: Public Affairs, 2005]). Of late, other journalists have followed suit, perhaps most notably John Heileman and Mark Halperin's *Game Change: Obama and the Clintons, McCain and Palin, and the Race of a Lifetime* ([New York, HarperCollins, 2010]; see also their "sequel," *Double Down: Game Change 2012* [New York: Penguin, 2013]). All of these accounts are informative and interesting, but they contain a level of detail best suited for all but the most politically interested.

Another approach to the study of campaigns and elections is what some term the "practitioner approach." This approach is similar to the journalistic tradition inasmuch as it relies on insider perspectives. The best example of this is the series sponsored by the John F. Kennedy School of Government Institute of Politics. The Kennedy School invites campaign managers to a symposium for what amounts to a debriefing about the strategies and tactics they employed during the previous campaign. The first of these books, titled *Campaign for President: The Managers Look at 1976*, Jonathan Moore and Janet Fraser (Cambridge, MA: Ballinger, 1977), was published in 1977 and has been produced every four years since. These books are also geared toward the politically interested and are also excellent insider accounts.

A final approach to the study of presidential campaigns and elections comes from the scholarly community. Many of these books are also produced immediately after a presidential election, and attempt to make some sense of what happened and why. Unlike the previous two traditions, the scholarly tradition is geared more toward scientific explanation rather than anecdotal and impressionistic conclusions. Most are, again, post-election quadrennial publications. James Ceaser and Andrew Busch have been authoring a post-election book since 1993 (*Upside Down and Inside Out: The 1992 Elections and American Politics* [Lanham, MD: Rowman & Littlefield, 1993]). Many are edited volumes. Michael Nelson has been editing a post-election collection every four years since 1985 (the latest, *The Elections of 2012* [Washington DC: CQ Press, 2014]). Other edited volumes include Gerald Pomper's collections (the last of which was *The Election of 2000: Reports and Interpretations* [New York, NY: Seven Bridges, 2001]), relative newcomer Larry Sabato, *The Year of Obama: How Barack Obama Won the White House* (New York: Pearson, 2009), and William Crotty, *Winning the Presidency 2008* (Boulder, CO: Paradigm, 2009). Some texts focus on upcoming elections (e.g., Michael Goldstein, *Guide to the 2004 Presidential Election* [Washington, DC: CQ Press, 2003]).

Other books are nonelection specific. The most notable of these are Nelson Polsby and Aaron Wildavsky's *Presidential Elections: Strategies and Structures of American Politics* (Lanham, MD: Rowman & Littlefield, 2011), in its thirteenth edition, and Stephen Wayne's *The Road to the White House 2016: The Politics of Presidential Elections* (Boston: Wadsworth Cengage, 2015), in its tenth edition. Yet other texts examine congressional elections, most notably, Gary Jacobson, *The Politics of Congressional Elections*, 8th ed. (New York: Pearson, 2012) and Paul Herrnson, *Congressional Elections: Campaigning at Home and in Washington*, 6th ed. (Washington, DC: CQ Press, 2013).

All of the books in these traditions are similar in that they take a fairly comprehensive look at campaigns and elections. Other books examine more specific aspects of the electoral process. For example, William Mayer's quadrennial edited book *The Making of the Presidential Candidates 2008* (Lanham, MD: Rowman & Littlefield, 2007) is an excellent text for understanding the presidential nomination process. Kathleen Hall Jamieson's *Packaging the Presidency: A History and Criticism of Presidential Campaign Advertising*, 3rd ed. (New York: Oxford University, 1996) is one of many that examine presidential campaign advertising. These, and many other books not listed here, are excellent sources for further reading on the subject.

Part I

VOTERS

Chapter 1

As Moderates Go, So Goes the Nation?
The Reality about the Decisive
"Independent" and "Swing Voter"

Despite decades of political science research, many commonly held assumptions about voting are not as simple as some political observers portray them to be. For example, during each election cycle, Americans are treated to any number of news accounts that discuss the growing numbers and power of two related blocs: the independent and the swing voter.[1] As one account proclaimed in 2014, "independent swing voters . . . may decide who wins" the election.[2]

The much-vaunted independent voters are those who have eschewed attachments to either of the two major parties. Popular accounts often portray these voters in a favorable light for shunning party labels and for making their voting decisions based on a thorough examination of the issues of the day and the candidates' stands on them. The independent voter is therefore the virtuous citizen, voting in a manner consistent with the model presented in high school civics courses. Swing voters are typically portrayed in a similar way, waiting to make their voting decisions until the last minute, after all of the information from the campaign has been received and processed. They too are reluctant to allow partisanship to dictate their vote.

A common theme throughout nearly every election cycle is that these voters comprise a growing percentage of the electorate.[3] Related stories focus on how this large and expanding segment of the electorate has the power to decide the election.[4] However, when political scientists examine how people actually cast their votes, rather than how voters see themselves, it becomes clear that partisanship within the electorate has actually *increased* in the past forty years. Indeed, there are few "true" or "pure" independents in the electorate who disregard political parties when casting their vote.

By focusing on the relatively small percentage of individuals who cast their votes independent of the influence of political parties, news accounts often tend to ignore the overwhelming number of those who *do* consider party in their voting decision. That is, to say independent and swing voters decide elections is misleading. In 2012, for example, Mitt Romney, who lost the presidential election to Barack Obama, won the vote of independents. In spite of hyperbole to the contrary, partisans typically decide elections. In the real world of presidential campaigns, much of the focus is on the mobilization of partisan voters rather than the persuasion of moderate independents.

THE INDEPENDENT VOTER

A widely held tenet of American politics is that since the 1950s the numbers of independent voters are growing. News accounts of the partisan preferences of American voters routinely reflect this belief. In recent years, the rise of the independent voter has been a popular subject, with headlines that scream that the number of "independent voters [is] burgeoning" and that "more voters are steering away from party labels."[5] Because they are growing in number, these so-called independents are presumably the most important bloc of voters in any given election.

Not surprisingly, those who cover or study American politics frequently equate the increased numbers of independent voters with the decline of political parties. One textbook is explicit, referring to the "decline of both parties and resultant upsurge of independents."[6] A book from the early 1970s sounded the alarmist note that "the party's over."[7] One of the leading texts on party politics is a bit less dramatic but still suggests that "the American electorate is somewhat less partisan now than it was prior to the 1960s."[8]

In fact, it is true that the number of people registering as independent has been increasing over the past several decades.[9] If we examine the traditional measurement of partisan identification, we could see that there has been a rise in independents since as far back as the 1950s. This is consistent with a trend toward what some refer to as partisan dealignment,[10] or a growing movement away from attachment to parties within the electorate. A good deal of research suggests that the public sees political parties as being less central to government and the political system. It is difficult for many people to see how political parties are relevant. Many, in other words, are not *non*partisans as much as they are *a*partisans.[11]

There is, however, more to the story. In 1952, the Survey Research Center and the Center for Political Studies of the Institute for Social Research at the University of Michigan conducted a wide-ranging national survey related to presidential and congressional elections. They conducted similar surveys in the thirteen presidential and midterm elections that followed. In 1977, the National Science Foundation began funding these surveys and, in the process, established the American National Election Studies (ANES).[12] The stated mission of the ANES "is to inform explanations of election outcomes by providing data that support rich hypothesis testing, maximize methodological excellence, measure many variables, and promote comparisons across people, contexts, and time."[13]

One of the many questions over the years that the ANES has asked concerns partisan identification, or the psychological attachment, if any, an individual feels toward a political party. For most political scientists studying American elections, the data provided by the ANES represent the gold standard. The interviewer asks respondents, "Generally speaking, do you usually think of yourself as a Republican, a Democrat, an Independent, or what?" Other choices include "other" and, starting in 1966, "no preference." If the respondent answers either "Republican" or "Democrat," there is a follow-up question: "Would you call yourself a strong (Republican/Democrat) or a not very strong (Republican/Democrat)?" If the respondent answers "independent," "other," or "no preference" to the first question, the question that follows is "Do you think of yourself as closer to the Republican or Democratic party?"[14]

The importance of the ANES surveys for the study of voting behavior would be difficult to overstate. After an initial study produced in 1954, the research team in 1960 produced what is arguably the most important work in the study of American voting behavior, *The American Voter*.[15] This book alone has spawned a veritable mountain of research since its publication, produced by several generations of scholars. For decades, political scientists have used ANES data. Indeed, it is impossible to study American voting behavior without coming face-to-face with the theories and conclusions of *The American Voter*.

One of the primary findings of the book is that the majority of voters cast their ballots based on their partisan identification. While some have challenged the central role of partisan identification in vote choice,[16] political science research has, over time, clearly demonstrated its powerful influence. This partisan identification develops primarily during childhood under the influence of one's parents.[17] While some have questioned the validity of the ANES partisan identification measure,[18] it has stood the test of time and is now a standard component of how political behavioralists model the study of voting. Other polling organizations (e.g., Gallup) ask similar questions measuring this concept.

The reason many claim that independent voters are growing in number and importance is that the number of people answering "independent" to the first party identification question has increased, and fairly significantly, since 1952. Measured in this way, the percentage of independents has almost doubled (from 23 percent to 38 percent) in the past half century (see Table 1.1).

However, if we examine this group of independents further and include their responses to the *second* question, we see that the percentage of people who claim to be closer to *neither* party is rather small. This fits with an intuitive understanding of what an independent actually is. Table 1.2 presents the data again, but this time divides the independents into three categories: those who claim to "lean" toward either one of the two major parties, as well as the "pure" independents. Although the percentage of these pure independents has fluctuated over the past fifty years, it has never constituted more than 15 percent (in

Table 1.1   Democratic, Republican, and Independent Identification by Year, 1952–2012 (in percentages)

Year	Democrats	Independents	Republicans
1952	47	23	28
1954	47	22	27
1956	44	23	29
1958	49	19	27
1960	47	23	30
1962	46	21	28
1964	52	23	25
1966	46	28	25
1968	45	30	25
1970	44	31	24
1972	41	34	23
1974	38	37	22
1976	40	37	23
1978	39	38	21
1980	41	34	23
1982	44	30	24
1984	37	34	27
1986	40	33	25
1988	35	36	28
1990	39	34	25
1992	36	38	25
1994	34	36	30
1996	37	35	27
1998	37	36	26
2000	34	40	24
2002	33	36	30
2004	32	39	28
2008	34	39	26
2012	35	38	27

From Harold W. Stanley and Richard Niemi (2013). *Vital Statistics on American Politics 2013–2014.* Washington DC: CQ Press, Table 3.1. Rows do not total 100 percent because those who expressed no preference or a preference other than those presented are excluded.

Table 1.2 Partisans, Independent "Leaners," and Pure Independents, 1952–2012 (in percentages)

Year	Democrats, and Independents "leaning" Democrat	Pure Independents	Republicans, and Independents "leaning" Republican
1952	57	6	35
1954	56	7	33
1956	50	9	37
1958	56	7	32
1960	53	10	37
1962	53	8	34
1964	61	8	31
1966	55	12	32
1968	55	11	34
1970	54	13	32
1972	52	13	33
1974	51	15	31
1976	52	15	33
1978	53	14	31
1980	52	13	33
1982	55	11	32
1984	48	11	39
1986	50	12	36
1988	47	11	41
1990	51	10	37
1992	50	12	37
1994	47	11	42
1996	51	9	39
1998	51	11	37
2000	49	12	37
2002	48	8	43
2004	49	10	40
2008	51	11	37
2012	47	14	39

From Harold W. Stanley and Richard Niemi (2013). *Vital Statistics on American Politics 2013–2014*. Washington DC: CQ Press, Table 3.1. Rows do not total 100 percent because those who expressed no preference or a preference other than those presented are excluded.

1974 and 1976) of the electorate (although there was a slight rise in 2012). Figure 1.1 shows the average percentage of partisans and "leaners" (independents who think of themselves as "closer to the Republican or Democratic party"), and pure independents, by decade. Again, while there is an increase in the percentage of independents during this time, it is hardly dramatic.

One conclusion to draw from these data is relatively straightforward: it is not necessarily the measure of partisan identification that is the culprit in propagating the myth of the rising independent voter, but rather how some have used the data from this measurement. A second problem is that an understanding of

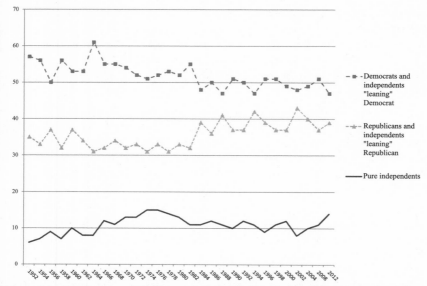

Figure 1.1　Percentage of Partisans, Independent Leaners, and Pure Independents, 1952–2012. *Source*: From Harold W. Stanley and Richard Niemi. 2013. Vital Statistics on American Politics 2013–2014. Washington DC: CQ Press, Table 3.1

how leaners and independents actually vote receives short shrift. For example, most leaners are actually partisans in their voting behavior. And, as suggested earlier, partisans tend to be loyal to candidates from their own party. Figure 1.2 shows that partisan loyalty in national elections has actually increased since the 1980s. By 2012, approximately 90 percent of partisan identifiers voted for their party's candidates in elections to the House, Senate, and the presidency. In only a very few cases does the number fall below 75 percent. In other words, partisanship clearly matters when it comes to voting.

Moreover, it is worth remembering the lessons of *The American Voter* and subsequent analyses (e.g., *Myth of the Independent Voter* by Keith et al.). Research strongly suggests that many independent voters are neither attentive to, nor involved in, politics. While they might be independent, many are not politically active, and they vote at much lower rates than partisans do.[19] It is a mistake, therefore, to focus disproportionate attention on how these individuals might vote in any given election, because many simply will not.

WHAT ABOUT SWING VOTERS?

Perhaps no other group of Americans is celebrated in news accounts throughout presidential campaigns more than the elusive[20] and all-powerful swing

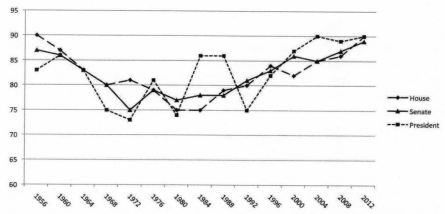

Figure 1.2 Party Line Voting in U.S. Elections, 1952–2012. *Source*: From Gary C. Jacobson (2014). "Barack Obama and the Nationalization of Electoral Politics in 2012." *Electoral Studies* (forthcoming), Figure 1.

voters. Accounts describe them as being nothing short of "supervoters,"[21] or individuals "that decide national elections."[22] In 2008, one popular website went so far as to include an "interactive calculator" to help readers determine for themselves if they belonged in this category.[23]

There are several problems with this focus on so-called swing voters. First, there is no common, agreed-upon definition or understanding of what a swing voter is. As one account surmises, "Political science has committed to neither a single term nor a common definition for this phenomenon."[24] Many, it seems, are actually the independents discussed earlier. Second, even using the most generous definition of a swing voter, they constitute only a minority of the voting public. Third, in terms of their actual voting behavior, many behave in a partisan manner. This too is consistent with the earlier discussion of independents. Finally, political science research indicates that swing voters actually "decide" very few elections. The little amount of research on the subject suggests that, in terms of demographics, the answer to this question varies from election to election.[25] It is, for example, entirely too simplistic to lump them into a single category like soccer moms, security moms, NASCAR dads, or "Joe Six-Packs" as some political observers have done over the years.[26]

So who is a swing voter? A basic definition would be that the swing voter is someone whose "candidate preference tends to be variable, and whose ultimate decisions will determine the outcome of the election."[27] Other possible definitions include individuals who are "relatively uncertain about who they will vote for," "persuadable" or "potentially persuadable" voters, voters who are "up for grabs," those who have "not developed a committed preference for one candidate," and those who are "undecided."[28] Political scientists have a few different concepts that seem to correspond, if only imperfectly, to this understanding. For example, Philip Converse identified a class of less engaged and informed individuals he termed "floating voters," or those who might be persuaded to vote for either party's candidate.[29] V. O. Key, Jr., identified a different group of (also less informed) voters he referred to as "party switchers," or those who might cast their ballot for the candidate from one party in one election and the other party's candidate in the next.[30] These two possibilities illustrate one of the problems in coming to a common definition of a swing voter: Does the concept refer to voting behavior in a single election (floating voters) or across multiple elections (party switchers)?

The way that most news organizations and polling firms define a swing voter is based on what are referred to as "strength of support" questions in preelection polling. Since 1944, Gallup has attempted to gauge the level of commitment poll respondents have toward their preferred (if any) candidate. For example, in 2004, those who expressed a preference for Bush in the standard question, "if the election were held tomorrow, for whom would you cast your vote," were then asked "are you certain now that you will vote for Bush for president, or do you think you may change your mind between now and the November election?" Those who claimed that their intention was to vote for Kerry were asked a similar question. Respondents who claimed that they might change their mind "between now and the November election" are usually classified as swing voters.[31]

It is also common to include as swing voters those who claim to be undecided at the time the survey asks the respondent to answer the question. The "undecided" category also often includes those who claim to be "leaning" toward one candidate or the other after expressing no preference. However, there is some evidence that the "undecided" vote may be overreported, perhaps due to the fact that respondents may be reluctant to tell the interviewer what their preference is.[32]

Like some other polling organizations, the Pew Research Center first asks people their presidential preference. In 2004, those expressing support for a candidate (e.g., Bush) were asked a follow-up question measuring the strength of that support: "Do you think there is a chance you might vote for John Kerry in November, or have you definitely decided not to vote for him?"[33] The same question was also asked of Kerry supporters. Supporters stating that there was a chance they might vote for the other candidate were typically classified as swing voters. Other survey firms employ similar strategies to measure strength of support for a candidate throughout the campaign, with the idea being that the weakly committed might be considered swing voters.[34] Here too, the undecided voters and those with no preference, but who are leaning toward a particular candidate, are often categorized as swing voters.

The point is that such strength of support questions help pollsters determine who the committed voters are. All others fall into the swing voter category. By this measure, swing voters sometimes can make up a sizable segment of the electorate, especially depending on which election it is and at what point during the campaign that the respondents answer the question. One problem is that this measure is so broad that it makes the concept almost meaningless. Swing voters cannot be a critical *subgroup* or *faction* if they constitute a large *majority* of the electorate. Moreover, as noted, there is no consensus that this is the proper way to determine what a swing voter is. Recent research by two political scientists using different methods suggests that the actual percentage of "persuadable" voters (those not firmly committed to either candidate) might be closer to one-fifth of the electorate.[35]

Some research suggests as well that many of the so-called swing voters are self-identified independents,[36] most of whom, as this chapter discussed earlier, exhibit partisan voting patterns. Others have found that many of the so-called persuadable swing voters—those who express only soft support for their candidate—vote for their preferred candidate in the end.[37] In 2004, as many as 85 percent of Bush supporters who said there was a chance they might vote for Kerry voted for Bush. The percentages for Kerry were similar.[38] While the percentages of soft supporters voting for their preferred candidate have been lower in previous elections, research suggests that election campaigns reinforce existing preferences, as opposed to changing minds.[39] Relatively few people, in other words, are actually persuaded during a campaign.

Finally, and this is perhaps the central question, do swing voters decide elections? As a group, these voters are less engaged in politics generally.[40] Moreover, most of these voters do not really start to focus on the campaign until the fall of the general election and their numbers decrease as the campaign wears on. In the end, many do not even vote.[41] In a fairly sophisticated analysis, a prominent political scientist who specializes in the dynamics of electoral choice and presidential elections determined that the only winning presidential candidate since 1952 who needed the swing vote bloc (as he defined and measured swing voters) to win was John Kennedy in 1960.[42] Swing voters, it seems, do not decide elections.

THE CORE CAMPAIGN: MOBILIZING THE BASE

How does the reality that most voters are partisans translate into actual campaign activity during a presidential campaign? It is certainly true that a great deal of time and money are spent throughout the campaign in an attempt to reach what campaigns refer to as "persuadables," the small percentage of likely voters who are undecided and who may be swayed. But, as the campaign draws to a close, attention shifts to turning out the vote. This entails efforts to register new voters, and subsequently to get them and the party faithful to the polls on Election Day. In previous times, party leaders went to great lengths to produce the number of votes needed for victory. For example, if the infamous Tammany Hall machine in New York City needed extra votes to put their candidate over the top, they would import extra voters from New Jersey or Pennsylvania.[43] Parties were also not averse to buying votes. Stephen Dorsey, one of the campaign managers of the 1880 Garfield campaign, reportedly bought 30,000 votes in Indiana for two dollars apiece.[44]

Modern get-out-the-vote (GOTV) efforts are very systematic and sophisticated, conducted at the state and local levels. Research demonstrates that voters are more likely to vote if they are contacted by political parties, candidate organizations, or other interested groups;[45] and voter turnout can be the critical difference in an election outcome. In 1968, for example, the Democratic Party did not heal its wounds after its bitter and divisive national convention until late October. This resulted in fewer Democrats registering and, thus, fewer votes for the party's presidential nominee Hubert Humphrey. The Democrats in 1976, with the help of organized labor, which plays a central role in Democratic GOTV efforts,[46] registered more voters than Republicans did. Jimmy Carter's 1976 win was also attributed to the party's successful drive to register African Americans. Republicans, who rely on volunteers, housewives, small business owners, religious conservatives, and retirees,[47] mounted a sophisticated, and largely successful, effort to increase turnout in 1984, contributing to Reagan's victory.[48]

The National Association for the Advancement of Colored People (NAACP) actively worked to raise voter turnout among African Americans in Florida, whose turnout in 2000 was almost double of what it was in 1996. Their campaign included recorded telephone messages from President Clinton and African American leaders urging people to vote, as well as reminders from the ministers of black churches of the importance of voting. In 2000, both parties engaged in intensive turnout efforts in battleground states. The Democratic Party had an estimated 40,000 volunteers making personal contacts with voters. Republicans were active as well. In the last week of the campaign, they made approximately eighty-five million telephone calls and sent over 110 million pieces of mail. During the final two weeks, they distributed roughly sixteen million pieces of campaign literature to people's doors, 1.2 million yard signs, and over one million bumper stickers. The National Rifle Association, pro-life, and other groups helped in this effort.[49]

Still, according to Bush's main strategist Karl Rove, some four million conservative voters stayed home in 2000. Rove subsequently built a GOTV operation designed to increase turnout in 2004. The effort focused on districts "where Republican candidates underperformed against the Democratic profile of the district."[50] The effort started with the purchase of commercial databases to pinpoint voters based on, among other things, shopping habits and magazine subscriptions. Gun owners, for example, were targets, as were subscribers to magazines like *Christianity Today.*[51] Republicans tested the operation in the 2002 congressional elections and increased turnout over 1998 by five million voters (as opposed to only two million for Democrats).[52] The commercial databases allowed the campaign to target appeals to members of thirty-two different subgroups in 2004.[53]

Rove also focused on increasing registration.[54] To mobilize young adults, Republicans dispatched a fifty-six-foot, eighteen-wheeled mobile voter registration center named Reggie the Registration Rig to various youth-oriented events such as MTV's "Total Request Live."[55] The Bush team registered approximately 3.4 million voters who had recently moved, also focusing on roughly seven million identified Republicans who did not consistently vote and another ten million unaffiliated voters.[56] In all, the campaign allocated approximately 125 million dollars for voter mobilization, more than three times the amount spent in 2000, with other groups (e.g., Progress for America Voter Fund,[57] various churches[58]) assisted in the effort as well.

As important as the more traditional registration efforts were, the aggressive and innovative use of new technologies by the Bush campaign in 2004 helped to build networks of people who canvassed neighborhoods.[59] This "one-on-one politics" effort was a throwback to an earlier era, with a modern twist. On the Bush website, individuals could type in their zip code and receive directions to their polling places as well as a list of five people in their immediate area and directions to their homes. One person would volunteer to recruit a few people, each of whom, in turn, recruited several more, resulting in a network of volunteers connected by e-mail to the national campaign organization. This resulted in approximately 1.4 million volunteers in key battleground states.[60] Daily messages and communications from national team leaders encouraged these local leaders and kept them informed.[61] The website also provided links to local talk radio, boilerplate letters to the editor, and other campaign materials.

Taken together, the Bush campaign reported that they made as many as 18 million attempts to contact voters in battleground states in the last four days of the campaign.[62] Democrats were active as well. The Kerry campaign reportedly spent sixty million dollars in voter mobilization efforts, more than twice the amount spent by Democrats in 2000. In addition, the American Federation of Labor and Congress of Industrial Organizations (AFL-CIO)

spent 45 million dollars in sixteen battleground states,[63] and America Coming
Together employed 2,500 people to register and contact new voters.[64] In the
last three weeks of the campaign alone, they claim to have made approximately sixteen million telephone calls, sent twenty-three million pieces of
mail, and delivered eleven million flyers.[65]

Although Barack Obama had an enormous amount of personal appeal, he
and his campaign team also understood that the presidency is won "on the
ground." His 2008 campaign was unprecedented in organization, execution,
and scope. Although closely based on the model Rove employed in 2004, it
went "well beyond even what Rove built. . . . [using] it's record-breaking
fundraising to open more than 700 offices in more than a dozen battleground
states, pay several thousand organizers, and manage tens of thousands of
volunteers."[66] In a summer 2008 editorial, Rove himself called Obama's
ground game "brilliant."[67] Like Bush, Obama used the Internet to recruit and
organize an army of volunteers for voter registration and turnout efforts. This
translated into a systematic grassroots effort. For example, Ohio was broken down into 1,231 "neighborhoods" which contained 8–10 precincts, and
importantly, also included rural areas that Kerry had ignored in 2004. While
the Obama campaign faced an "enthusiasm gap" four years later in 2012, in
which polling data showed supporters were less enthusiastic than they had
been in 2008, it was still able to overcome this by focusing, again, on turnout
efforts.[68] In virtually every demographic group, Obama's vote totals exceeded
polling expectations as the result of these efforts.

CONCLUSION

The conventional wisdom that independent and swing voters are a growing segment of the electorate and decide elections oversimplifies the more
complex reality of American election campaigns. As this chapter has illustrated, despite increases in the percentage of self-identified independents,
independent leaners are quite partisan at the polls, casting legitimate doubts
as to whether independents are truly increasing in number and importance.
Similarly, even if we could identify who swing voters are with any precision,
there are probably fewer than is popularly believed, and, in almost all cases
they do not, as a bloc, decide elections.

In short, two of the most widely discussed aspects about American
voters—the rise of the independent voter and the importance of the swing
voter—require several caveats and a more nuanced discussion than the conventional wisdom typically provides. The plain fact is that party identification
still heavily influences most voters in midterm and presidential elections.

Indeed, the mobilization of partisan voters is a matter of high priority in modern campaign strategy.

NOTES

1. We wish to acknowledge the contributions to this chapter made by Bruce Keith et al., *The Myth of the Independent Voter* (Berkeley: University of California Press, 1992), and the contributors to the volume, William G. Mayer, ed., *The Swing Voter in American Politics* (Washington, DC: Brookings Institution, 2008).

2. Linda Killian, "Yes, Independent Swing Voters Are Real. And May Decide Who Wins Elections," *The Daily Beast*, November 3, 2014, http://www.thedailybeast.com/articles/2014/11/03/how-swing-voters-keep-washington-divided.html.

3. For recent examples, see Catalina Camia, "More Voters Choose Indie Label, Buck Democrats and GOP," *USA Today*, December 12, 2013, http://www.usatoday.com/story/news/politics/2013/12/11/independent-voters-registration-third-way/3988351; Richard Wolf, "Voters Leaving Republican, Democratic Parties in Droves," *USA Today*, December 22, 2011, http://usatoday30.usatoday.com/news/politics/story/2011-12-22/voters-political-parties/52171688/1.

4. Janet Hook, "Votes of Independents Could Be Key," *The Wall Street Journal*, November 5, 2012, http://www.wsj.com/articles/SB10001424052970204755404578099141834504374.

5. Kate Dailey, "The American Independent: A Voter on the Rise," BBC News, January 11, 2012, http://www.bbc.com/news/magazine-16480070; "Pew Poll Notes Rise in Independent Voters," NPR, May 21, 2009, http://www.npr.org/templates/story/story.php?storyId=104406480; John P. Avlon, "Independent Voters Burgeoning," *New York Sun*, April 28, 2006, www.nysun.com/article/31852; Rhodes Cook, "Moving On: More Voters Are Steering Away from Party Labels," *Washington Post*, June 27, 2004, B01.

6. George C. Edwards III, Martin P. Wattenberg, and Robert L. Lineberry, *Government in America: People, Politics, and Policy, Study Edition, Brief Version* (New York: Longman, 2002), emphasis in original. Among others, see also "The Election: Turbulence and Tranquility," in *The Elections of 1996*, ed. Michael Nelson (Washington, DC: CQ Press, 1997), 63–4.

7. David Broder, *The Party's Over: The Failure of Politics in America* (New York: Harper, 1972).

8. Paul Allen Beck and Marjorie Random Hershey, *Party Politics in America*, 9th ed. (New York: Longman, 2001), 118. To be fair, some parties', campaigns', and elections' texts have not been taken with the notion of growing numbers of independents. See, for example, Nelson Polsby and Aaron Wildavsky, *Presidential Elections*, 10th ed. (Chatham, NJ: Chatham House, 2000), 18; William J. Keefe and Marc J. Hetherington, *Parties, Politics, and Public Policy in America*, 9th ed. (Washington, DC: CQ Press, 2003), 173–6.

9. Jeffrey M. Jones, "Record-High 42% of Americans Identify as Independents," Gallup, January 8, 2014, http://www.gallup.com/poll/166763/

record-high-americans-identify-independents.aspx; Barry C. Burden and Steven Greene, "Party Attachments and State Election Laws," *Political Research Quarterly* 53 (2000): 63–76; Steven E. Finkel and Howard A. Scarrow, "Party Identification and Party Enrollment: The Difference and the Consequences," *Journal of Politics* 47 (1985): 620–42.

10. See Russell J. Dalton, *Citizen Politics: Public Opinion and Political Parties in Advanced Industrial Democracies*, 3rd ed. (New York: Chatham House, 2002), 183–6.

11. For the classic formulation of this theory, see Martin P. Wattenberg, *The Decline of American Political Parties, 1952–1996* (Cambridge, MA: Harvard University Press, 1998) and Dalton, *Citizen Politics: Public Opinion and Political Parties in Advanced Industrial Democracies.*

12. See "The Origins of NES," www.electionstudies.org/overview/origins.htm.

13. See "About ANES, 2006–2009," www.electionstudies.org/overview/overview. htm.

14. For those inclined to investigate further, this question is variable VCF0301 in the 2004 NES Cumulative Data File data set. See "Party Identification 7-Point Scale 1952–2004," www.electionstudies.org/nesguide/toptable/tab2a_1.htm.

15. Angus Campbell, Gerald Gurin, and Warren E. Miller, *The Voter Decides* (Evanston, Ill.: Row, Peterson, 1954); Angus Campbell, Philip E. Converse, Warren E. Miller, and Donald E. Stokes, *The American Voter* (New York: Wiley, 1960).

16. Anthony Downs, in *An Economic Theory of Democracy* (New York: Harper, 1957), suggested that citizens select candidates or parties based on proximity to their own preferences. V. O. Key, Jr., in *The Responsible Electorate: Rationality in Presidential Voting 1936–1960* (Cambridge, MA: Belknap, 1966), argued that voters are more rational than *The American Voter* suggests. Samuel L. Popkin, in *The Reasoning Voter: Communication and Persuasion in Presidential Campaigns* (Chicago: University of Chicago Press, 1991), updates Key's theory with particular attention to the effects of the media. Morris P. Fiorina argued in *Retrospective Voting in American National Elections* (New Haven, Conn.: Yale University Press, 1981) that citizens base their voting choices on the past performance of politicians and parties.

17. See Paul Allen Beck, "A Socialization Theory of Partisan Realignment," in *The Politics of Future Citizens*, ed. Richard G. Niemi (San Francisco: Jossey-Bass, 1974); Philip E. Converse, *The Dynamics of Party Support: Cohort-Analyzing Party Identification* (Beverly Hills, Calif.: Sage, 1976); Paul R. Abramson, "Developing Party Identification: A Further Examination of Life-cycle, Generational, and Period Effects," *American Journal of Political Science* 23 (1979): 78–96; and Paul Allen Beck and M. Kent Jennings, "Family Traditions, Political Periods, and the Development of Partisan Orientations," *Journal of Politics* 53 (1991): 742–63.

18. Barry C. Burden and Casey A. Klofstad, "Affect and Cognition in Party Identification," *Political Psychology* 26 (2005): 869–86.

19. Martin P. Wattenberg, "Turnout Decline in the U.S. and Other Advanced Industrial Democracies," Center for the Study of Democracy, University of California, Irvine, 1998, www.democ.uci.edu/publications/papersseriespre2001/marty.html.

20. David Shribman, "Hunting The Elusive Swing Vote," *Globe and Mail*, September 6, 2008, A23.

21. Carl M. Cannon and Carol Kaufmann, "Meet the 2008 Supervoters," ReadersDigest.com, 2008, www.rd.com/your-america-inspiring-people-and-stories/2008-swing-voters-at-the-ballots--election-/article98943.html.

22. Al From and Victoria Lynch, "Who Are the Swing Voters? Key Groups That Decide National Elections," Democratic Leadership Council Political Study, September 25, 2008, www.dlc.org/print.cfm?contentid=254754.

23. Chris Wilson, "Are You a Swing Voter? A Slate Interactive Calculator," *Slate. com*, October 27, 2008, www.slate.com/id/2203144.

24. Daron R. Shaw, "Swing Voting and U.S. Presidential Elections," in *The Swing Voter in American Politics*, ed. William G. Mayer (Washington, DC: Brookings Institution, 2008), 77.

25. Mayer, *The Swing Voter*.

26. For a summary of the many different fad categorizations of swing voters, see Christopher Beam, "One-Armed Vegetarian Live-In Boyfriends: The Quest for This Year's Sexy Swing Demographic," Slate, July 16, 2008, http://www.slate.com/articles/news_and_politics/politics/2008/07/onearmed_vegetarian_livein_boyfriends.html.

27. Shaw, "Swing Voting," 77.

28. Quoted in William G. Mayer and Ruy Teixeira, "Conclusion: The State of the Discussion," in *The Swing Voter in American Politics*, ed. William G. Mayer (Washington, DC: Brookings Institution, 2008), 134.

29. Philip Converse, "Information Flow and the Stability of Partisan Attitudes," *Public Opinion* Quarterly 26 (1962): 578–99.

30. V. O. Key, Jr., *The Responsible Electorate: Rationality in Presidential Voting, 1936–1960* (Cambridge, MA: Harvard University, 1966).

31. Over the years, Gallup's questions wording has changed; see Jeffrey M. Jones, "Swing Voters in the Gallup Poll, 1944 to 2004," in *The Swing Voter in American Politics*, ed. William G. Mayer (Washington, DC: Brookings Institution, 2008), 35.

32. Mayer, *The Swing Voter*.

33. Michael Dimock, April Clark, and Juliana Menasce Horowitz, "Campaign Dynamics and the Swing Vote in the 2004 Election," in *The Swing Voter in American Politics*, ed. William G. Mayer (Washington, DC: Brookings Institution, 2008), 61.

34. See Adam Clymer and Ken Winneg, "Swing Voters? Hah! The Not Very 'Persuadables' and the Not Really 'Undecideds' in 2004," in *The Swing Voter in American Politics*, ed. William G. Mayer (Washington, DC: Brookings Institution, 2008) for Annenberg's question wording.

35. In both of these cases the identification of swing voters was made by using what are known in the NES data set as candidate "thermometer" scores, which measure how warmly (positively) an individual feels toward candidates. See William G. Mayer, "What Exactly Is a Swing Voter? Definition and Measurement," in *The Swing Voter in American Politics*, ed. William G. Mayer (Washington, DC: Brookings Institution, 2008); James Campbell, "Do Swing Voters Swing Elections?" in *The Swing Voter in*

American Politics, ed. William G. Mayer (Washington, DC: Brookings Institution, 2008).

36. Shaw, "Swing Voting."

37. Clymer and Winneg, "Swing Voters?"; Dimock, Clark, and Menasce Horowitz, "Campaign Dynamics and the Swing Vote"; Jones, "Swing Voters in the Gallup Poll."

38. Clymer and Winneg, "Swing Voters?"

39. Dimock, Clark, and Menasce Horowitz, "Campaign Dynamics and the Swing Vote"; Jones, "Swing Voters in the Gallup Poll"; Campbell, "Do Swing Voters Swing Elections?"

40. Shaw, "Swing Voting."

41. Dimock, Clark, and Menasce Horowitz, "Campaign Dynamics and the Swing Vote"; Jones, "Swing Voters in the Gallup Poll."

42. Campbell, "Do Swing Voters Swing Elections?"

43. Robert J. Dinkin, *Campaigning in America: A History of Election Practices* (New York: Greenwood, 1989), 74.

44. Allan Peskin, *Garfield* (Kent, Ohio: Kent State University Press, 1978), 504.

45. Paul R. Abramson, John H. Aldrich, and David W. Rohde, *Change and Continuity in the 2004 Elections* (Washington, DC: CQ Press, 2006), 100–1.

46. Peter L. Francia, *The Future of Organized Labor in American Politics* (New York: Columbia University Press, 2006).

47. Evan Thomas, *Election 2004: How Bush Won and What You Can Expect in the Future* (New York: PublicAffairs, 2004), 168.

48. Wayne, *Road to the White House*, 216–17.

49. Ibid. 217.

50. James W. Ceaser and Andrew E. Busch, *Red over Blue: The 2004 Elections and American Politics* (Lanham, MD: Rowman & Littlefield, 2005), 133.

51. Richard Lowry, "Bush's Well-Mapped Road to Victory: How Rove et al. Pulled It Off," *National Review*, November 29, 2004, 40–5; Ceaser and Busch, *Red over Blue*, 133–4.

52. Rhodes Cook, "Voter Turnout and Congressional Change," Pew Research Center, November 1, 2006, pewresearch.org/pubs/83/voter-turnout-and-congressional-change.

53. William Saletan, "Conclusion," in *Divided States of America: The Slash and Burn Politics of the 2004 Presidential Election*, ed. Larry J. Sabato (New York: Longman, 2006), 269–78.

54. Thomas, Election 2004, 168.

55. "Reggie the Registration Rig Ready to Rock with MTV's 'TRL'," Republican National Committee, www.gop.com/News/Read.aspx?ID=4040.

56. Lowry, "Bush's Well-Mapped Road to Victory," 40–5.

57. Abramson, Aldrich, and Rohde, *Change and Continuity in the 2004 Elections*, 45.

58. David D. Kirkpatrick, "Bush Campaign Seeks Help from Congregations," *New York Times*, June 3, 2004, www.nytimes.com/2004/06/03/politics/campaign/03CHUR.html.

59. Ceaser and Busch, *Red over Blue*, 133–4.

60. Ryan Lizza, "Head Count: How the GOP Learned Voter Turnout," *New Republic*, November 18, 2002, 14.

61. Lowry, "Bush's Well-Mapped Road to Victory."

62. Ibid.

63. Vanessa Williams, "Democrats Aim to Organize the Union Vote," *Washington Post*, October 23, 2004, A8.

64. Glen Justice, "Advocacy Groups Reflect on Their Role in the Election" *The New York Times*, November 5, 2004, http://www.nytimes.com/2004/11/05/politics/campaign/05money.html.

65. Ibid.

66. Alec MacGillis, "Obama Camp Relying Heavily on Ground Effort," *Washington Post*, October 12, 2008, A4.

67. Karl Rove, "Barack's Brilliant Ground Game," *Wall Street Journal*, July 10, 2008, online.wsj.com/article/SB121564804985640977.html.

68. James W. Caeser, Andrew E. Busch, and John J. Pitney Jr. 2013. *After Hope and Change: The 2012 Elections and American Politics* (Lanham MD: Rowman & Littlefield).

FOR MORE READING

Keith, Bruce, et al. *The Myth of the Independent Voter*. Berkeley: University of California, 1992.

Magleby, David B., ed. *The Change Election: Money, Mobilization, and Persuasion in the 2008 Federal Elections*. Philadelphia: Temple University Press, 2011.

Mayer, William G., ed. *The Swing Voter in American Politics*. Washington, DC: Brookings Institution, 2008.

Chapter 2

Data-Crunching Wizards

The New Masters of the Campaign Universe? What "Big" Data Can and Cannot Do for Campaigns

In the aftermath of the 2012 presidential election, several headlines trumpeted how "big data" had helped President Obama "win" reelection.[1] Obama's team of data analysts captured the attention of not only the press but also the Republican National Committee (RNC), which vowed to win the "space race" for data supremacy in future elections.[2] As an RNC official explained in 2014, "They put up Sputnik. We believe we can put a man on the moon."[3] Yet, the attention and accolades afforded to these data-crunching wizards for "revolutionizing"[4] campaigns are deserved in some respects, but overhyped in others. Our purpose in this chapter is to wade through evidence from political scientists and observations from campaign practitioners to present a clearer picture of the consequences of the "big" data revolution.

As we will show, the use of "big" data (i.e., terabytes of data with information about voters, including their voting history, party affiliation, and even spending habits) to tailor and "microtarget" specific messages to certain types of voters has transformed the traditional campaign "war room." Whereas professional consultants once relied heavily on their own intuition and gut instincts for major strategic decisions, big data analysis now makes it possible for campaign operatives to make data-driven choices about how and where best to target money and resources. However, the claim that big data analysis was the key to President Obama's reelection victory seems highly dubious. As political science research has documented, the use of big data seems likely to have played no more than a marginal role in determining the outcome of the 2012 election.

SOURCES AND USES OF BIG DATA

Political parties and campaign organizations have long kept computerized databases of information about citizens. However, before the big data revolution, campaigns relied on more simplistic techniques to target voters. For example, campaigns tried to determine the likelihood that an individual would turn out to vote based simply on that individual's previous voting history over the four most recent elections.[5] The assumption was that voters who consistently turned out to vote in the past were likely to vote again in the next election. Campaigns gauged voter intentions in a similarly straightforward fashion. A registered Democrat was presumed likely to vote for Democratic candidates, whereas it was assumed that someone registered as a Republican would vote for Republican candidates.

It was not until the 2002 midterm election that the first serious effort at building a big database with multiple layers of voter information came about. George W. Bush's chief political strategist, Karl Rove, helped build the "Voter Vault" to assist Republican efforts (see also Chapter 1).[6] Several years later, the Democratic National Committee (DNC) and the for-profit company Catalist, run by Democratic operative Harold Ickes, compiled their own extensive voter databank to compete with Republicans.[7] Both national parties and their allied organizations have continued to expand their collection of voter data since that time.

Much like the simpler voter databases of the past, today's big databases begin with publicly available voter information gathered from state records that typically come from the Office of the Secretary of State. This information includes a person's past voting history, such as whether a person voted in a particular election and if so, whether they voted with an absentee ballot or at their designated polling location. It also includes the voter's party affiliation, and in some states, some basic demographic information such as date of birth and gender. This type of information became easier to obtain and access following the Help America Vote Act of 2002, which required states to produce a "single, uniform, official, centralized, interactive computerized statewide voter registration list."[8]

Today's databases have earned the label "big" because they have grown well beyond this basic information. With advances in personal computer technology (processor speed and storage capacity), political parties and other organizations have begun collecting additional data about voters. It is now common for voter databanks to include not only an individual's voting history and party affiliation, but also census and precinct data about their place of residence, as well as their spending habits, which campaigns can purchase from consumer data firms. Consumer data may include information on whether the voter owns a home, the car he or she drives, the specific magazines to which the voter subscribes, restaurants he or she frequents, and much more.[9] More recently, big databases have begun to include voter information taken from the Internet and social media websites such as Twitter feeds and Facebook posts.[10] Advances in computer software have also improved the capabilities of campaign organizations to update information in real time, whether from online sources (such as a campaign website) or information collected from volunteers in the field, who can update voter information using the latest mobile app technology.

Campaigns utilize all of this information with the assistance of analysts (also referred to in slang as "quants") who create statistical models that can help predict individual behavior. The ultimate goal is to determine the most efficient and effective ways to reach and target different types of voters. Referred to as "microtargeting," this effort helps campaigns identify which individuals are most likely to turn out to vote and support the campaign's candidate. Microtargeting not only helps identify whom to target but the message that is most likely to resonate with certain voters. By knowing in advance which voters to target (and, on the flip side, which voters to ignore) and how best to target them, big data practitioners can reap major savings and efficiency gains for campaigns in terms of both time and money. Over the course of the campaign, a small efficiency gain associated with even a single mass mailing gets multiplied to add up to a significant sum. These developments have had a major effect on the decision-making process of most campaign organizations. The strategic actions and responses of any major modern campaign now rely, at least to some degree, on big data for answers.

THE OBAMA CAMPAIGN AND BIG DATA IN THE 2012 ELECTION

Heading into the 2012 campaign, President Obama's re-election campaigns faced some considerable challenges. For the first eight months of 2012, the unemployment rate stood at 8 percent or higher, a level that was relatively high, by historical standards, for an incumbent president seeking reelection.[11] Obama's approval ratings were below 50 percent for much of 2012, dipping below his *disapproval* numbers at certain points throughout the year.[12] A few polls showed even some highly partisan Democrats expressing disappointment with his overall job performance as president.[13] The campaign, in other words, faced considerable challenges.

Despite these challenges, Obama's reelection team built what at least one political observer called the "most technologically advanced [campaign team] in American history."[14] At campaign headquarters in Chicago was what staffers nicknamed "the Cave," a technological command post that was the brainchild of campaign manager Jim Messina. His vision was for a sophisticated and data-driven operation that could capitalize on research, testing, and analysis to help inform nearly all major decisions.[15] Working with Messina were White House senior strategist David Axelrod, senior adviser David Plouffe, and deputy campaign manager, Jen O'Malley Dillon. The campaign also hired a "chief scientist," Rayid Ghani, an expert in supermarket sales promotions, and a "dream team" of political scientists, psychologists, and behavioral economists to help execute their data-driven approach.[16] According to one account, the Obama campaign had the look of a "tech startup" company.[17]

The Obama team entered 2012 with the goal of acquiring as much information as possible about voters and potential voters in order to improve efforts to identify, register, persuade, and turn out voters. The campaign began by first analyzing "after-action" reports based on the effectiveness of mobilization efforts in battleground states in the months immediately after the 2008 election. These reports analyzed nearly every aspect and detail of the campaign's grassroots and volunteer efforts in 2008 and summarized the findings in a 500-page report. The objective was to get a better understanding of the methods and examples that worked best in the field in 2008.[18]

The campaign looked forward to 2012 by incorporating the latest technological advances into its larger campaign plan. The Obama website utilized a tool called "Dashboard," which brought traditional campaign fieldwork together with online organizing. Harper Reed, the campaign's chief technology officer referred to Dashboard as an online organizing tool to "create that offline field experience online."[19] Dashboard included a "Volunteer" button that allowed Obama supporters to do traditional phone-banking activities online. It also helped Obama supporters coordinate and organize events. When an Obama supporter logged into Dashboard and entered information about where he or she lived, the Dashboard platform connected that supporter to a "neighborhood team."[20] From there supporters could plan local events or other activities. The campaign encouraged volunteers to contact their own friends and family members. A volunteer, for instance, may have had friends listed on his or her Facebook page who were not registered voters. If a volunteer logged-in to Dashboard through his or her Facebook account, the campaign (with the volunteer's permission) could instantly identify his or her Facebook friends and the voter registration status of those friends. With this information, the Obama campaign was able to encourage the volunteer to contact their unregistered friends. This would presumably be more effective than having a stranger from the campaign contact the individual. The system then tracked all of this information, keeping cumulative totals on how much activity (e.g., calls made or team meetings attended) each volunteer had completed.[21]

Another major goal of the campaign effort was the integration of various data. Rather than keeping separate lists and files for donors, volunteers, and voters, the campaign built a single comprehensive database with the ability to provide real-time updates as new data became available either from the field or online. This was an enormous challenge, in large part, because the fifty different state offices (and various departments) did not always use the same software or even collect data in the same way.

The infrastructure that brought everything together was what the Obama campaign called "Narwhal," the name of a rare Arctic whale. Narwhal integrated the data platforms of various software vendors and provided a mechanism to merge information from the campaign's website, Twitter, and from other digital communications data with field data into one master database, all in "real time."[22] With Narwhal, campaign staff from anywhere in the nation had access to all of the voter information that the campaign had collected from any source and from any platform. This not only provided campaign staff with updated and detailed information about the voters in their precinct or state, but also simplified and streamlined communication between field directors, volunteers, state campaign directors, and others. What began for the Obama reelection campaign as a ten-terabyte (one terabyte equals 1,000 gigabytes) database quickly grew to 50 terabytes by the end of the 2012 election.[23] With this massive amount of data, analysts were able to build statistical models that generated predictive political behavior scores about each individual in the database. These models generated the probability that any given individual would participate in various activities (e.g., making a phone call, contributing, volunteering time) to help the campaign.[24]

Beyond predictions about what individuals might do, the models also gave the campaign team information about citizens' candidate and issue preferences. To do this, analysts generated "support scores" using a scale from 0 to 100 (a "0" meant that no one would support a particular candidate or issue, while a score of "100" meant that 100 people out of 100 would support the candidate or issue). These scores were then combined with scores that predicted the probability the individual would vote. So when, on the one hand, a person had a high support score but a low turnout score, the campaign made a concerted effort to register that voter and ensure he or she voted early (in states that allowed early voting) or got to the polls on Election Day. On the other hand, when a person had a high turnout score but a persuasion score between 40 and 60 (where a higher score is a high probability of voting for Obama), the campaign focused its efforts on persuading that voter. Persuasion efforts were most intense in the final weeks of the campaign.[25]

To understand which persuasion materials were likely to have the greatest effect, the Obama campaign conducted random experiments to see which communications and messages worked best. Perhaps most notable was the so-called "Optimizer," which guided television advertising strategies.[26] Combining information about the television viewing habits and political and socioeconomic data of individuals, the Optimizer identified blocs of persuadable voters and the television programs that they were most likely to watch. Instead of simply advertising on the television programs that had the highest television ratings or those programs that reached a particular age demographic, the Obama campaign targeted networks such as TV Land, which its database revealed had a large number of undecided viewers who were amenable to persuasion.[27] Armed with this information, the campaign was able to maximize its resources, and in the end, was probably more effective.

The Romney campaign attempted to counter the Obama campaign's data operation with its own high-tech effort to mobilize supporters. Referred to as Project Orca—so named because orca whales are one of the few predators of the narwhal—the Romney campaign kept their own operation secret until the end of the campaign. Orca was a web application designed to help the campaign use its own information and analyses to maximize its get-out-the-vote efforts. Volunteers in the field tracked which voters had and had not voted and entered that information into an Orca Web portal. This gave the campaign the ability to update its voter turnout data in real time to Romney headquarters in Boston. In this way, the campaign could avoid contacting voters who had already cast their ballots and could maximize time in the field by volunteers to contact only likely supporters who had not yet voted.

Romney officials reported after the election that Orca generated information from 91 percent of its targeted counties, totaling 14 million voters in key battleground states.[28] However, the program encountered some difficulties. For example, several Romney campaign workers had personal identification numbers that did not work. Heavy volume overloaded the system with incoming information, forcing it to shut down for more than 90 minutes on Election Day. Numerous Romney campaign workers expressed frustration with Orca on social media throughout Election Day. In a post-election interview, one Romney volunteer called Orca an "unmitigated disaster."[29]

Perhaps not surprisingly, Republicans and their allies, who perceived the Romney campaign as having failed to keep pace with the Obama campaign, wasted little time in expanding their big data efforts for 2014. Both parties also announced plans to continue investing huge sums of money into more big data collection for the 2016 election. Yet while Obama's "cave," with its intensely data-driven campaign operation, unquestionably transformed the traditional "war room," its effect on voting and the actual outcome of the election is less certain.

EVALUATING OBAMA'S BIG DATA ADVANTAGE
AND OTHER LIMITATIONS OF BIG DATA

The internal dynamics of the Obama campaign's "cave" were fundamentally different from the ways in which traditional campaign war rooms functioned. However, several aspects of the big data revolution have been less consequential. In a recent study of 38 media markets nationwide representing 42 million voters, two political scientists found that the Obama campaign's highly touted advantage over the Romney campaign in mobilizing voters was, in fact, quite modest.[30] Their research estimated a net gain of only 1.6 percentage points for the Obama campaign over the Romney campaign in terms of turning out its respective party's registered voters.[31]

This is not to suggest that Obama's mobilization effects were unimportant. Indeed, the authors found that the Obama campaign's voter mobilization efforts yielded an impressive gain of 15.4 percentage points in turnout among registered Democrats who received targeted appeals in battleground states.[32] However, the authors also found similar effects for the Romney campaign. Republican turnout increased by an estimated 13.8 percentage points as a result of the Romney campaign's targeted voter mobilization efforts in those same battleground states.[33] Despite the reported problems on Election Day with the Romney campaign's Orca web application, the Republicans' overall technological disadvantage in mobilizing its own voters proved to be minimal.

In short, the Obama campaign's technological efforts were superior to those of the Romney campaign, but not by much, and certainly not by enough to have decided the outcome of the election. As the authors conclude, "the praise for Obama's 2012 campaign may be overblown. Both campaigns appear to have been effective in mobilizing voters, and the 2012 Obama campaign was not dramatically more effective than Romney's campaign."[34]

Additional misconceptions exist about the big data revolution. Several media reports have pointed to consumer information as the essential element in voter databases and have suggested it is central to microtargeting voters. In the words of one article,

> Political strategists buy consumer information from data brokers, mash it up with voting records and online behavior, then run the seemingly-mundane minutiae of modern life—most-visited websites, which soda's in the fridge—through complicated algorithms and: pow! They know with "amazing" accuracy not only if, but *why*, someone supports Barack Obama or Romney.[35]

However, the reality of what consumer data can actually do for a campaign comes up well short of such claims. In most instances, consumer information adds only a minimal amount of predictive power to the various statistical models that traditional campaigns have developed and utilized.

Alex Lundry of the Republican microtargeting firm, TargetPoint, remarked in an interview, "Despite its sex appeal to the media, for the most part consumer data is only helpful on the margins."[36] In a similar vein, Justin Gargiulo, CEO and founder of VoterTrove, explained, "Learning that there are seven non-primary voters . . . who read *Field and Stream* is not going to help a candidate get elected."[37]

Political scientists cast further doubt on the importance of consumer data in predictive models on voting behavior.[38] For example, numerous studies make clear that the best predictor of whether a person will vote is not what he or she buys, but rather whether that person has voted in the past.[39] The same is true for how one casts his or her vote. The products a person buys have considerably less predictive power than a voter's party affiliation (see previous chapter). As one account summarizes, "In reality, consumer data is of limited utility. With the data campaigns have, the best predictor of whether you will vote in an election is whether you voted in past elections. And the best predictor of how you'll vote is not your choice of beer but your party registration. Consumer data adds little beyond basic demographics."[40]

Indeed, for all of the hype about consumer data, it is expensive to purchase and available for only a few individuals. With so many gaps in the data, consumer information is simply not a critical piece to most predictive voting behavior models. Another research team concludes, "Information on magazine subscriptions, car purchases, and other consumer tastes . . . tends not to be useful in constructing predictive scores for the entire population. The vast majority of these variables literally do nothing to increase the predictive power of models of mass behavior once prior behavior is accounted for."[41] They conclude, "in short, many of the claims about the information that campaigns purchase about individuals is overblown; little of the information that is most useful to campaigns is purchased. Official voter files are public records, census and precinct-level information are also freely available, and individual citizens themselves volunteer a wealth of data that can be used to develop scores that predict all citizens' behaviors and preferences."[42]

Aside from the limitations of consumer data, collecting reliable and accurate data on critically important factors such as an individual's race and religion is not always easy for a campaign. Only some states collect information about a voter's race, and even here there are challenges in collecting it on potential first-time voters who have yet to register. Without hard information, analysts must instead rely on their statistical models to make an intelligent guess about a voter's race. There is even less publicly available information on most individuals about religion, thereby forcing data analysts to rely even more on statistics to complete voter profiles.

Predictions about an individual's race and religion are often far from precise. One political scientist noted that data in the Catalist voter file, one of the largest and most comprehensive voter databases, was 90 percent accurate in determining the race of an individual who was white, but only 73 percent accurate for Latinos and just 68 percent accurate for African Americans.[43] Model estimates on an individual's religion were even less exact. Identifying a voter as Catholic was accurate 38 percent of the time, while identifying a voter as Jewish was accurate just 25 percent of the time.[44] Given the well-known effect of race and religion on voting behavior, this means that big data files have gaps and inaccuracies in critical areas of a voter's profile. This further complicates the ability of a campaign to microtarget its message. This can have significant consequences. Mistargeted campaign communications may not only fail to mobilize or persuade voters, but they can also have the reverse effect of turning off the voter. One study, for example, found that mailings designed to target Latino voters harmed a candidate when received by non-Latino voters.[45]

In addition, even when there is complete and accurate information on a likely voter, the use of the data for microtargeting may not be as effective as the new "conventional wisdom" suggests.[46] This is consistent with the observations of some political practitioners. Jeremy Bird, the national field director for the Obama reelection campaign, stated in an interview that in "almost every test I saw, the broad economic message was winning."[47]

Yet, even when a campaign finds a "winning" message, there are additional hurdles for a campaign to overcome. Analysts inside the Obama reelection campaign have discussed how e-mails that recruited volunteers successfully and solicited donations in the early months of 2012 did not work well in the later months of the election.[48] An e-mail, for example, that worked well in February or March of an election year often did not generate much impact in September or October, suggesting that data-driven targeting often requires frequent testing and retesting to be effective.

Finally, for all of the reports about how the Obama campaign was obsessive about basing its strategic decisions on testing and numbers, the reality is that this was simply not possible. Of particular note, the campaign conducted few tests on the effectiveness of its television advertising.[49] The main obstacle in conducting such tests is the difficulty in establishing a control group, or a group of people who did not see any television ads at all. This would have required the Obama campaign to refrain from running ads in at least one battleground state, a decision that they reasonably feared could hurt their chances of winning the election. While the campaign did make a breakthrough with its use of the "Optimizer," the campaign did not know which voters actually saw their ads or whether any of the messages in those ads had an effect on them. Thus, for the largest expense and most critical aspects of the campaign, television advertising, the Obama campaign's reliance on big data and testing were quite limited.

Ultimately, the outcome of the 2012 election likely rested on factors outside of the control of the campaign. As political science research has long shown, economic factors typically have a disproportionately strong effect on presidential election outcomes.[50] In 2012, while the overall unemployment rate remained high, the rate of unemployment had begun to decline as Election Day approached.[51] Indeed, the overwhelming majority of forecasting models from political scientists, many of them relying on indicators largely unrelated to the decisions and actions of the Obama and Romney campaigns, predicted months in advance that Obama would win the election (and in some cases by a predicted margin that was remarkably accurate).[52] All of this suggests that the Obama campaign's much vaunted use of big data had a minimal impact on the results of the 2012 election and almost certainly was not responsible for determining the election's outcome.

FUTURE OF BIG DATA IN CAMPAIGNS

Despite some of the inflated claims about the significance of big data in determining the outcome of the 2012 presidential election, the Obama campaign's use of big data and extensive testing did successfully mobilize millions of voters. Romney's campaign, however, did much the same and was able to wash out any major gains that Obama may have generated from its operation. Of course, the fact that each campaign neutralized the other does not mean that the use of big data is unimportant. Indeed, big data and its use in campaigns are here to stay.

Following the 2012 election, the Republican Party and its allies immediately began to invest large sums of money into improving its data operations. One company, BehaviorMatrix, in partnership with the company CrowdVerb, currently tracks online information that voters leave on Facebook, Twitter, blogs, and other Internet forums. After combining this information with data from state voter files, it generates models to predict the voter's political opinions and emotions. The algorithms they generate also help to identify which individuals lead and influence friends, family, and others. These "influencers" can be valuable to a campaign, as research overwhelmingly shows that voters respond best to political messages that come from people they know.[53] In 2014, Behavior Matrix used its technology to assist Senator Mitch McConnell of Kentucky in his surprisingly comfortable 15.5 percentage point margin of victory over Democrat Alison Lundergan Grimes.[54]

Heading into the 2016 election, major candidates for president have already begun their efforts to compile data. Ready PAC (formerly Ready for Hillary), a super PAC created to help elect Hillary Clinton to the White House, was active as early as the 2014 midterm election in sharing data on its donors and supporters in exchange for data on donors and supporters in the databases of Democratic House, Senate, and gubernatorial candidates, as well as several Democratic committees and allied organizations.[55] These "list swaps" are designed to build goodwill with fellow Democrats, particularly with major state party leaders whose lists are typically not as extensive as the lists that a major national campaign can build. More importantly, these exchanges may give the Clinton campaign an edge in the "big data" race, an edge that, as the 2012 Obama campaign proved, can indeed help to mobilize voters, donors, and volunteers.

Republicans pledged their own strong commitment to big data collection and technological sophistication in 2016. The RNC announced it would make its database available to all Republican candidates during the entire election cycle, including the nomination phase.[56] More significantly, it promised major upgrades and refinements to its voter databases, including investments in updating all data on voters, expanding data collection, and improving voter scores and analytics.[57] In addition, the RNC announced plans to improve its social media outreach and to equip its volunteers with improved mobile applications so that voter information can be easily accessed and updated for those in the field.[58]

SUMMARY AND CONCLUSION

The role of big data was one of the most discussed aspects of the 2012 presidential election. Some of this hype was deserved. As the first half of this chapter made clear, the Obama reelection campaign organization and its "cave" did not resemble a traditional presidential campaign "war room." Advanced data collection techniques and sophisticated testing yielded additional and sometimes extremely valuable information, which, in turn, played a major role in influencing many of the campaign's key strategic decisions.

However, despite these advances, the advantage the Obama campaign may have had in the 2012 election over the Romney campaign appears to have been rather minimal, and was almost certainly not responsible for determining the outcome of the election. While voter databases contain more information than ever, a good deal of this information is of limited value, particularly consumer spending data. Even the purported advantages of microtargeting, which predates the Obama reelection campaign, may not yield any advantages, as recent evidence suggests that broadly targeted messages appear to be more effective.

The big data revolution, nonetheless, was still important in improving the overall ability of both the Obama and Romney campaigns to target voters more efficiently and effectively. In fact, one of the major takeaways from the 2012 election was not that big data did not matter at all, but rather that the Romney campaign was not nearly as ineffective as many popular accounts suggested. In the end, Obama's purported big data and technological superiority provided him with less than a two-point net advantage in Democratic turnout—not because his campaign efforts were ineffective, but rather because the Romney campaign did a reasonably effective job itself with its own big data operation.

Entering the 2016 election, big data and data analytics will continue to play a major role for every major presidential campaign. Efforts such as list swaps and improved data integration investments started as early as the 2014 midterm election. Beyond more data, more analytical testing is also likely. As one Obama analyst explained, "I don't think the next big step will be about a new source of data. It will be about better understanding the data we have."[59] Yet, all of these efforts are likely to affect the election only at the margins. Campaign-related effects, as a large body of political science research has long shown, are likely to be consequential only in the event of extremely competitive elections.

NOTES

1. Michael Scherer, "Inside the Secret World of the Data Crunchers Who Helped Obama Win," *Time*, November 7, 2012, http://swampland.time.com/2012/11/07/inside-the-secret-world-of-quants-and-data-crunchers-who-helped-obama-win and Michael Scherer, "How Obama's Data Crunchers Helped Him Win," CNN, November 8, 2012, http://www.cnn.com/2012/11/07/tech/web/obama-campaign-tech-team.

2. Cameron Joseph, "RNC Pushing to Win Tech 'Space Race'," *The Hill*, January 15, 2014, http://thehill.com/blogs/ballot-box/campaign-committees/195526-rnc-pushing-to-win-tech-space-race.

3. Joseph, "RNC Pushing to Win Tech 'Space Race'."

4. Patrick O'Connor, "Political Ads Take Targeting to the Next Level," *The Wall Street Journal*, July 14, 2014, http://www.wsj.com/articles/political-ads-take-targeting-to-the-next-level-1405381606.

5. David W. Nickerson and Todd Rogers, "Political Campaigns and Big Data," *Journal of Economic Perspectives* 28 (2014): 51–74.

6. Yochi J. Dreazen, "Democrats, Playing Catch-Up, Tap Database to Woo Potential Voters," *The Wall Street Journal*, October 31, 2006, http://www.wsj.com/articles/SB116226051099508453 and Costas Panagopoulos and Peter L. Francia, "Grassroots Mobilization in the 2008 Presidential Election," *Journal of Political Marketing* 8 (2009): 315–33.

7. David B. Magleby, "A Change Election," in *The Change Election: Money, Mobilization, and Persuasion in the 2008 Federal Elections*, ed. David B. Magleby

(Philadelphia: Temple University Press, 2011) and Panagopoulos and Francia, "Grassroots Mobilization in the 2008 Presidential Election."

8. Robert S. Montjoy, "HAVA and the States," in *Election Reform: Politics and Policy*, ed. Daniel J. Palazzolo and James W. Ceaser (Lanham, MD: Lexington Books, 2005), 25.

9. Nickerson and Rogers, "Political Campaigns and Big Data" and Sasha Issenberg, *The Victory Lab: The Secret Science of Winning Campaigns* (New York: Broadway Books, 2012).

10. Micah Cohen, "From Campaign War Room to Big-Data Broom," *The New York Times*, June 19, 2013, http://bits.blogs.nytimes.com/2013/06/19/from-campaign-war-room-to-big-data-broom.

11. Jenny Marlar, "U.S. Adjusted Unemployment Rate at 8.1% in August," Gallup, September 6, 2012, http://www.gallup.com/poll/157289/unadjusted-unemployment-rate-august.aspx and Bruce E. Caswell, "Obama By the Numbers," in *The Obama Presidency: Promise and Performance*, ed. William Crotty (Lanham, MD: Lexington Books, 2012).

12. Gallup, "Presidential Approval Ratings—Barack Obama," http://www.gallup.com/poll/116479/barack-obama-presidential-job-approval.aspx and Real Clear Politics, "President Obama Job Approval," http://www.realclearpolitics.com/epolls/other/president_obama_job_approval-1044.html.

13. Gary Younge, "The Struggle for Obama's Voters: 'I Just Wish He Could Have Been Better'," *The Guardian*, October 10, 2012, http://www.theguardian.com/world/2012/oct/10/struggle-obama-voters-wish-better and Bryan Moore, "Four Years Later, Some Iowa Democrats Have Mixed Feelings About Obama," CNN, January 3, 2012, http://www.cnn.com/2012/01/02/politics/iowa-obama-four-years-later/index.html.

14. Cohen, "From Campaign War Room to Big-Data Broom."

15. Dan Balz, "How the Obama Campaign Won the Race for Voter Data," *The Washington Post*, July 28, 2013, http://www.washingtonpost.com/politics/how-the-obama-campaign-won-the-race-for-voter-data/2013/07/28/ad32c7b4-ee4e-11e2-a1f9-ea873b7e0424_story.html and Sasha Issenberg, "How President Obama's Campaign Used Big Data to Rally Individual Voters," *MIT Technology Review*, December 19, 2012, http://www.technologyreview.com/featuredstory/509026/how-obamas-team-used-big-data-to-rally-voters.

16. Scherer, "Inside the Secret World of the Data Crunchers Who Helped Obama Win" and Balz, "How the Obama Campaign Won the Race for Voter Data."

17. Balz, "How the Obama Campaign Won the Race for Voter Data."

18. Ibid.

19. Ibid.

20. Nancy Scola, "With 'Dashboard,' Obama Campaign Aims to Bridge Online and Off," *The Atlantic*, May 24, 2012, http://www.theatlantic.com/politics/archive/2012/05/with-dashboard-obama-campaign-aims-to-bridge-online-and-off/257606.

21. Scola, "With 'Dashboard,' Obama Campaign Aims to Bridge Online and Off."

22. Balz, "How the Obama Campaign Won the Race for Voter Data." See also Issenberg, "How President Obama's Campaign Used Big Data to Rally Individual

Voters" and Scherer, "Inside the Secret World of the Data Crunchers Who Helped Obama Win."

23. Nickerson and Rogers, "Political Campaigns and Big Data."

24. Nickerson and Rogers, "Political Campaigns and Big Data" and Balz, "How the Obama Campaign Won the Race for Voter Data."

25. Ibid.

26. Issenberg, "How President Obama's Campaign Used Big Data to Rally Individual Voters." See also John Sides and Lynn Vavreck, "Obama's Not-So-Big Data," *Pacific Standard*, January 21, 2014, http://www.psmag.com/politics-and-law/obamas-big-data-inconclusive-results-political-campaigns-72687 and Andrew Lampitt, "The Real Story of How Big Analytics Helped Obama Win," InfoWorld, February 14, 2013, http://www.infoworld.com/article/2613587/big-data/the-real-story-of-how-big-data-analytics-helped-obama-win.html.

27. Issenberg, "How President Obama's Campaign Used Big Data to Rally Individual Voters" and Sides and Vavreck, "Obama's Not-So-Big Data."

28. Maggie Haberman and Alexander Burns, "Mitt Romney's ORCA Program Couldn't Stay Afloat," Politico, November 9, 2012, http://www.politico.com/news/stories/1112/83653.html and Michael Kranish, "ORCA, Mitt Romney's High-Tech Get-Out-the-Vote Program, Crashed on Election Day," Boston.com, November 10, 2012, http://www.boston.com/news/politics/2012/president/candidates/romney/2012/11/10/orca-mitt-romney-high-tech-get-out-the-vote-program-crashed-election-day/gfIS8VkzDcJcXCrHoV0nsI/story.html.

29. Stephanie Marcus, "Mitt Romney's Project ORCA Failure: Broken ORCA App Cost Him Thousands of Votes," *The Huffington Post*, November 10, 2012, http://www.huffingtonpost.com/2012/11/10/mitt-romney-project-orca-broken-app-cost-thousands-votes_n_2109986.html.

30. Ryan D. Enos and Anthony Fowler, "Aggregate Effects of Large-Scale Campaigns on Voter Turnout," http://people.hmdc.harvard.edu/~renos/papers/EnosFowlerGOTV/EnosFowler_AggregateGOTV.pdf. See also Brian Fung, "The Diminishing Returns of Big-Data Campaigning," *The National Journal*, May 8, 2013, http://www.nationaljournal.com/tech/the-diminishing-returns-of-big-data-campaigning-20130508.

31. Enos and Fowler, "Aggregate Effects of Large-Scale Campaigns on Voter Turnout." The findings are also summarized in Fung, "The Diminishing Returns of Big-Data Campaigning."

32. See Fung, "The Diminishing Returns of Big-Data Campaigning."

33. Ibid.

34. John Sides, "Obama's Voter Mobilization Was Barely More Effective Than Romney's," The Monkey Cage, May 7, 2013, http://themonkeycage.org/2013/05/07/obamas-voter-mobilization-was-barely-more-effective-than-romneys.

35. Terrence McCoy, "The Creepiness Factor: How Obama and Romney Are Getting to Know You," *The Atlantic*, April 10, 2012, http://www.theatlantic.com/politics/archive/2012/04/the-creepiness-factor-how-obama-and-romney-are-getting-to-know-you/255499.

36. Quoted in Sides and Vavreck, "Obama's Not-So-Big Data."

37. Justin Gargiulo, "Why the Best Data in the World Won't Win You an Election," *Campaigns & Elections*, July 27, 2014, http://www.campaignsandelections.com/magazine/1690/why-the-best-data-in-the-world-won-t-win-you-an-election.

38. John Sides and Lynn Vavreck, *The Gamble: Choice and Chance in the 2012 Presidential Election* (Princeton, NJ: Princeton University Press, 2013) and Sides and Vavreck, "Obama's Not-So-Big Data."

39. Donald P. Green and Ron Shachar, "Habit Formation and Political Behaviour: Evidence of Consuetude in Voter Turnout," *British Journal of Political Science* 30 (2000): 561–73, and Eric Plutzer, "Becoming a Habitual Voter: Inertia, Resources, and Growth in Young Adulthood," *American Political Science Review* 96 (2002): 41–56.

40. Sides and Vavreck, "Obama's Not-So-Big Data."

41. Nickerson and Todd Rogers, "Political Campaigns and Big Data."

42. Ibid.

43. Eitan D. Hersh, *Hacking the Electorate: How Campaigns Perceive Voters* (New York: Cambridge University Press, 2015), Table 6.2, p. 127. These findings are also discussed in Sides and Vavreck, "Obama's Not-So-Big Data."

44. Hersh, *Hacking the Electorate*, Table 8.1, p. 172.

45. Eitan D. Hersh and Brian F. Schaffner, "Targeted Campaign Appeals and the Value of Ambiguity," *Journal of Politics* 75 (2013): 520–34.

46. Hersh and Schaffner, "Targeted Campaign Appeals and the Value of Ambiguity" and Sides and Vavreck, "Obama's Not-So-Big Data."

47. Quoted in Sides and Vavreck, "Obama's Not-So-Big Data."

48. Sides and Vavreck, "Obama's Not-So-Big Data."

49. Ibid.

50. See for a good summary of the literature on this subject, see Michael S. Lewis-Beck and Mary Stegmaier, "Economic Determinants of Electoral Outcomes," *Annual Review of Political Science* 3 (2000): 183–219.

51. Michael Falcone, "Timing Is Everything: Unemployment Drops Below 8 Percent With One Month to Go," ABC News, October 5, 2012, http://abcnews.go.com/blogs/politics/2012/10/timing-is-everything-unemployment-drops-below-8-percent-with-one-month-to-go-the-note.

52. See the special issue of *PS: Political Science and Politics* 45 (October 2012).

53. Cohen, "From Campaign War Room to Big-Data Broom."

54. Ibid.

55. Dan Merica, "Hoping for '16 Payoff, Ready for Hillary Greases Midterm Wheels," CNN, September 10, 2014, http://www.cnn.com/2014/09/10/politics/clinton-email-swaps-2016.

56. Patrick O'Connor, "RNC, GOP Candidates, Super PACs to Share Voter Data," *The Wall Street Journal*, May 7, 2015, http://blogs.wsj.com/washwire/2015/05/07/rnc-gop-candidates-super-pacs-to-share-voter-data.

57. David M. Drucker, "RNC Soups Up 2016 Voter-Turnout Program," *Washington Examiner*, January 28, 2015, http://www.washingtonexaminer.com/rnc-soups-up-2016-voter-turnout-program/article/2559419.

58. Jennifer G. Hickey, "RNC Embraces Social Media, Launches New Facebook App," NewsMax, June 13, 2015, http://www.newsmax.com/Politics/

Republican-National-Committee-social-media-Facebook/2014/09/22/id/596058. See also the RNC's Growth and Opportunity Project, http://goproject.gop.com/RNC_Growth_Opportunity_Book_2013.pdf.

    59. Quoted in Cohen, "From Campaign War Room to Big-Data Broom."

FOR MORE READING

Hersh, Eitan D. *Hacking the Electorate: How Campaigns Perceive Voters*. New York: Cambridge University Press, 2015.

Issenberg, Sasha. *The Victory Lab: The Secret Science of Winning Campaigns*. New York: Broadway Books, 2012.

Nickerson, David W. and Todd Rogers. 2014. "Political Campaigns and Big Data." *Journal of Economic Perspectives* 28(2): 51–74.

Sides, John and Lynn Vavreck. *The Gamble: Choice and Chance in the 2012 Presidential Election*. Princeton, NJ: Princeton University Press, 2013.

Chapter 3

Democracy in Crisis? Myths and Misunderstandings about Voter Turnout and Election Fraud

Voter turnout is one of the most thoroughly studied subjects in political science. One could literally fill entire rooms with the amount of scholarship that has been devoted to understanding how and why voters and potential voters exercise their most fundamental of democratic freedoms. The reason for this is simple: voting is essential to democratic citizenship. If one accepts the Founding Fathers' belief that government derives its legitimacy from the consent of the governed, then participation by citizens in free, fair, and regular elections is necessary for a functioning democracy to exist.

Historians and political scientists frequently trace the evolution of American democracy in terms of when and how certain groups like women, African Americans, and young adults received the right to vote. Indeed, political observers and scholars often view expanding democratic participation and increasing voter turnout as a measure of democratic success. However, in spite of the fact that voter turnout is so often under the microscope, several commonly held assumptions about the subject are questionable.

Perhaps the most common misconception about voter turnout is the belief that American voter turnout has been in general decline. Some have gone as far as to label the situation a "turnout crisis."[1] But the latest research on the subject has called this idea into question, concluding that the decline in turnout might not be as serious as many observers had suggested.[2] Moreover, discussions about declining voter turnout in the United States typically ignore the fact that the modest voter turnout decline that does exist appears to parallel a decline in most established democracies as well.

A more recent controversy regarding voter turnout revolves around discussion of alleged voter fraud and voter identification laws. In what has developed into a divisive partisan issue, rhetoric surrounding these issues has become heated and often exaggerated. On the one side, we hear claims of rampant voter fraud, used as justification for stricter voter identification laws. As one account surmises, "Unfortunately, in some U.S. cities, voter fraud has been so common and so pervasive for so long that it's more likely to be a punch line than a felony."[3] On the other side, we hear charges that voter identification laws are unnecessary and serve only to suppress the vote, particularly among young and minority voters. Implementing these laws across the 50 states would presumably result in "catastrophic consequences."[4]

There is very little evidence to support either contention. Voter fraud, especially fraud perpetrated by impersonation or stealing another's identification, is exceptionally rare. Indeed, it is almost nonexistent. Likewise, voter identification laws have had only a very modest effect on voter turnout, with some studies suggesting that they have had no significant impact at all.

Given the importance of voter turnout, electoral integrity, and voting rights to a healthy democracy, these issues warrant serious attention and objective discussion. In the pages that follow, we first review the factors that political science research has suggested can affect voter turnout. We then seek to cut through the sometimes wild claims that suggest American democracy is in crisis, whether because of low turnout, election fraud, or voter suppression.

WHAT AFFECTS VOTER TURNOUT?

Discussions about voting behavior in the United States often begin with the premise that Americans do not vote in percentages equal to the past or that they do not vote in numbers proportionate to citizens in other democracies. Most American government textbooks frame the discussion of voting in the United States in terms of low voter turnout, noting correctly that the United States ranks near the bottom of the world in voter turnout.[5] During the campaign of 2014, a number of stories featured discussion about the "abysmally low turnout" in the United States."[6] The picture these accounts present, at least implicitly, is that our democracy is in decline.[7]

Many scholars echo similar sentiments. Works such as *The Disappearing American Voter*, *Why Americans Don't Vote*, *Why Americans* Still *Don't Vote* (emphasis added), *Why America Stopped Voting*, and *Where Have All the Voters Gone?* all suggest in their titles that American turnout is in decline.[8] One author, for example, explicitly refers to "the turnout problem."[9] Another summarizes, "In ever larger numbers over the past three decades, Americans have been tuning out campaigns and staying home on Election Day. Turnout has fallen in virtually every type of American election."[10]

There are a variety of explanations offered for the decline in voter turnout in this research. We can divide these explanations into two broad categories, institutional and noninstitutional factors. Institutional factors focus, simply, on the rules governing the administration of elections. Noninstitutional factors include various characteristics of individual citizens. As it happens, some types of people are more likely than others to vote. Noninstitutional factors also include various aspects of the campaign itself. We will discuss each of these in turn.

Institutional Factors: The Rules

The act of voting in the United States is more difficult than in other democracies. This, many believe, drives turnout down. Borrowing from economists, some political scientists hold that individuals are "rational actors" who weigh the costs of voting against its perceived benefits. For example, filling out a registration form, traveling long distances to reach a polling place, and then waiting in a line to cast a ballot might be too much of a cost when compared with the perceived benefit of casting one vote.

Institutional factors may be important because they can reduce the costs of voting by making the process more accessible and convenient for citizens. Most voting laws and the rules that determine voting requirements are made by the states. Beyond complying with antidiscrimination provisions contained in the Voting Rights Act of 1965, states are free to create their own standards for voter registration, determine the location of polling places, decide how long these polling places will be open, set absentee ballot requirements, and more.[11]

Despite the idiosyncrasies of each state's voting laws and requirements, several general aspects of election law in the United States are important to understand in a discussion of possible reasons as to why people do not vote. Many studies suggest that restrictive laws, such as registration requirements, or in particular, deadlines that force citizens to register early in the election season, result in decreased levels of voter turnout.[12] For example, in most states, people are required to register to vote before Election Day. The length of time varies from state to state, but it is usually at least a few weeks prior to the election. This is not the case in other established democracies, where voter registration is the responsibility of the national government. Some people, even the best intentioned, simply forget to register until it is too late or to reregister after moving. The result is that they cannot vote.

In most other democracies in the world, voting takes place on weekends or special holidays dedicated to voting. In the United States, Election Day is on a Tuesday. This is significant because most people work on Tuesdays. In order to vote, people have several inconvenient options. They can rise early and go to the polls before work, or they can vote during a lunch break, during work (after having boss's permission), or after work. This added inconvenience (or cost, in the language of rational choice theory) may reduce the likelihood of voting.

There are also more elections in the United States than in any other country. In most European democracies there are only a few elections (e.g., representative to parliament, representative to the European Union, and a scattering of local offices) held in any given four- or five-year period. By comparison, the U.S. system offers a bewildering array of elections almost every year. There are, for example, primary and general elections for the U.S. House of Representatives and other offices every two years (all even-numbered years). In some states and cities, citizens vote in primary and general elections for governor, state legislature, mayor, city council, and so on, during odd-numbered years. Elections to decide on ballot propositions also can occur in any year and at different times of the year. In some rare instances, citizens might even have to vote in a recall election. Put simply, the decentralized system of elections in the United States asks Americans to vote with great frequency.

Additionally, voting in the United States can be a somewhat complicated affair. In most democracies, citizens might be asked to cast a vote for a political party and maybe for a single member of Parliament from their district, and perhaps for a few other offices. Our system of federalism and separated government means there are a multiplicity of offices that voters must decide on, from president down to county commissioner, local sheriff, circuit court judges, and more. In total, there are over one million elective offices in the United States, and ballots rarely simplify matters by giving voters the option of voting a straight-party ticket for all offices.[13] It is the rare individual who has taken the time to research each candidate running for each office. The array of choices citizens face at the voting booth can be intimidating, especially to first-time voters, who are inexperienced and more likely to be lacking in information about the process and the choices facing them. In fact, it may be so intimidating that they decide to stay home.

Finally, with respect to the rules governing elections, plurality-winner rules in single-member districts decide nearly all elections for federal office in the United States. This is unlike electoral systems in most other democracies, which employ a system of proportional representation, either completely or combined with plurality-winner/single-member districts. Some research has suggested that voter turnout is lower in plurality-winner/single-member district systems because they tend to produce two-party systems, which provide citizens with fewer choices, presumably reducing the incentive for citizens who support minor-party candidates to vote.[14]

Citizens can become especially frustrated with only two choices because candidates in a two-party system often blur their differences in an attempt to capture the "median voter," who falls in the middle of the ideological spectrum.[15] For voters aged between 18 and 24, this may be especially problematic. Young voters are less likely to perceive differences between the two major parties and often express dissatisfaction with the major-party candidates running for office.[16] In short, the choices facing citizens on Election Day may not seem as clear as they would like them to be, which reduces the incentive to vote.

While some of these rules may depress voter turnout, there have been several efforts in recent years to ease the burden on citizens to vote. The first, and perhaps most prominent, was the National Voter Registration Act of 1993 (the Motor Voter Bill) that requires motor vehicle offices nationwide to accept voter registration applications, and allows other government agencies and programs to do so as well. Mail-in voter registration also has become common in many states. As of 2015, a dozen states and the District of Columbia further allow same day (Election Day) registration.

Many states are doing more to reduce the burden of voting itself. All states have absentee ballots that allow individuals to vote from a location other than their designated polling place and at a time that is convenient to them. A total of 22 states conduct at least some of their elections entirely by mail; three (Oregon, Washington, and Colorado) hold all of their elections by mail; and 27 states and the District of Columbia allow "no excuse" absentee voting, meaning that individuals do not have to have a reason for requesting an absentee ballot.[17] Finally, more than half of the states require that private businesses give employees time off to vote, and many provide that the employee be paid for this time (at least in some cases).[18] However, in the end, the evidence is mixed about whether these institutional reforms have had significant and substantive effects on voter turnout.[19]

Non-institutional Factors

Beyond institutional arrangements, numerous other influences can affect voter turnout. The first set of factors deals with individuals themselves. For example, one argument is that voting is a habit: the more a person does it, the more likely he or she is to keep doing it.[20] This helps explain why younger citizens are less likely to vote than their older counterparts.[21] People who feel connected to their communities are also more likely to vote, if only because they have something to protect or advocate (e.g., lower property taxes for homeowners).

Another reason why people do not vote is that many are either not interested in, or are cynical about, government, politics, and politicians. It is common, for example, to hear people complain that campaigns are too long, too negative, and focus too much on personality rather than on the issues. This is significant because these negative perceptions can lead to cynicism about campaign politics, the political system, and the belief that voting has the potential to affect change. These feelings are important because an individual's sense of political efficacy (the confidence an individual has in their own political understanding and abilities), trust in government, and sense of duty associated with citizenship are often significant predictors of voting.[22] Along these lines, people who identify with, or feel attached to a political party are more apt to vote than people who claim they are independents.[23]

Related to these general attitudes about politics and the individual's place in the political system is knowledge about politics. Those who are more knowledgeable about politics are more likely to vote. In fact, formal education itself has a similar effect on an individual's likelihood of voting. The more educated one is in terms of formal schooling, the more likely that individual is to vote.[24] This may be the result of the fact that our system of government, like the institutional arrangements governing elections, is fairly complex. Individuals can easily become confused about their choices and the implications of those choices.

In addition to education, the academic literature overwhelmingly confirms that other socioeconomic, demographic, and background variables can affect turnout, including income, gender, race, marital status, residential mobility, religiosity, and organizational memberships.[25] Age also has been the focus in a few studies.[26] In the late 1960s and early 1970s, at the height of the Vietnam War, young people, who opposed the military draft, mobilized around the slogan, "old enough to fight, old enough to vote." Eventually, this led to ratification of the Twenty-sixth Amendment in 1971, which lowered the voting age from 18 to 21. In 1972, the first election after the amendment's ratification, youth turnout reached an impressive rate of 54.6 percent.[27] However, in the years that followed, youth turnout rates have been consistently lower than the turnout rates for older Americans (see Figure 3.1). In spite of this persistent age gap in voter turnout rates, commentators often predict that the coming election will be the "big year" for young voters. However, these expectations nearly always fall short.[28]

A final set of factors that affect voter turnout has to do with the campaign itself. Competitive elections tend to see higher voter turnout, quite likely

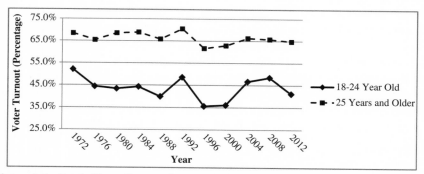

Figure 3.1 Youth Voter Turnout in Presidential Elections, 1972–2012. *Source*: The Center for Information & Research on Civic Learning and Engagement. http://www.civic youth.org/wp-content/uploads/2007/10/72_12_cps_voting_WithLogos.xls.

because individuals are more likely to believe their vote will make a difference. This may be one reason why voter turnout was so low in 1996, a year few thought Bob Dole had a real chance to defeat the incumbent President Bill Clinton. In addition, elections that generate more media coverage tend to stimulate greater interest, which, in turn, leads to greater turnout.[29] Similarly, candidates, parties, interest groups, and ordinary citizens can play a role in stimulating interest in the campaign as well, by talking to other citizens. Individuals who meet or are contacted by a candidate are far more likely to get involved than those who have not.[30] One especially interesting recent research finding is that personalized campaign messages and appeals are a particularly effective method of generating increased turnout.[31] This is especially true with regard to person-to-person contact, which can be extremely effective in getting people to vote. In other words, one person can make a difference by simply talking to friends, family, coworkers, or associates.[32]

In sum, there are a multiplicity of factors that affect whether individuals will exercise their most fundamental of democratic freedoms. They are important to understand because, as noted earlier, voter turnout confers the "consent of the governed"—a vital component to the legitimacy of democratic government. In the next section we turn our attention to the myth of the "vanishing voter," focusing on how voter turnout is measured and reported.

VOTER TURNOUT IN THE UNITED STATES

What can we make of the claim that American democracy is in peril because of ever-lower and dangerous levels of voter turnout? Is voter turnout in the United States in decline? On the face of it this claim is problematic if we consider the past three presidential elections. In 2004 the Republicans were very successful in mobilizing their supporters to turn out and vote, while the same was true of Democrats in 2008 and to some lesser extent in 2012. By one measure turnout in 2008 was higher than in any presidential election since 1968. Even over a longer period of time, to suggest that voters in the United States are vanishing overstates the case. The fact is that when measured correctly, voter turnout has remained relatively constant over the past few decades. Moreover, any decline in voter turnout in the United States is quite consistent with developments in other countries.

Voter Turnout: A Statistic in Search of a Standard

Determining voter turnout would seem to be a fairly straightforward calculation: the number of votes cast (the numerator) is divided by the number of potential voters (the denominator). On the one hand, it is relatively easy to tabulate the number of votes counted in any given election. On the other hand, tabulating the number of potential voters is not as simple a task as one might think. Voter turnout statistics typically utilize census data, which counts all those living in the United States who are eighteen or older. This is referred to as the voting age population (VAP).

Until fairly recently, the VAP measure was the accepted standard in calculating voter turnout rates. However, political scientists Michael McDonald and Samuel Popkin have noted that the VAP measure is problematic because it fails to tabulate the number of *eligible* voters accurately. Age, they note, is not the only criterion for a person to be considered eligible to vote. Noncitizens are ineligible to vote, as are prisoners and felons in many states. Several states even prohibit ex-felons from voting. Most accounts of voter turnout throughout American history fail to consider the actual eligible population.

McDonald and Popkin suggest that the decline in voter turnout in the past fifty to sixty years has been systematically overestimated because of the increase in the number of those eighteen years of age or older who are noncitizens or felons. In addition, some states do not allow the mentally incompetent to vote, although this is only a tiny fraction of the population (perhaps one-tenth of one percent). McDonald and Popkin also examine residency requirements in various states, which they estimate disenfranchise approximately 1 percent of the VAP in any given election.[33] Finally, they note that the census has become more accurate over the past half century. In 1940, the Census Bureau estimated that their count missed approximately 5.8 percent of the population. Many of these "missed" citizens were likely to be poor and less educated, and therefore less likely to vote, resulting in potentially biased turnout statistics. This number shrank to 1.8 percent in 1990.

More simply, the number of people incorrectly counted as potential voters—the voting-age population—has grown relative to those who have reported voting. These discrepancies have collectively created a situation whereby the statistics have *overestimated* the number of people eligible to vote, thus *underestimating* voter turnout. This explains much of the reason that previous estimates using the VAP statistic appear to have overstated declines in voter turnout.

A final aspect of our discussion centers around the calculation of the number of votes cast. Many experts believe that one of the reasons voter turnout was so high in the late 1800s is that there was a good deal of election fraud in various states and localities.[34] For example, some research suggests that in certain areas of the country corrupt election officials "stuffed" ballot boxes or deliberately reported false returns, often inflating the vote totals for the candidate of the party in power.[35] This would, of course, lead to inflated rates of voter turnout. Unfortunately, no complete data are available to estimate the effects of vote fraud on voter turnout.

McDonald and Popkin's research points to another fact worth considering. The numerator in the voter turnout equation relies on the number of votes cast for president (during presidential election years) or the number of votes cast for members of Congress (during midterm election years). However, this method systematically undercounts the number of votes cast because some citizens, albeit a small percentage (approximately 2 percent), show up to the polls to vote for ballot propositions or local offices but abstain from casting votes for higher offices.[36] This would not have been possible until the widespread adoption of the Australian ballot in the 1890s, a period that corresponds with yet another fairly sharp decline in turnout.[37]

Table 3.1 shows estimates of the turnout rate using the VAP as well as voting eligible population (VEP). Importantly, the VEP calculation only corrects for felons and noncitizens who are ineligible, not for the mentally incompetent, those disenfranchised by residency requirements, or census undercounting. In other words, the corrections are conservative. The final column shows a fairly significant increase in the difference using these two methods to calculate the turnout rate. The point is that VEP estimates of turnout suggest a less dramatic decline than do those based on VAP.

Regardless of whether one calculates voter turnout using VAP or VEP, it is still true that turnout in the United States has declined slightly over the past

Table 3.1   VAP vs. VEP: Voter Turnout Rates in U.S. Elections, 1972–2012

Year	VAP Turnout Rate	VEP Turnout Rate	Difference
1972	55.2	56.2	1.0
1974	38.2	39.1	0.9
1976	53.5	54.8	1.3
1978	37.9	39.0	1.1
1980	52.8	54.7	1.9
1982	40.6	43.0	2.4
1984	53.3	57.2	3.9
1986	36.5	39.0	2.5
1988	50.3	54.2	3.9
1990	36.5	39.8	3.3
1992	55.0	60.6	5.6
1994	38.9	41.8	2.9
1996	48.9	52.6	3.7
1998	36.1	39.0	2.9
2000	51.2	55.6	4.4
2002	36.3	40.5	4.2
2004	55.4	60.7	5.3
2006	37.1	41.3	4.2
2008	56.9	62.3	5.4
2012	53.6	58.6	5.0

Source: See Michael P. McDonald's "United States Election Project" at http://www.electproject.org/home/voter-turnout/voter-turnout-data.

century and remains lower when compared with turnout in other established democracies. Yet, the way in which some political observers present this fact often makes the situation appear bleaker than it actually is. For example, Figure 3.2 presents turnout rates (using VAP) in the United States from 1824 to 2012. Here, the decline in voter turnout appears to be dramatic.

However, Figure 3.3 presents data measuring voter turnout from 1920 (when the size of the electorate effectively doubled) to 2012. Here a decline is apparent as well, but a comparison of the trend lines in each figure suggest that the recent decline might be less serious than some portray it to be. In fact, since 1976, when turnout was 55.2 percent (using VAP statistics), it has hovered consistently in the low 50 percent range. This only reinforces the point that voters do not appear to be "vanishing."

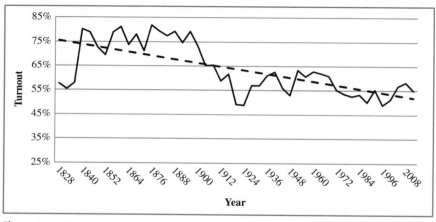

Figure 3.2 Voter Turnout in Presidential Elections, 1828–2012. *Source*: Gerhard Peters and John Woolley, "Voter Turnout in Presidential Elections," American Presidency Project, at http://www.presidency.ucsb.edu/data/turnout.php.

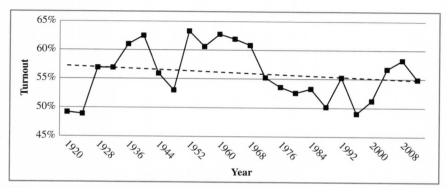

Figure 3.3 Voter Turnout in Presidential Elections, 1920–2012.

While turnout has dropped modestly over the course of the past century or so, U.S. rates are consistently lower when measured against turnout in other established democracies. It is also true, however, that voter turnout has been declining in other nations over the past fifty years.[38] As Figure 3.4 indicates, average voter turnout from 1950 to 2012 has declined significantly in other established democracies. In fact, while U.S. voter turnout is lower than all of the others, the decline in the United States during this period is less than in any of these countries (see Table 3.2).

It is worth noting, however, that the voter turnout rate in the 2014 election was unusually low in the United States at just 35.9 percent of the VEP.[39] This has only reinforced the alarmist tone that American democracy is in trouble.[40] However, we would urge a broader view of recent turnout trends. Just two years earlier in the 2012 presidential election, the turnout rate was a

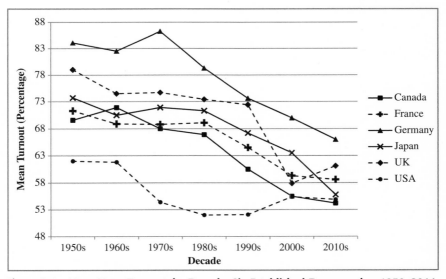

Figure 3.4   Mean Voter Turnout, by Decade, Six Established Democracies, 1950–2014.
Source: "Voter Turnout." International Institute for Democracy and Electoral Assistance (International IDEA), http://www.idea.int/vt/. All figures are calculated based on voting age population.

Table 3.2   Decline in Voter Turnout, Six Established Democracies, 1950–2014

	Canada	France	Germany	Japan	U.K.	U.S.
Mean, 1950s	69.6%	71.3%	84.1%	73.7%	79.1%	59.3%
Mean, 2010s	54.2%	58.6%	66.0%	55.8%	61.1%	55.9%
Decline	15.4	12.7	18.1	17.9	17.9	7.1

Source: International Institute for Democracy and Electoral Assistance, http://www.idea.int/vt. All figures are calculated based on VAP.

respectable 58.6 percent of the VEP—a rate slightly higher than in the hyper-competitive 2000 presidential election when turnout was 55.3 percent of the VEP.[41] The 2014 election notwithstanding, it seems difficult to argue that voter turnout in the United States has reached crisis levels.

VOTER FRAUD, VOTER ID LAWS AND OTHER
CONTROVERSIES SURROUNDING THE RIGHT TO VOTE

Much was made in the aftermath of the hotly contested presidential election of 2000 about African Americans waiting in long lines to vote or being denied the vote in certain areas of northern Florida. Typically, Democrats were the source of these claims. Others, mainly Republicans, asserted that many absentee ballots from members of the military were unjustly disqualified.[42] In 2004, there were problems with voting machines and long lines at many inner city polling stations in Ohio, a state that was expected to be critical to victory for both candidates. Democrats complained that these long lines likely decreased voter turnout in these areas, which may have cost its presidential nominee, John Kerry, critical votes.[43] In 2008, there was much ado made about the activities of the pro-Obama group Association of Community Organizations for Reform Now (ACORN). Republicans claimed the group was organizing registration and voting efforts for individuals who were not actually eligible to vote.[44]

By 2012, rhetoric concerning alleged disenfranchisement and voter fraud had evolved to the point where there are now two easily identifiable sets of charges and claims, each associated with either Democratic or Republican supporters. Republicans, claiming they have evidence of widespread voter fraud, insist on the need to secure the "integrity" of elections by enacting laws that demand citizens produce photo identification in order to vote.[45] Democrats counter these claims by asserting that evidence of voter impersonation—the type of fraud that identification laws intend to eliminate—is exceedingly rare. They further claim that voter identification (voter ID) laws are actually a ploy by Republicans to suppress turnout among lower income and minority citizens who traditionally support the Democratic Party.[46]

Is there any merit to these claims? Is voter fraud a problem? Do voter identification laws suppress turnout, particularly among minorities and lower income citizens? The systematic evidence, based on available research, suggests that both charges are exaggerated. While anecdotes of fraud and of disenfranchisement due to identification requirements abound, and while suggestions of widespread abuse of fraud or voter suppression make for good partisan rhetoric, these claims are not supported by the evidence.

There have been several systematic studies during the past decade examining the extent to which voter fraud may be a problem in national elections, and all come to the same conclusion. In-person voter fraud, where an individual claims to be someone he or she is not in order to vote, does occur, but is exceedingly rare. Documented cases of voter fraud in any given national election rarely number higher than a few dozen.[47] In one of the most comprehensive studies on voter fraud, Justin Levitt of the Brennan Center for Justice at New York University's School of Law reported that "there have been a handful of substantiated cases of individual ineligible voters attempting to defraud the election system. But by any measure, voter fraud is extraordinarily rare."[48] Levitt notes the lack of incentive to commit voter fraud given the harsh federal penalties (five years in prison and a $10,000 fine) and additional state penalties for the inconsequential benefit of an additional vote. Instead, Levitt concludes that purported cases of voter fraud can be typically traced to benign errors, such as clerical and typographical errors. He explains, "Often, what appears to be voter fraud—a person attempting to vote under a false name, for example—can be traced back to a typo. . . . For example, despite having died in 1997, Alan J. Mandel was alleged to have voted in 1998; upon further investigation, Alan J. Mandell (two "l"s), who was very much alive and voting at the time, explained that local election workers simply checked the wrong name off of the list."[49]

In North Carolina, a story broke that appeared to indicate a clear case of voter fraud. A report from the conservative think tank, Civitas, presented evidence showing that some 2,214 voters in the state cast ballots at the ripe age of 110.[50] However, upon further investigation it was shown that these numbers were the artifact of an old voter registration law, which, before 1960, only required people to provide proof that they were of legal age to vote. A person did not have to provide an exact date of birth. For those who did not report a date of birth, the state entered a default year of 1900. Of course, none of those voters were actually born in 1900. All proved to be alive and eligible voters. What appeared to be voter fraud was not.[51]

If there is no evidence of widespread or systematic voter fraud, why the push for identification laws? Part of the reason is that they were included as one of the recommendations of the blue ribbon Commission on Federal Election Reform, formed after the 2000 presidential election and chaired by former President Jimmy Carter and former Secretary of State James Baker III.[52] Critics, of course, as noted earlier, allege more cynical reasons which they believe are rooted in efforts by Republicans to gain an electoral advantage by disenfranchising young and minority voters who disproportionately vote for Democrats. In fact, some Republicans have added fuel to this suspicion by admitting to this motivation publicly, as one North Carolina Republican did on the *Daily Show with Jon Stewart* in 2013.[53] Democrats not only question

Republican motives but predict that voter identification laws could have a significant impact in reducing voter turnout.[54] However, while some preliminary research suggests that they may have a small negative effect on voter turnout,[55] other studies find no effect.[56] In reviewing a summary of the research on the effects of voter identification laws on voter turnout, one political scientist concludes, "None of this is to say that voter identification laws are unproblematic. It is just difficult to prove that they are associated with lower turnout."[57]

CONCLUSION

Over the past several decades, a myriad of claims have pushed the notion that American democracy is in crisis whether due to low voter turnout or most recently, voter fraud and voter suppression. Yet, as this chapter makes clear, American democracy is not in crisis. Voter turnout is not in serious decline, even in the aftermath of several states passing voter identification laws, and voter fraud is nearly nonexistent.

Of course, this is not to suggest that American democracy is perfect, nor that voter fraud or voter suppression are not important issues worthy of our attention. A democracy requires fairness in the electoral process for citizens to respect election outcomes and the legitimacy of government. But proper and informed perspective on these issues is critical.

NOTES

1. John Nichols, "What to Do About Record Low Voter Turnout? Call a Holiday!" *The Nation*, November 17, 2014, http://www.thenation.com/blog/190769/what-do-about-record-low-voter-turnout-call-holiday#.

2. We wish to acknowledge the contribution to this chapter made by Michael P. McDonald and Samuel Popkin, "The Myth of the Vanishing Voter," *American Political Science Review* 95 (2001): 963–74.

3. Horace Cooper, "Voter Fraud Is Real: Why the Voting Rights Act Should Be Used to Fight Election Fraud," The National Center for Public Policy Research, August 2012, http://www.nationalcenter.org/NPA636.html.

4. "Judge Strikes Photo ID Requirement for PA Voters," WPXI News, January 17, 2014, http://www.wpxi.com/news/news/local/judge-strikes-photo-id-requirement-pa-voters/ncr7m/.

5. See, for example, Morris P. Fiorina, Paul E. Peterson, with Bertram Johnson, *The New American Democracy*, 3rd ed. (New York: Longman, 2003), 164–5.

6. "The Worst Voter Turnout in 72 Years," *The New York Times*, November 11, 2014, http://www.nytimes.com/2014/11/12/opinion/the-worst-voter-turnout-in-72-years.html.

7. See Bryan Mercurio, "Democracy in Decline: Can Internet Voting Save the Electoral Process?" *John Marshall Journal of Computer & Information Law* 22 (2004), papers.ssrn.com/sol3/papers.cfm?abstract_id=590441.

8. Ruy A. Teixeira, *Why Americans Don't Vote: Turnout Decline in the United States, 1960–1984* (Westport, Conn.: Greenwood, 1987); Ruy A. Teixeira, *The Disappearing American Voter* (Washington, DC: Brookings Institution, 1992); Frances Fox Piven and Richard A. Cloward, *Why Americans Don't Vote* (New York: Pantheon, 1988); Frances Fox Piven and Richard A. Cloward, *Why Americans Still Don't Vote: And Why Politicians Want It That Way* (Boston: Beacon, 2000); Mark Lawrence Kornbluh, *Why America Stopped Voting: The Decline of Participatory Democracy and the Emergence of Modern American Politics* (New York: New York University, 2000); Martin P. Wattenberg, *Where Have All the Voters Gone?* (Cambridge, MA: Harvard University Press, 2002); Lisa Hill, "Low Voter Turnout in the United States: Is Compulsory Voting a Viable Solution?" *Journal of Theoretical Politics* 18 (2006): 207–32; Arend Lijphart, "Unequal Participation: Democracy's Unresolved Dilemma," *American Political Science Review* 91 (1997): 1–14.

9. Walter Dean Burnham, "The Turnout Problem," in *Elections American Style*, ed. A. James Reichley (Washington, DC: Brookings Institution, 1987).

10. "About the Project," Vanishing Voter Project, www.vanishingvoter.org/about.shtml.

11. This section draws heavily on David Lee Hill, *American Voter Turnout: An Institutional Approach* (Boulder, Colo.: Westview, 2006).

12. For a more complete treatment of this subject, see Mark N. Franklin, *Voter Turnout and the Dynamics of Electoral Competition in Established Democracies since 1945* (New York: Cambridge University Press, 2004).

13. In almost all elections in the United States, the Australian ballot is used, which lists each office separately. Another balloting system is used in parliamentary elections, where citizens are presented with a list of party candidates, from which they choose one party list.

14. Jeffrey A. Karp and Susan A. Banducci, "Political Efficacy and Participation in Twenty-Seven Democracies: How Electoral Systems Shape Political Behavior," *British Journal of Political Science* 38 (2008): 311–34. See also G. Bingham Powell, "American Voter Turnout in Comparative Perspective," *American Political Science Review* 80 (1986): 17–43; Robert Jackman, "Political Institutions and Voter Turnout in the Industrial Democracies," *American Political Science Review* 81 (1987): 405–24.

15. Anthony Downs, *An Economic Theory of Democracy* (New York: Harper & Row, 1957).

16. Ted Halstead, "A Politics for Generation X," *Atlantic Monthly*, August 1999; Institute of Politics, "Attitudes towards Politics and Public Service."

17. Data are from the National Conference of State Legislatures, http://www.ncsl.org/research/elections-and-campaigns/election-administration.aspx.

18. State-by-State Time Off to Vote Laws. Findlaw.com. Accessed January 22, 2015. Available at http://www.findlaw.com/voting-rights-law.html.

19. For information on the effects of early voting, see Robert M. Stein and Patricia A. Garcia-Monet, "Voting Early but Not Often," *Social Science Quarterly* 78

(1997): 657–71; Paul Gronke, Eva Galanes-Rosenbaum, and Peter A. Miller, "Early Voting and Turnout," *PS: Politics & Political Science* (October 2007): 639–45. For information on the effects of motor-voter laws, see Daniel P. Franklin and Eric E. Grier, "Effects of Motor Voter Legislation: Voter Turnout, Registration, and Partisan Advantage in the 1992 Presidential Election," *American Politics Research* 25 (1997): 104–17; Stephen Knack, "Does 'Motor Voter' Work? Evidence from State-Level Data," *Journal of Politics* 57 (1995): 796–811. Michael D. Martinez and David Hill, "Did Motor Voter Work?" *American Politics Research* 27 (1999): 296–315.

20. Donald P. Green and Ron Shachar, "Habit Formation and Political Behaviour: Evidence of Consuetude in Voter Turnout," *British Journal of Political Science* 30 (2000): 561–73.

21. Eric Plutzer, "Becoming a Habitual Voter: Inertia, Resources, and Growth in Young Adulthood," *American Political Science Review* 96 (2002): 41–56.

22. John P. Katosh and Michael W. Traugott, "Costs and Values in the Calculus of Voting," *American Journal of Political Science* 26 (1982): 361–76; for more information about trust in government, see Joseph S. Nye Jr., Philip D. Zelikow, and David C. King, ed., *Why People Don't Trust Government* (Cambridge, MA: Harvard University Press, 1997).

23. Steven J. Rosenstone and John Mark Hanson, *Mobilization, Participation, and Democracy in America* (New York: Macmillan, 1993); Cornelius P. Cotter, James L. Gibson, John F. Bibby, and Robert J. Huckshorn, *Party Organizations in American Politics* (New York: Praeger, 1984).

24. William H. Flanigan and Nancy H. Zingale, *Political Behavior of the American Electorate*, 11th ed. (Washington DC: CQ Press, 2005).

25. Some of the landmark works in this area are by Sidney Verba, Kay Lehman Schlozman, and Henry E. Brady, *Voice and Equality* (Cambridge: Harvard University Press, 1995); Raymond E. Wolfinger and Steven J. Rosenstone, *Who Votes?* (New Haven, CT: Yale University Press, 1980); Sidney Verba and Norman H. Nie, *Participation in America: Political Democracy and Social Equality* (New York: Harper & Row, 1972). See also Jan E. Leighley and Jonathan Nagler, *Who Votes Now? Demographics, Issues, Inequality, and Turnout in the United States* (Princeton, NJ: Princeton Univesity Press, 2014).

26. Martin P. Wattenberg, *Is Voting For Young People?* (New York: Pearson Longman, 2007); Mark Bauerlein, *The Dumbest Generation: How the Digital Age Stupefies Young Americans and Jeopardizes Our Future (Or, Don't Trust Anyone Under 30)* (New York: Tarcher Penguin, 2008).

27. Statistics reported in this section are derived by a method similar to deriving VEP statistics. See Mark Hugo Lopez, Emily Kirby, and Jared Sagoff, "The Youth Vote 2004, with a Historical Look at Youth Voting Patterns, 1972–2004," *Working Paper* 35, Center for Information and Research on Civic Learning and Engagement, July 2005.

28. Jody C Baumgartner and Peter L. Francia, *Conventional Wisdom and American Elections: Exploding Myths, Exploring Misconceptions*, 1st ed. (Lanham, MD: Roman & Littlefield, 2008), chapter 1.

29. Flanigan and Zingale, *Political Behavior of the American Electorate*.

30. Peter W. Wielhouwer and Brad Lockerbie, "Party Contacting and Political Participation, 1952–90," *American Journal of Political Science* 38 (1994): 211–29; Costas Panagopoulos and Peter L. Francia, "Grassroots Mobilization in the 2008 Presidential Election," *Journal of Political Marketing* 8 (2009): 315–33.

31. Diana Burgess, Beth Haney, Mark Snyder, John L. Sullivan, and John E. Transue, "Rocking the Vote: Using Personalized Messages to Motivate Voting among Young Adults," *Public Opinion Quarterly* 64 (2000): 29–52.

32. Alan Gerber and Donald Green, "The Effects of Canvassing, Telephone Calls, and Direct Mail on Voter Turnout: A Field Experiment," *American Political Science Review* 94 (2000): 653–63.

33. McDonald and Popkin, "The Myth of the Vanishing Voter."

34. Philip E. Converse, "Change in the American Electorate," in *The Human Meaning of Social Change*, ed. Angus Campbell and Philip E. Converse (New York: Russell Sage, 1972).

35. For an excellent review of voter fraud in the 1800s, see Peter H. Argersinger, "New Perspectives on Election Fraud in the Gilded Age," *Political Science Quarterly* 100 (Winter 1985–1986): 669–87.

36. McDonald and Popkin, "The Myth of the Vanishing Voter," 964.

37. Jerrold G. Rusk, "The Effect of the Australian Ballot Reform on Split Ticket Voting: 1876–1908," *American Political Science Review* 64 (1970): 1220–38.

38. Russell J. Dalton, *Citizen Politics: Public Opinion and Political Parties in Advanced Industrial Democracies*, 3rd ed. (New York: Chatham House, 2002).

39. "2014 November General Election Turnout Rates," United States Elections Project, http://www.electproject.org/2014g. See also Jose A. DelReal, "Voter Turnout in 2014 Was the Lowest Since WWII," *The Washington Post*, November 10, 2014, http://www.washingtonpost.com/blogs/post-politics/wp/2014/11/10/voter-turnout-in-2014-was-the-lowest-since-wwii.

40. "The Worst Voter Turnout in 72 Years," *The New York Times*, November 11, 2014, http://www.nytimes.com/2014/11/12/opinion/the-worst-voter-turnout-in-72-years.html.

41. "2012 November General Election Turnout Rates" United States Elections Project, http://www.electproject.org/2012g; "2000 November General Election Turnout Rates" United States Elections Project, http://www.electproject.org/2000g.

42. See James W. Caeser and Andrew E. Busch, *The Perfect Tie: The True Story of the 2000 Presidential Election* (Lanham MD: Rowman & Littlefield, 2001); James W. Caeser and Andrew E. Busch, *Red Over Blue: The 2004 Elections and American Politics* (Lanham MD: Rowman & Littlefield, 2005); James W. Caeser and Andrew E. Busch, *Epic Journey: The 2008 Elections and American Politics* (Lanham MD: Rowman & Littlefield, 2009).

43. Adam Liptak, "Voting Problems in Ohio Set Off an Alarm," *The New York Times*, November 7, 2004, http://www.nytimes.com/2004/11/07/politics/campaign/07elect.html. See also Adam Cohen, "No One Should Have to Stand in Line for 10 Hours to Vote," *The New York Times*, August 25, 2008, http://www.nytimes.com/2008/08/26/opinion/26tue4.html.

44. "Thousands of Voter Registration Forms Faked, Officials Say," *CNN*, October 10, 2008, http://www.cnn.com/2008/POLITICS/10/09/acorn.fraud.claims.

45. See Hans Von Spakovsky, "Here Comes the 2014 Voter Fraud," *The Wall Street Journal*, October 27, 2014, http://www.wsj.com/articles/hans-von-spakovsky-here-comes-the-2014-voter-fraud-1414450805; John Fund, "Voter Fraud: We've Got Proof, It's Easy," *The National Review*, January 12, 2014, http://www.nationalreview.com/article/368234/voter-fraud-weve-got-proof-its-easy-john-fund.

46. Kevin Drum, "The Dog That Voted and Other Election Fraud Yarns," *Mother Jones*, July/August 2012, http://www.motherjones.com/politics/2012/07/voter-suppression-kevin-drum. Jonathan Weiler, "The Last Refuge of Scoundrels—Republicans and Voter Suppression," *The Huffington Post*, November 5, 2012, http://www.huffingtonpost.com/jonathan-weiler/the-last-refuge-of-scound_b_2079941.html.

47. Eric Lipton and Ian Urbana, "In 5-Year Effort, Scant Evidence of Voter Fraud," *The New York Times*. April 12, 2007. Available at http://www.nytimes.com/2007/04/12/washington/12fraud.html; Lorraine C. Minnite. "The Politics of Voter Fraud." *Project Vote*, March 5, 2007. Available at http://www.projectvote.org/images/publications/Policy%20Reports%20and%20Guides/Politics_of_Voter_Fraud_Final.pdf; Philip Bump. "The Fix: The Disconnect Between Voter ID Laws and Voter Fraud." *Washington Post*. October 13, 2014. Available at http://www.washingtonpost.com/blogs/the-fix/wp/2014/10/13/the-disconnect-between-voter-id-laws-and-voter-fraud/; Jane Mayer. "The Voter-Fraud Myth." *The New Yorker*, October 29, 2012. Available at http://www.newyorker.com/magazine/2012/10/29/the-voter-fraud-myth; Sarah Childress. "Why Voter ID Laws Aren't Really about Fraud." *Frontline*. October 20, 2014. Available at http://www.pbs.org/wgbh/pages/frontline/government-elections-politics/why-voter-id-laws-arent-really-about-fraud/; Natasha Khan and Corbin Carson. "Comprehensive Database of U.S. Voter Fraud Uncovers No Evidence That Photo ID Is Needed." *News21*, August 12, 2012. Available at http://votingrights.news21.com/article/election-fraud/.

48. Justin Levitt, "The Truth About Voter Fraud," Brennan Center for Justice, 2007, http://www.brennancenter.org/sites/default/files/analysis/The%20Truth%20About%20Voter%20Fraud.pdf.

49. Ibid.

50. Susan Myrick, "110 Year Olds Vote Strong in NC," *Civitas Review*, http://civitasreview.com/elections-campaigns/110-year-olds-vote-strong-in-nc.

51. "Are There Really 112 Year Old Voters on the State's Voter Rolls," *North Carolina State Board of Elections*, http://www.wral.com/asset/news/state/nccapitol/2012/10/31/11722418/SBOE_Response_to_Civitas_Report.pdf.

52. See http://www.eac.gov/assets/1/AssetManager/Exhibit%20M.PDF.

53. "Suppressing the Vote," *The Daily Show with Jon Stewart*, October 23, 2013, http://thedailyshow.cc.com/videos/dxhtvk/suppressing-the-vote.

54. Manny Fernandez, "Party Predictions Differ in Texas on Impact of New Voter ID Law," *The New York Times*, February 5, 2014, http://www.nytimes.com/2014/02/06/us/party-predictions-differ-in-texas-on-impact-of-new-voter-id-law.html.

55. Lonna Rae Atkeson, Lisa Ann Bryant, Thad E. Hall, Kyle Saunders, and Michael R. Alvarez, "A New Barrier to Participation: Heterogeneous Application

of Voter Identification Policies," *Electoral Studies* 29 (2010): 66–73; United States Government Accountability Office. "Issues Related to State Voter Identification Laws." GAO-14-634. September 2014, http://www.gao.gov/assets/670/665966.pdf.

56. Jason D. Mycoff, Michael W. Wagner, and David C. Wilson, "The Effect of Voter Identification Laws on Aggregate and Individual Level Turnout." Paper prepared for presentation at the Annual meeting of the American Political Science Association (Chicago, IL, August, 2007); John R. Lott, Jr. "Evidence of Voter Fraud and the Impact that Regulations to Reduce Fraud have on Voter Participation Rates." Brennan Center for Justice. August 18, 2006. Available at http://www.brennancenter.org/sites/default/files/legal-work/3386f09ec84f302074_hum6bqnxj.pdf; Stephen Ansolabehere, "Effects of Identification Requirements on Voting: Evidence from the Experiences of Voters on Election Day." *PS: Politics & Politicsl Science*, January 2009, 127–30.

57. John Sides, "Do Voter Identification Laws Depress Turnout?" *The Monkey Cage*, October 3, 2011, http://themonkeycage.org/2011/10/03/do-voter-identification-laws-depress-turnout-redux.

FOR MORE READING

Hill, David Lee. *American Voter Turnout: An Institutional Approach*. Boulder, Colo.: Westview, 2006.

Leighley, Jan E. and Jonathan Nagler. *Who Votes Now? Demographics, Issues, Inequality, and Turnout in the United States*. Princeton, NJ: Princeton University Press, 2014.

Verba, Sidney, Kay Lehman Schlozman, and Henry E. Brady. *Voice and Equality*. Cambridge: Harvard University Press, 1995.

Wolfinger, Raymond E. and Steven J. Rosenstone. *Who Votes?* New Haven, Conn.: Yale University Press, 1980.

Part II

CAMPAIGNS

Chapter 4

End of the Two-Party System?
The Myth of the Rise of Third Parties

In 1968, former Alabama governor George Wallace ran for president as candidate of the American Independent Party, famously declaring, "there's not a dime's worth of difference" between the Democratic and Republican Parties.[1] A recent book uses Wallace's statement in its title,[2] and presidential candidate Ralph Nader repeated this claim during his 2000 and 2004 campaigns.[3] Nader, among others, is known for referring to the two major parties as "Tweedledum and Tweedledee," a reference to the twins in Lewis Carroll's *Through the Looking-Glass and What Alice Found There*.[4] Many Americans agree with this assessment of the two major political parties in America. For example, in one survey, 39 percent of respondents agreed with the statement, "There is little difference between the candidates and policies of the Republican Party and the candidates and policies of the Democratic Party."[5] In fact, many voters not only fail to see differences between the parties, but also often respond favorably to poll questions about the need for a third party.[6]

Of course, Americans have always been somewhat ambivalent to political parties. This may be in part due to the fact that most learn at an early age that George Washington warned of the destructive and divisive potential of political parties in his 1796 Farewell Address.[7] However, dissatisfaction with the two major parties may be at an all-time high. A 2013 Gallup poll found that 60 percent of Americans believed that "a third major political party is needed because the Democratic and Republican parties 'do a poor job' representing the American people." This percentage represents a record high mark since Gallup has been asking the question. Indeed, over the past decade, support for a third party has averaged over 50 percent. Of those polled, "only about four in 10" have a positive view of the Republican and Democratic parties, reflecting a rather "tepid" view of each "for much of the last decade."[8] One observer put it simply, "The American people have finally had enough of a two-party system."[9]

Citing the perceived similarities and declining popularity that voters express toward the Democratic and Republican parties in public opinion polls, political pundits frequently trumpet the notion that a viable third party is on its way and will soon advance itself into a position where it can seriously compete with the two major parties. These predictions of third-party success, however, almost never materialize, and, in the rare cases when they do, prove to be short lived.

In this chapter, we review the two structural reasons why the rise of a third party in the United States is unlikely to occur in any significant and sustained way despite the declining popularity of the two major parties. First, the American electorate is predominately moderate, meaning that parties and candidates are competing for a large share of votes in the middle of the ideological spectrum. While it might be possible for a third party to emerge in such an electoral environment, it is more likely that competition would, over time, settle into one between two parties—and a weaker party would be left behind.

Yet, a moderate electorate is not enough to ensure the stability of a two-party system. The second reason we are unlikely to see a third party succeed in the long term is the electoral system. In particular, rules that specify that only one winner will be selected from each electoral district and that the winner will be the individual who receives the most (not the majority of) votes, all serve as powerful disincentives for supporters of third or minor parties.

PARTY SYSTEMS IN COMPARATIVE PERSPECTIVE

Most democracies have multiparty systems, and parties in these systems represent a broad range of the ideological spectrum. For example, in most European democracies there is a significant socialist or social democratic party on the left. Great Britain has the Labour Party, France has its Socialist Party, and Germany has the Social Democratic Party.[10] These same countries also have conservative or Christian democratic parties that oppose them from the right side of the ideological spectrum. Examples include Great Britain's Conservative Party, France's Rally for the Republic, and Germany's Christian Democratic Union (with their smaller sister party, the Christian Socialist Union). In addition to these main parties of the left and right, most European democracies (as well as other established democracies) have minor parties that win a significant share of the vote in national and local elections (for a listing of some of these parties, see Table 4.1).[11] An impressive show of minor party strength occurred in France where ultranationalist candidate Jean-Marie Le Pen of the National Front Party finished a surprising second in the presidential election of 2002. A decade later in 2012, Le Pen's daughter,

Table 4.1   Minor Parties in European Democracies

Party Type	Examples
Classic Liberal	Free Democratic Party (Germany), Liberal Democrats (Great Britain)
Green	German Green Party, Green Party (France)
Regional	Scottish National Party (Great Britain), Northern League (Italy)
Ultra-Nationalist	National Front (France), Austrian Freedom Party
Radical Socialist/Communist	The Left (Germany), French Communist Party

Marine, ran a strong presidential campaign herself, finishing with 18 percent of the vote, slightly higher than the vote share received by her father in the first round of balloting in 2002.[12]

By comparison, the United States has always had a two-party system, and the same two parties have dominated national politics since 1860. Both of these parties occupy a relatively small space on the spectrum of major political ideologies of the world. To be more specific, both American political parties come from the same classic liberal tradition. Both embrace, as a matter of faith, classic liberal ideas about individual freedoms. These ideas find acceptance in the economic realm of a market economy and in the political realm of democratic governance. In this narrow sense, it is true that there is not a "dime's worth of difference" between the Republican and Democratic parties.

It is within this relatively small ideological slice of classic liberalism that American politics takes place. However, there is a wide gulf separating the two parties when it comes to their prescriptions for American society. Party activists, members, and supporters hold sharply different opinions on most issues of public policy.[13] Members of Congress have grown more polarized over time as well, suggesting that elites in the two parties find few issues on which to agree.[14] The two major American political parties are, in fact, quite different from each other in terms of the positions they take on any variety of issues. Yet, the differences between the Republicans and the Democrats are not as great as the differences between major parties in some other democracies.

Several theories have been advanced to explain the stability of the two-party system in the United States. Political scientist V.O. Key suggests that there is a lasting duality of interests in American society that, while shifting (East-West, North-South, urban-rural), naturally coalesces to form a two-party system.[15] Another theory is the social consensus theory, which suggests that because the United States did not have a feudal past, there has historically been agreement on the basic values that provide the foundation for the republic (democratic government, a market economy). Therefore, two parties have always been needed to forge compromise.[16] These theories are centered primarily on the idea that parties are an outgrowth of social forces.

Our discussion first takes this "bottom-up" approach, focusing on the idea that American electorate is a generally moderate one.

A RELATIVELY MODERATE ELECTORATE
AND THE MEDIAN VOTER THEORY

Compared to citizens in many other countries, research suggests that the American electorate is fairly moderate.[17] Although some issues, such as abortion or gay marriage, can be fairly divisive, relatively few people claim to be extremely liberal or extremely conservative on most issues.[18] If we accept that aggregate opinion is moderate on most issues, it can be depicted as a bell-shaped curve, or normal distribution. In Figure 4.1, the horizontal axis represents the hypothetical positions that can be taken on any given issue, ranging from extremely liberal (Democratic) on the left to extremely conservative (Republican) on the right. The vertical axis represents the number of people who take these positions. For example, at the extreme right end of the *x*-axis, there are relatively few individuals classified as extremely conservative Republicans. A majority clustered in the middle area of the spectrum indicates that most people are relatively moderate. The shaded area of the figure represents the number of voters who are one standard deviation off the mean, or the midpoint, and are the individuals who are closest to the middle. This shaded area represents 68.3 percent of the distribution, or the total area of the figure—a clear majority.

Parties competing for votes among a moderate electorate will attempt to moderate their program and message, or "move to the center," in order to capture the greatest number of votes. This is known as the "median voter

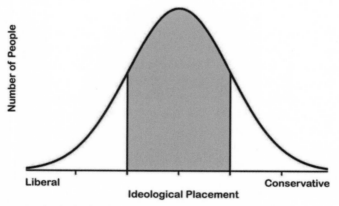

Figure 4.1   Hypothetical Distribution of a Moderate Electorate.

theory." Originally, the work of economists, it was first articulated in an article by Duncan Black and subsequently expanded upon in Anthony Downs's influential *An Economic Theory of Democracy*.[19] Downs's theorem suggests individuals will vote for the party or candidate that is closest to them on the ideological spectrum. Because voters in the United States cluster in the middle of the spectrum (in statistical terms, are normally distributed), parties and candidates naturally moderate their message and move to the center. This tendency has the effect of reducing the effective number of parties, as only a limited number can reasonably compete for the same bloc of votes.

The notion that there are few discernible differences between the two major parties is based on the fact that candidates sometimes moderate their party's policy positions when campaigning for office. This then explains the myth of Tweedledum and Tweedledee. As candidates from both parties moderate their messages or issue positions, their resulting messages will appear to be, or might actually be, quite similar.

ELECTORAL SYSTEMS: RULES AND THEIR EFFECTS

Electoral systems are a set of rules that govern how votes will translate into seats in government office. While it might be tempting to believe that one could simply count votes and award seats to those who received the most votes, this might not always be the answer. For example, imagine a scenario in which three candidates, Smith, Jones, and Brown, were running for president. The election is held and the votes were distributed as follows:

- Smith: 35 percent,
- Jones: 33 percent,
- Brown: 32 percent.

In this scenario, we might simply award the presidency to Smith, as she received more votes than either of the other two candidates. But this would also mean that she would take office in spite of the fact that 65 percent of the voting public (almost two-thirds) did *not* vote for her. Electoral systems must deal with sometimes complex issues like this and others.

Electoral systems address two main questions: how many winners will there be, and how will winners be determined? With regard to the number of winners, a number of alternatives may be used. For example, at-large elections often determine city council races. Under such a system, voters select a list of candidates for *all* of the seats on the council, and the seats are then awarded to those individuals who receive the most votes. Alternatively, some city and town councils, and even a few state legislatures, have so-called multimember districts, where voters elect at least two candidates to represent the district. Philadelphia, Cincinnati, and Seattle are a few cities that use an at-large system to select their city councils, while the state of Maryland uses the multimember district system to select members to the state legislature.[20]

However, in most elections in the United States, including all elections to federal office, there is only one election winner per district. In U.S. House elections, only one candidate wins a seat in Congress in each of the 435 districts. Similarly, while each state has two senators, elections to the Senate are staggered so that no state elects both its senators in the same election year. Finally, in every state except Maine and Nebraska, the winner of the popular vote for president receives all of the Electoral College votes awarded to that state.[21] This system, where there is only one winner from each election district, is known as a single-member district (SMD) system.

A second aspect of an electoral system deals with the rules that determine a winner. Does the winner require a plurality (the most), a majority, or some other minimal threshold of the vote to win office? In parliamentary systems, it is common to select multiple representatives from the entire country or a region according to the principle of proportionality. Under this system, known as proportional representation, citizens vote for a party. Each party then receives seats in parliament based on the proportion of votes it earns in the election. For example, in a national legislature with one hundred seats, a party that receives 30 percent of the vote would win thirty seats. The formulas governing proportional representation rules are typically much more complex,[22] but the proportional principle still applies.

In the United States, plurality-winner rules determine the winners in federal elections. Referred to by some as "winner takes all" or "first past the post," the winner is the candidate who receives the most votes, even if no candidate receives a majority of the votes. In the example election used above between Smith, Jones, and Brown, Smith won a plurality of the votes with 35 percent. With the exception of Louisiana and Georgia, plurality-winner rules apply to all elections to the U.S. House and Senate.

It is important to understand how different electoral systems work because they have a direct effect on the political system in general, and the party system in particular. The French political scientist Maurice Duverger suggested long ago that countries with SMD, plurality-winner electoral systems tend to have two-party systems.[23] There are some exceptions. For example, while the British use an SMD, plurality-winner electoral system, there is a significant third party (the Liberal Democrats) and several significant regional parties (the Scottish National Party, the Welsh Plaid Cymru).

To illustrate the difficulties that third parties confront, consider the following hypothetical example. Figure 4.2 shows the geographic distribution of party support in a "country" for three political parties. The figure shows that Republicans enjoy the support of all of the inhabitants who live in the outer region of the country, delineated as "A." Democrats are supported by those who live in the inner ring of the circle, labeled as "B." Finally, those who live in the center ("C") support the New Party. Support for Republicans amounts to 44 percent of the electorate, Democrats 41 percent, and for the New Party, 15 percent.

Imagine now that this country elects a 100-person legislature under a straight proportional representation (multimember district) system. In other words, each party will be awarded seats in the legislature directly proportional to the percentage of votes it receives. Republicans, with 44 percent of the vote, receive 44 seats; Democrats, 41 seats. Although the New Party is clearly the smallest of the three parties, it receives 15 seats in the legislature, allowing it some voice in governance. In fact, depending on the ideological orientation of the New Party, either the Republicans or the Democrats will attempt to align with the New Party in order to gain majority (greater than 50 percent) status in the legislature.[24] They might offer to select a few of the New Party's leaders for prominent positions in the administration or adopt an issue position important to the New Party. In such a case, we might even be justified

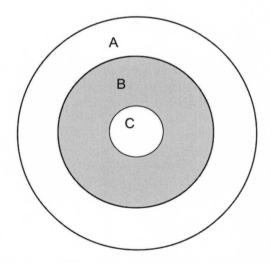

Area	All Inhabitants Support	Percentage of Vote
A	Republican Party	44%
B	Democratic Party	41%
C	New Party	15%

Figure 4.2   Hypothetical Example #1: Geographic Distribution of Party support.

in claiming that the New Party is easily as powerful as the two larger parties, because without New Party's cooperation neither has a majority. The point is that the New Party has every incentive to continue on its course, as do its supporters (voters, donors, volunteers, candidates).

Imagine now that this same country has determined to elect its legislature by way of SMD–plurality-winner rules. The same regions of the country support the same parties, and by the same percentages. For simplicity, let us reduce the size of the legislature in this second hypothetical example to ten seats. Voters in each electoral district will select one representative in the legislature, and that individual will be the one who receives the most votes in that district (see Figure 4.3). In district one (-1-), the Republican candidate, with 44 percent of the vote, wins the election and a seat in the legislature. District two sees similar results.

In fact, with their 44 percent of the vote in each district, Republicans win all districts. As this example illustrates, the SMD–plurality-winner electoral system exaggerates the margin of victory for the winner (and the margin of loss for the loser). With only 44 percent of the vote nationwide, Republicans win 100 percent of the seats (10) in the legislature. In 2014, Republicans secured 56.8 percent of the seats in the House of Representatives with 50.9 percent of the national vote total. Democrats won 43.2 percent of the seats with 45.3 percent of the vote. Most elections to the House follow a similar pattern, as do elections in other countries that use SMD–plurality-winner rules (e.g., Great Britain).

In our hypothetical example, it is not hard to imagine a swing in the percentage of votes between the Democrats and the Republicans in at least a few districts from one election to the next. Democrats, in other words, are unlikely to be locked out of the legislature in the long term. In contrast, the New Party, with only 15 percent of the vote, is unlikely ever to be able to get enough votes in any of these districts to win a seat in the legislature.

Over time—after repeated elections—voters, candidates, and supporters of the New Party will begin to see that it is politically expedient and strategically wise to align with one of the larger two parties. Politically, there might be a variety of incentives for the New Party to do so. First, it faces an obvious choice: align with one of the two major parties and share power or be consigned to an eternity in the political wilderness. It has no prospect of gaining *any* power otherwise. Second, the larger parties could offer incentives to the New Party to join forces. These might include adopting a focus on a policy important to the New Party, modifying a position on an existing issue to account for the New Party's position, offering legislative leadership positions to prominent members of the New Party, and more.

Beyond what the party itself does, voters and supporters will move over time toward one of the two major parties as well. Duverger identifies what

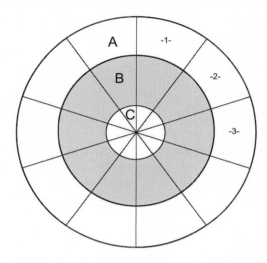

Area	All Inhabitants Support	Percentage of Vote
A	Republican Party	44%
B	Democratic Party	41%
C	New Party	15%

Figure 4.3   Hypothetical Example #2: Geographic Distribution of Party Support with 10 Single Member Districts.

he calls a "psychological factor" that pushes out third parties. According to this explanation, voters do not want to waste or "throw away" their votes on a likely loser. In the end, SMD, plurality-winner electoral systems erode the ability of third parties to compete and survive. This is Duverger's Law: in SMD, plurality-winner electoral systems, third parties are practically squeezed out of the systems.

If the effects of the electoral system were not enough to discourage the formation and long-term viability of third or minor parties, other election-related laws have that effect as well. For example, debates between political candidates at all levels of government during the general election season regularly feature a Democrat and a Republican. Only rarely do debate sponsors or the major-party candidates themselves consent to allow a minor party or independent candidate to join. In 1992, independent presidential Ross Perot debated the Republican President George H.W. Bush in his reelection bid and his Democratic challenger, Bill Clinton. This was an exception. In 1996, as the Reform Party candidate, Perot was not included in the presidential debates. In 2000, Reform Party candidate Pat Buchanan was excluded, as was Green Party candidate Ralph Nader.

Campaign finance laws, at least for presidential elections, are also designed to privilege major parties and their candidates. Candidates for their party's nomination may receive what are known as federal "matching" funds from the government. This means that the government will "match" the first $250 of an individual's contributions to a candidate.[25] The total amount a candidate receives in matching funds is also capped at a certain limit (in 2012 that number was approximately $22.8 million).[26] In order to be eligible to receive this money a candidate must raise at least $5,000 in 20 different states. For a major-party candidate, the campaign can draw on the resources of state and local party activists, making it much easier to meet this requirement than for a candidate not affiliated with the two established parties.

Major-party candidates are also entitled to receive money for the general election campaign (in 2012, approximately $91 million).[27] A third-party or independent candidate is eligible to receive public funding if the third party's nominee from the previous presidential election managed to garner 5 percent of the national vote in the general election. While this may seem a small percentage, the reality is that very few third-party candidates ever reach this threshold. In 2000, Ralph Nader, as the Green Party candidate, narrowly missed it, meaning that the Green Party was not eligible for public funds in that or the next election.[28] Without public funds, third-party candidates must self-finance their campaigns or raise funds privately—a difficult task given that few donors are interested in giving to a candidate who will almost always assuredly lose.[29] Consequently, third-party candidates can only rarely generate the tens to hundreds of millions of dollars necessary to wage a viable presidential campaign, making it difficult to win even 5 percent of the vote in the general election and thereby qualify for public funds.

Finally, laws in several states make it difficult for minor-party candidates to appear on the ballot. To be fair, the rationale for this is not necessarily to ensure the continued duopoly of the Democratic and Republican parties. Instead, these laws are designed to discourage frivolous candidacies that could result in a lengthy and unmanageable ballot for voters. Elections, including the printing of ballots, cost money. In addition, presenting voters with too many choices may be confusing and lead to lengthy waiting times at the polls. A cluttered ballot might even be so confusing that it turns away potential voters, reducing turnout. Each of the states have their own individual ballot access rules, with some states providing stricter requirements for third-party candidates than others (see Box 4.1).

A number of states have third parties that are officially recognized. In a few cases, third parties can be marginally competitive in some areas. Nonetheless, electoral rules, particularly the electoral system, make it all but impossible for a third party to enjoy long-term national success.

Box 4.1   Various State Measures Governing Ballot Access for Minor Parties and Independent Candidates

Filing Fees: Most states require that candidates pay a fee to get their name on the ballot. In some cases, the amount is a minimal flat fee. In 2015, Pennsylvania charged $200 for individuals running for president.[1] In other states this flat fee can be a few thousand dollars. Other states charge a percentage of the salary associated with the office being sought. In 2014, South Carolina charged one percent of the $174,000 annual salary for a member of Congress (either representative or senator) multiplied by the length of the term. Candidates for the U.S. Senate, for example, paid $1,740 times six, for a total of $10,440.[2] Because minor parties and independent candidates typically have fewer resources than do the major and their candidates, these fees can be troublesome.

Filing Dates: All states have deadlines that all candidates and parties must adhere to in order to have their names on the ballot. For the major parties accustomed to these deadlines and with organizations in each state, this is typically not a problem. However, minor parties and independent candidates must not only find out when these dates are, but also in many cases gather petition signatures to allow them on the ballot prior to the deadline.[3]

Petition Signature Requirements: Many states require that minor party and independent candidates submit a petition in order to gain access to the ballot. Like filing fees (if any) these rules vary greatly. Some states demand a minimal absolute number of signatures be submitted. Hawaii, for example, only requires 25 signatures for candidates to either house of Congress. To run for the Senate in Virginia, an individual must collect 10,000 signatures; in Iowa, 1,500 from ten different counties. Here too the major parties have an organizational advantage.

Political Parties: Here the questions are more basic. Do the rules for independent candidates vary from those governing access for political party candidates? And how do minor parties automatically gain access to the ballot? In Arkansas, a party that wins three percent of the vote in the most recent presidential or gubernatorial election has officially recognized party status, and thus ballot access for its candidates in the next election.

Fusion: Some few states (e.g., Connecticut, Delaware, New York, and South Carolina) allow for a greater competitive advantage for minor party and independent candidates by providing for fusion voting, where two parties nominate the same candidate.

(Continued)

Box 4.1   *(Continued)*

Sore Loser Laws: These laws prohibit candidates who lost in their party's primary to run again in the general election as an independent or under a different party label. These statutes were intended to privilege the two major parties by not allowing intra-party dissent to morph into the formation and success of a new party.

See generally, "Getting on the Ballot: What It Takes." 2012. *The Canvas: States and Election Reform*. National Conference of State Legislatures. Issue 27, February 2012. Available at http://www.ncsl.org/documents/legismgt/elect/Canvass_Feb_2012_No_27.pdf; Winger, Richard. n.d. Ballot Access News. Available at http:// http://ballot-access.org/; Conor M. Dowling. 2008. "The Cost of Running for Office: How Electoral Campaign Laws Structure Candidate Entry in U.S. Elections." Unpublished dissertation, Binghampton University (SUNY); Oliver Hall, "Death by a Thousand Signatures: The Rise of Restrictive Ballot Access Laws and the Decline of Electoral Competition in the United States," 29 *Seattle U. L. Rev.* 407 (2005).

1. Office of the Philadelphia City Commissioners. n.d. "Nomination Petitions and Filing Fees." Available at http://www.philadelphiavotes.com/en/candidates-a-campaigns/nominating-petitions.
2. South Carolina State Election Commission. n.d. "Filing Fees." Available at http://scvotes.org/candidate_information/filing_fees.
3. See, for example, The Federal Election Commission. n.d. "2010 Congressional Primary Dates and Candidate Filing Deadlines for Ballot Access." Available at http://www.fec.gov/pubrec/fe2010/2010pdates.pdf.

IS A THIRD PARTY REALLY NEEDED?

Dissatisfaction with the two major parties often is—although not always—grounded in the idea that there are few discernible differences between them. As noted at the outset of this chapter, many believe that the major parties simply do not offer enough actual choice, and that a third party could and would add fresh ideas, new perspectives, to policy debates. This assumption, however, bears closer examination. Are there actual meaningful differences between the Republican and Democratic parties? The short answer is a resounding "yes."

As evidence, we can look first to the platforms of the parties themselves. A party platform is a document that outlines, often very specifically, the positions the party takes on a variety of issues. The platform is the party's official policy document, and it is here that we can see numerous differences between the parties themselves.

Much of the difference between the two parties in the past two decades is in the positions each takes on social and cultural issues, such as abortion and civil rights.[30] The Republican Party has consistently held the more conservative or traditional positions on these so-called cultural issues. For example, Republicans generally oppose abortion rights, gay marriage, and embryonic stem-cell research, and favor school prayer. Most Democrats, conversely, favor a women's right to choose an abortion, legal marriage for same-sex couples, and embryonic stem-cell research, and oppose school prayer.

Many Republicans oppose affirmative action, while a large percentage of Democrats favor programs that serve to redress past discrimination. Democrats usually support hate crime legislation, while Republicans typically (with some exceptions, such as when President George H. W. Bush signed the Hate Crimes Statistic Act in 1990) oppose it. Additionally, many Democrats favor legislation regulating certain aspects of gun ownership (e.g., waiting periods for the purchase of handguns). Most Republicans perceive these laws as an infringement on their Second Amendment rights and oppose them.

On issues related to education, Democrats generally advocate putting more money into public schools, whereas a large number of Republicans believe that the problem of failing schools should be addressed by some measure of privatization (namely, school vouchers). Democrats are more likely to be in favor of legislation and regulation to protect the environment, Republicans less so. The George W. Bush administration's withdrawal from the Kyoto Protocol on greenhouse gas emissions, and Al Gore's scathing criticism of this decision in his documentary "An Inconvenient Truth," are examples of this difference. Democrats are generally in favor of greater government involvement in the realm of health care in order to reduce the number of uninsured and underinsured. Republicans typically oppose government involvement in managing the nation's health-care system. The fierce partisan battles waged in Congress and the deep public divisions that continue to exist over the Affordable Care Act (Obamacare) exemplify these sharp divisions.

On economic matters, Republicans tend to favor policies that emphasize individual initiative and limited government intervention, whereas Democrats are more inclined to see a role for government regulation. For example, Republicans are generally in favor of tax cuts (broadly defined) while many Democrats prefer using tax revenues to reduce the federal deficit or to increase federal spending on programs addressing social needs. Democrats often call for increases in the minimum wage to assist the working poor. Many Republicans believe that this is harmful to business and ultimately to workers because wage increases may force business to cut costs with layoffs. Finally, Republicans have historically been the party that takes a more hawkish stand on foreign policy disputes and favor greater military spending when compared to those in the Democratic Party. Democrats, led by President Obama, have generally favored gradual troop withdrawal from recent wars in Iraq and Afghanistan, whereas some Republicans have supported "staying the course" or even troop increases in trouble spots in the Middle East.

In short, there are significant differences between the issue positions of the two parties. While it is true that candidates sometimes do stray from the official party line, presidential candidates have always been central to the process of drafting these documents.[31] The first party platform was written in 1832 when the first Democratic National Convention met to re-nominate Andrew Jackson.[32] The document was actually written as an address for Jackson to deliver to the convention, making it a very candidate-specific document. This has been the case throughout history. However, because direct primaries and caucuses—rather than the party itself—effectively decide the party nomination, presidential candidates are free to ignore the platform if they so chose. A rather obvious example occurred in 1996, when Republican presidential hopeful Bob Dole freely admitted that he had not even read the Republican Platform.[33]

Another reason for the blurred differences between the two parties on the presidential campaign trail is that both candidates are attempting to appeal to the middle of the electorate. This blurring of the lines by presidential candidates, however, should not lead one to conclude that the parties themselves are similar. Most research overwhelmingly demonstrates that the moderate rhetoric of presidential candidates is a poor indicator of how members of the two parties actually govern, especially in the U.S. Congress. Increasingly, the evidence shows that Democrats and Republicans find very little upon which to agree when casting their roll-call votes on legislation in Congress.[34] Evidence makes clear that the Democratic and Republican parties do not look alike, as some have suggested.[35] Political activists, individual donors, and interest groups all exert pressure on elected officials to stand firm on certain core party principles, making moderation more difficult.[36] In addition, elected officials often represent districts with heavy concentrations of voters from their own political parties, creating little incentive to reach across party lines and develop a more pragmatic approach to governing.[37] According to political scientist Keith Poole, "Moderates have virtually disappeared during the thirty years between the 93rd and 108th Congresses and the parties have pulled apart."[38]

The result is growing polarization in Congress, underscoring that there are clearer and more pronounced differences between the parties than at any time in recent memory. The statements of presidential candidates should not be confused with the positions of the parties they claim to represent. Candidates are not parties. There is a party line (or to be more precise, two party lines), even if candidates do not always follow that party line. Each party's platform reflects fundamental differences in the positions of both parties. It is also important to remember that these differences are not simply words in some irrelevant party platform that are ignored by elected officials. Members of the two major parties do govern differently—even if the rhetoric of their presidential candidates can sometimes make the parties seem very similar.

CONCLUSION

There are a number of minor or third parties in the United States today, a few of which sometimes attract a moderately respectable following. These include the Green Party, which stands for grassroots democracy, social justice, "ecological wisdom," diversity and equity, and economic decentralization.[39] Libertarians, "America's third largest political party," hold a "vision for a world in which all individuals can freely exercise the natural right of sole dominion over their own lives, liberty and property."[40] Other parties (e.g., the Constitution Party) are popular in selected areas, while many states have state-specific minor parties (e.g., Hawaii Independence Party). But, with very few exceptions (Sen. Angus King of Maine, Sen. Bernie Sander of Vermont, Governor Bill Walker of Alaska), these parties do not win higher elective office.

The reason for this is very straightforward: the rules of the game work against them. The reality is that the SMD–plurality-winner electoral system creates a powerful incentive for candidates, supporters, and parties to move eventually to one of the two existing major parties. In addition, other electoral rules work to marginalize or disadvantage minor parties. While the desire for a third party—more choice—is legitimate, it is extraordinarily unlikely that the United State will ever have anything but a two-party system.

NOTES

1. William J. Keefe and Marc J. Hetherington, *Parties, Politics, and Public Policy in America*, 9th ed. (Washington, DC: CQ Press, 2003), 49.

2. Alexander Cockburn and Jeffrey St. Clair, eds., *Dime's Worth of Difference: Beyond the Lesser of Two Evils* (Oakland, Calif.: AK Press, 2004).

3. Eric Boehlert, "Nader's Nadir," *Salon*, February 21, 2004, archive.salon.com/news/feature/2004/02/21/nader/index_np.html.

4. Eric Alterman, "Bush's Useful Idiot," *Nation*, October 4, 2004, www.thenation.com/doc/20041004/alterman.

5. Larry J. Sabato and Bruce Larson, *The Party's Just Begun: Shaping Political Parties for America's Future*, 2nd ed. (New York: Longman, 2002), 127.

6. Jeffrey M. Jones, "Americans Continue to Say a Third Political party is Needed," *Gallup*, September 24, 2014, http://www.gallup.com/poll/177284/americans-continue-say-third-political-party-needed.aspx.

7. See http://avalon.law.yale.edu/18th_century/washing.asp.

8. Jones, "Americans Continue to Say a Third Political party is Needed."

9. Evans Lynn, as quoted in Allison Hammond, "Many Students Would Welcome a Third Major Political Party," *USA Today*, October 19, 2013, http://www.usatoday.com/story/news/nation/2013/10/19/millennials-want-political-reorganization/3013343/.

10. Great Britain's Labour Party and Germany's Social Democratic Party, however, have received significant attention recently for adopting what some call "third way" positions that defy traditional left-wing policy prescriptions. See Knut Roder, *Social Democracy and Labour Market Policy: Developments in Britain and Germany* (New York: Routledge, 2003).

11. Alan Ware, *Political Parties and Party Systems* (New York: Oxford University Press, 1996).

12. Jamie Coomarasamy, "Marine and Jean-Marie Le Pen Fight Over French National Front," *BBC*, May 22, 2015, http://www.bbc.com/news/world-europe-32809900.

13. Alan I. Abramowitz, *The Polarized Public: Why Government Is So Dysfunctional* (New York: Pearson, 2013).

14. Keith T. Poole and Howard Rosenthal, *Ideology and Congress* (New Brunswick, NJ: Transaction Publishers, 2007).

15. V. O. Key Jr., *Politics, Parties, and Pressure Groups*, 5th ed. (New York: Crowell, 1964).

16. Louis Hartz, *The Liberal Tradition in America* (New York: Harcourt, Brace, and World, 1955).

17. Morris P. Fiorina, Samuel J. Abrams, and Jeremy C. Pope, *Culture War? The Myth of a Polarized America* (New York: Longman, 2005).

18. Fiorina, Abrams, and Pope, *Culture War?*

19. Duncan Black, "On the Rationale of Group Decision-Making," *Journal of Political Economy* 56 (1948): 23–34; Anthony Downs, *An Economic Theory of Democracy* (New York: Harper, 1957).

20. "City Council Election Methods," FairVote: The Center for Voting and Democracy, www.fairvote.org/media/documents/City_Council_Manual.pdf.

21. Individual electors in Maine and Nebraska are awarded based on the winner of the presidential vote in each House district. In practice, all typically end up being allocated to the winner of the popular vote. See Stephen J. Wayne, *The Road to the White House 2004: The Politics of Presidential Elections* (Belmont, Calif.: Wadsworth, 2004), 323.

22. Examples include stipulating that a party must receive a minimum percentage of votes (say, 5 percent) to receive any seats, or accounting for partial seats.

23. Maurice Duverger, *Political Parties: Their Organization and Activity in the Modern State*, trans. Barbara North and Robert North, 2nd ed. (New York: Wiley, 1965). See also Arend Lijphart, *Electoral Systems and Party Systems: A Study of Twenty-seven Democracies, 1945–1990* (Oxford: Oxford University Press, 1994).

24. The Republicans and Democrats are unlikely to try and align with each other. Why? According to the "minimal winning coalition" rule posited by William Riker, parties or groups have no incentive to build a majority that is larger than necessary to win. See William H. Riker, *The Theory of Political Coalitions* (New Haven, Conn.: Yale University Press, 1962).

25. That is, any individual contribution total of $250 or less is matched dollar for dollar, while a $251 donation or higher would receive no more than a $250 match.

26. For more information, see the website of the Federal Election Commission at http://www.fec.gov/press/bkgnd/fund.shtml.

27. For more information, see the website of the Federal Election Commission at http://www.fec.gov/press/bkgnd/fund.shtml.

28. "Presidential Election Campaign Fund." 2014. Federal Election Commission. April 9, 2014. Available at http://www.fec.gov/press/bkgnd/fund.shtml.

29. Clifford W. Brown, Lynda W. Powell, and Clyde Wilcox, *Serious Money: Fundraising and Contributing in Presidential Nomination Campaigns* (New York: Cambridge University Press, 1995).

30. See James D. Hunter, *Culture Wars* (New York: Basic Books, 1991), for one of the first treatments of the culture war phenomenon.

31. Judith Parris, *The Convention Problem: Issues in Reform of Presidential Nominating Procedures* (Washington, DC: Brookings Institution, 1972).

32. Larry Smith, "The Party Platforms as Institutional Discourse: The Democrats and Republicans of 1988," *Presidential Studies Quarterly* 22 (1992): 531.

33. "Republicans: Convention Notes," *Time*, August 26, 1996, 21.

34. Poole and Rosenthal, *Ideology and Congress*.

35. Mathew I. Pinzur, "Nader Mounts Attack at UNF on Major 'Look-Alike' Parties," *Florida Times Union*, October 13, 2000, A09.

36. See Jacob S. Hacker and Paul Pierson, *Off Center: The Republican Revolution and the Erosion of American Democracy* (New Haven, Conn.: Yale University Press, 2006). See also Geoffrey Layman, *The Great Divide: Religious and Cultural Conflict in American Party Politics* (New York: Columbia University Press, 2001).

37. Thomas E. Mann, "Redistricting Reform: What Is Desirable? Possible?" in *Party Lines: Competition, Partisanship, and Congressional Redistricting*, ed. Thomas E. Mann and Bruce E. Cain (Washington, DC: Brookings Institution Press, 2005), 92–114.

38. Keith T. Poole, "The Decline and Rise of Party Polarization in Congress during the Twentieth Century," *Extensions* (Fall 2005): 9.

39. For more information, see the website of the Green Party at http://www.gp.org.

40. For more information, see the website of the Libertarian Party at http://www.lp.org.

FOR MORE READING

Hershey, Marjorie Random. *Party Politics in America*. 16th ed. New York: Pearson, 2014.

McCarty, Nolan, Keith T. Poole, and Howard Rosenthal. *Polarized America: The Dance of Ideology and Unequal Riches*. Cambridge: MIT Press, 2006.

Reichley, A. James. *The Life of the Parties: A History of American Political Parties*. Lanham, Md.: Rowman & Littlefield, 1992.

White, John Kenneth and Daniel M. Shea. *New Party Politics: From Jefferson and Hamilton to the Information Age*. Boston: Bedford/St. Martin's, 2000.

Zeigler, L. Harmon. *Political Parties in Industrial Democracies*. Itasca, Ill.: F. E. Peacock, 1993.

Chapter 5

Buying Elections? Misconceptions about Campaign Finance and the *Citizens United* Case

In January of 2010, the U.S. Supreme Court made headlines when it issued its ruling in *Citizens United v. Federal Election Commission*. The case centered on the question of whether a corporation could directly finance political communications through a film without running afoul of federal campaign finance law. In a 5-4 ruling, the Court sided with the rights of corporations on First Amendment grounds. Justice Anthony Kennedy, writing for the majority, declared that federal campaign finance law had unconstitutionally denied Citizens United, a nonprofit corporation, its right to free speech. He summarized his argument by asserting, "If the First Amendment has any force, it prohibits Congress from fining or jailing citizens, or *associations of citizens*, for simply engaging in political speech" [italics added].[1]

The Court's ruling received near-instant condemnation from those in the campaign finance reform community. Fred Wertheimer of the pro-campaign finance reform group Democracy 21 labeled the decision "the most radical and destructive campaign finance decision in Supreme Court history."[2] Keith Olbermann, then a host on MSNBC, went as far as to claim that the case "might actually have more dire implications than *Dred Scott v. Sandford*."[3] And in his 2010 State of the Union Address, just weeks after the *Citizens United* decision, President Obama told a national audience that "the Supreme Court reversed a century of law that I believe will open the floodgates for special interests—including foreign corporations—to spend without limit in our elections."[4]

An opinion piece in the conservative *National Review* saw matters differently. It countered that the "floodgates are now open . . . for free speech."[5] Likewise, the former Solicitor General of the United States under President George W. Bush, Theodore Olson, claimed that the decision, "may be the most important case in history because what that decision said is that individuals, under the First Amendment, cannot be inhibited, cannot be restrained, cannot be threatened, cannot be censored by the government when they wish to speak about elections and the political process."[6]

With its *Citizens United* decision, the Court clearly evoked strong reactions from both sides of the debate surrounding campaign finance reform. Perhaps not surprisingly, misconceptions about the ruling and its consequences still persist. In this chapter, we try to make some sense of what this landmark case actually changed and how it has actually affected campaign finance. To set the stage, we begin with a brief history of campaign finance reform, focusing on the intentions of reformers. Following that, we examine how the *Citizens United* decision has and has not altered the campaign finance system.

FRAMEWORK OF THE MODERN CAMPAIGN FINANCE SYSTEM

Stories about wealthy industrialists contributing vast sums of money to political candidates go back more than a century. William McKinley (who served as Governor of Ohio from 1891 to 1895 and as President from 1897 to 1901), for instance, was helped throughout his political career by Ohio millionaire, Mark Hanna. According to various accounts, Hanna contributed $100,000 (approximately $2.5 million today) to McKinley for his 1896 campaign for president.[7] McKinley also had the financial backing of big corporations, business owners, and executives, including Standard Oil and J. P. Morgan, each of which gave $250,000 ($6 million today) to the campaign.[8] Corporate interests helped McKinley outspend his opponent, William Jennings Bryan, a populist who held positions at odds with big business, by as much as ten-to-one.[9] The large sums of money donated to the McKinley campaign from the corporate sector prompted some of the earliest calls for Congress to institute rules and restrictions on campaign finance.

Indeed, political cartoons frequently cast leading political figures from the period as corrupt. James G. Blaine, a U.S. Senator and 1884 presidential contender, was famously depicted as a "tattooed man" with each tattoo representing an expression of corruption (see Figure 5.1). Cartoonist Thomas Nast was also well known for his work highlighting bribery, fraud, and graft in government (see Figure 5.2).

Congress took its first major steps to reform the nation's campaign finance system following charges that President Theodore Roosevelt exchanged favors with corporate and banking interests for their financial support of his 1904 presidential campaign.[10] Unable to quell the suspicion of improper dealings, Roosevelt proposed a federal law in 1905 eliminating all corporate campaign contributions and requiring disclosure of campaign expenditures.

Figure 5.1 Big Money's Grip on Government: Bernhard Gillam's "Phryne Before the Chicago Tribunal" (A Depiction of James Blaine Covered in his Scandals, Originally Published in *Puck*, June 4, 1884). *Source*: This image is in the public domain.

Congress responded by passing the Tillman Act of 1907. The law banned corporations and interstate banks from contributing directly to candidates for federal office.

In later years, Congress passed further regulations on campaign contributions. The first federal disclosure requirements (i.e., public reporting of campaign contributions and expenditures) took effect in 1910 (for U.S. House elections) and in 1911 (for U.S. Senate elections). Congress also set limits on campaign expenditures for all congressional candidates. The Federal Corrupt Practices Act of 1925, which served as the primary law regulating federal campaign finance for much of the twentieth century, attempted to strengthen these disclosure requirements and expenditure limits.[11]

One major drawback of early reform efforts was the failure to establish a regulatory agency to monitor and enforce campaign finance law. Instead, the various measures relied on congressional oversight, which proved to be highly ineffective. Early reforms also failed to establish a clear and comprehensive set of penalties for those who violated the law. Moreover, candidates could avoid charges of violating spending limits and disclosure requirements simply by claiming to have had no knowledge of spending on their behalf. As a result, campaign finance effectively remained unregulated and lacked proper disclosure.

Decades later, the use of television to air campaign ads increased the pressure on political candidates to raise money. With campaign costs escalating,

Figure 5.2   Big money's Grip on Government: Thomas Nast's "The Brains" (A Depiction of Boss Tweed of the Tammany Ring, Originally Published in *Harper's Weekly,* October 21, 1871). *Source*: This image is in the public domain.

Congress passed the Federal Election Campaign Act (FECA) and the Revenue Act in 1971. The laws instituted a system of public financing of presidential elections, set contribution and spending limits, and required full reporting of the money that federal campaigns raised and spent.[12]

The FECA also laid the foundation for the creation of political action committees (PACs). Although corporations and labor unions had long been barred from contributing money to candidates for federal office,[13] the new law allowed them to form "separate segregated funds" (i.e., a PAC) through donations raised from stockholders and employees of a corporation or members of a union. They could then use donations from these "separate segregated funds"—or PACs—to spend in federal elections.

Strangely, given the sentiment for campaign finance reform at the time, Congress failed to provide for an adequate enforcement mechanism of the new laws. Consequently, few cases ever reached litigation. Pressure built to strengthen campaign finance laws when news surfaced that Richard Nixon's Committee to Re-Elect the President laundered unreported campaign funds to pay for the silence and perjury of those responsible for breaking into the Watergate hotel in 1972.[14] The Watergate scandal moved Congress to strengthen FECA in 1974, and included the creation of the Federal Election Commission (FEC) to oversee and enforce federal campaign finance law. The 1971 and 1974 laws serve as the foundation of the modern campaign finance system, one with enforceable laws that set limits on campaign contributions and spending, disclosure of contributions and expenditures, and public financing of presidential elections.

In 1976, however, the U.S. Supreme Court partially weakened these reforms with its ruling in *Buckley v. Valeo*. The Court ruled that although limits on campaign contributions were constitutional (to help prevent corruption or the appearance of corruption), spending money independent of a candidate and the candidate's campaign was a form of free speech protected by the First Amendment. This invalidated limits on so-called "independent" expenditures described in FECA. The ruling gave PACs and individuals the right to spend unlimited amounts of money advocating for the election or defeat of a federal candidate if—and only if—the coordination of such expenditures remained independent of the candidate's campaign organization. The Court declared, "The First Amendment denies government the power to determine that spending to promote one's political views is wasteful, excessive, or unwise. In the free society ordained by our Constitution, it is not the government, but the people—individually, as citizens and candidates, and collectively, as associations and political committees—who must retain control over the quantity and range of debate on public issues in a political campaign."[15]

In 1979, Congress further amended FECA to allow individuals and interest groups to give unlimited amounts to political parties for the purpose of "party-building activities" (e.g., buying office equipment, building mailing lists) and to help state and local candidates. This unregulated "soft money" soon became a way for companies, labor unions, and wealthy individuals to make contributions to parties that sometimes exceeded hundreds of thousands of dollars. Parties often earmarked this money to use in particular races for generic party advertising and issue advocacy (i.e., political ads promoting a particular cause—not a candidate).[16] When the Court ruled in *Colorado Republican Federal Campaign Committee v. FEC* (1996) that parties could spend unlimited amounts of money on behalf of a candidate for federal office, provided that the expenditures were made without consulting the candidate, party leaders intensified efforts to solicit soft money contributions from businesses and wealthy individuals.[17]

In a later case, the Court ruled that interest groups could bypass setting up a PAC to pay for so-called "issue advertisements," provided they did not expressly advocate the election or defeat of any candidate for federal office.

This meant that corporate profits and union membership dues could be used to finance issue advertisements if they avoided such "express advocacy." Shortly afterward, groups began to produce and air issue advocacy ads that were in fact thinly veiled campaign ads, but which carefully avoided the words "vote for" or "vote against."[18]

With the rise of issue advertisements and soft money contributions in the mid to late 1990s, concerned groups and citizens argued that large soft money contributions, which average citizens could not afford to give, amplified the voices of the wealthiest Americans and created an environment ripe for corruption.[19] Equally troubling for reformers was the fact that many organized groups were now using issue ads instead of campaign ads. And, because issue ads did not fall under the provisions of FECA, it was difficult and often impossible to trace how they had been financed. Organized interests were able to create new organizations with innocuous sounding names such as "Citizens for Reform," disguising who was actually funding them.[20] Pressure began to build for a new round of reforms during the 1990s. Following the financial scandal and subsequent collapse of the Enron Corporation, reports surfaced that its executives had used soft money donations to help the company avoid federal regulations.[21] Finally, in 2002, Congress passed the Bipartisan Campaign Reform Act (BCRA).

BCRA banned soft money contributions to political parties in an effort to eliminate the large six-figure donations that had become increasingly common throughout the 1990s. However, the law increased the amount that individuals could give to political parties to help compensate for their loss of soft money funds. BCRA also attempted to close the loophole that had allowed for the surge of issue advocacy ads throughout the second half of the 1990s. Under the new law, any ad[22] that referred to a clearly identified candidate for federal office within 60 days of the general election or 30 days of a primary election qualified as "electioneering communications." BCRA required that interest groups pay for these electioneering communications with PAC funds as opposed to general treasury funds.

Senator Mitch McConnell, a staunch opponent of BCRA, led the first major legal challenge to the new law, and in 2003, the Supreme Court heard *McConnell v. FEC*. In a major victory for BCRA supporters, the Court upheld the ban on the use of soft money by national party committees, ruling that there was sufficient governmental interest in "preventing the actual or apparent corruption of federal candidates and officeholders"[23] to justify the restriction. The Court also upheld regulations on electioneering communications, reasoning that because corporations and unions could still finance electioneering communications through their PAC funds, BCRA did not result in an outright ban on expression. According to the Court, issue ads aired in the final days of the election were the "functional equivalent of express advocacy."[24]

The ruling thereby left the law relatively intact, and it appeared as if BCRA had survived its major constitutional challenge.

ROBERTS COURT AND THE CASE OF
CITIZENS UNITED V. FEC

In 2007, the Supreme Court, now under Chief Justice John Roberts, signaled a major shift in campaign finance regulations in the case of *Wisconsin Right to Life, Inc. v. FEC*, which reversed some of BCRA's core provisions. The Court ruled that ads which did not contain express advocacy (or its functional equivalent), even if aired within 60 days of the general election or 30 days prior to a primary, were not sufficiently corruptive to outweigh the free-speech rights of Wisconsin Right to Life, Inc.[25] This ruling signaled the emerging antiregulatory direction of the Roberts Court.

The decision in *Wisconsin Right to Life, Inc. v. FEC*, however, created only a minor stir compared to its later ruling in *Citizens United v. FEC*. The *Citizens United* case traces its history back to the 2008 Democratic presidential nomination season. Citizens United, a conservative nonprofit organization, sought to promote its ideas through books such as *Prince Albert: The Life and Lies of Al Gore* (2000) and *The Many Faces of John Kerry: Why This Massachusetts Liberal is Wrong for America* (2004). The group later expanded its efforts to include the production of documentary films, and for the 2008 election, had planned to release *Hillary: The Movie*. The film featured a scathing attack on then-Senator Hillary Clinton, who at the time was running for the Democratic presidential nomination. The documentary highlighted Clinton's involvement in various scandals during her years of public service in Arkansas and Washington.[26]

To make the film widely available, Citizens United sought to sell the film as a DVD directly to consumers and to show the film in a small number of selected theaters. It also offered to pay $1.2 million to a consortium of cable operators for the documentary to be offered through an "on demand" service at no charge to cable subscribers.[27] However, as noted earlier, federal law under BCRA barred corporations from funding electioneering communications from their general treasuries, a provision upheld in *McConnell v. FEC*.[28] Citizens United financed *Hillary* from various corporate sources and sought to pay for its distribution and advertising with funds in its general treasury, not from its political action committee (Citizens United Political Victory Fund). This raised a host of legal questions, notably whether *Hillary* was equivalent to a lengthy negative campaign advertisement, and if so, whether Citizens United was thereby subject to the electioneering communication financing requirements as specified in BCRA.

Fearing criminal and civil penalties, Citizens United went to district court to seek a preliminary injunction to prevent the FEC from applying and enforcing its interpretation of BCRA's electioneering communication requirements on the film based on the legal argument that the law violated its members' First Amendment rights. Given the Supreme Court's earlier willingness to weaken BCRA's electioneering restrictions in *Wisconsin Right to Life*, the group sought to challenge the law further. The U.S. District Court, however, ruled against Citizens United and denied the injunction, arguing that *Hillary: The Movie* amounted to express advocacy and therefore *Wisconsin Right to Life* did not apply (that case had only involved *nonexpress* issue advocacy). It also noted that previous court rulings, notably *McConnell v. FEC*, had upheld BCRA's communication provisions.[29]

Citizens United appealed the ruling to the U.S. Supreme Court. During oral arguments, Justice Samuel Alito questioned U.S. Deputy Solicitor General, Malcolm Stewart, about the extent to which BCRA applied to communications beyond advertisements, including books and other printed material. The following exchange then took place:

Justice Alito: What's your answer to Mr. Olson's point that there isn't any constitutional difference between the distribution of this movie on video demand and providing access on the Internet, providing DVDs, either through a commercial service or maybe in a public library, providing the same thing in a book? Would the Constitution permit the restriction of all of those as well?

Mr. Stewart: I think the—the Constitution would have permitted Congress to apply the electioneering communication restrictions to the extent that they were otherwise constitutional under *Wisconsin Right to Life*. Those could have been applied to additional media as well. And it's worth remembering that the preexisting Federal Election Campaign Act restrictions on corporate electioneering, which have been limited by this Court's decisions to express advocacy—

Justice Alito: That's pretty incredible. You think that if a book was published—a campaign biography that was the functional equivalent of express advocacy—that could be banned?

Mr. Stewart: I'm not saying it could be banned, I'm saying that Congress could prohibit the use of corporate treasury funds and could require a corporation to publish it using its PAC—

Justice Alito: Well, most publishers are corporations. A publisher that is a corporation could be prohibited from selling a book?

Mr. Stewart: Well, of course the statute contains its own media exemption, for media—

Justice Alito: No, I'm not asking what the statute says. The government's position is that the First Amendment allows the banning of a book if it's published by a corporation?

Later in the exchange, Justice Kennedy asks about the government's position concerning a 500-page book with a single line of express advocacy at the end of it.

Justice Kennedy: If it's a 500 page book and at the end it says "And so vote for X," the government could ban that?

Mr. Stewart: Well, if it says "vote for X," it would be express advocacy, and it would be covered by the pre-existing Federal Election Campaign Act provisions—

Justice Kennedy: No, I'm talking about under the Constitution—what we've been discussing—if it's a book.

Mr. Stewart: If it's a book, and it is produced—and again, to leave—to leave to one side, the question of—

Justice Kennedy: Right, right, forget the—

Mr. Stewart: —possible media exemption—if you had Citizens United, or General Motors, using general treasury funds to publish a book that said at the outset, for instance, "Hillary Clinton's election would be a disaster for this"—

Justice Kennedy: No, no, take my hypothetical. It doesn't say at the outset. It runs—here is a—whatever it is. "This is a discussion of the American political system," and at the end it says "Vote for X."

Mr. Stewart: Yes. Our position would be that the corporation could be required to use PAC funds rather than general treasury funds.

Justice Kennedy: And if they didn't you could ban it?

Mr. Stewart: If they didn't, we could prohibit the publication of the book . . . [for] using the corporate treasury funds.[30]

This exchange expanded the scope of the case from one that merely involved corporate funding of a documentary to the much broader issue of speech rights for corporations. When a decision was finally reached, the Court overturned (by 5-4) the lower court's ruling on First Amendment grounds, and FECA's prohibition on corporations from using general treasury funds to finance electioneering and express advocacy communications. Similar to the rationale in *Buckley v. Valeo*, the majority wrote, "independent expenditures, including those made by corporations, do not give rise to corruption or the appearance of corruption."[31] In the absence of corruption, the Court reasoned that the government had no compelling interest or justification to curb the free speech rights of Citizens United or any corporation or political organization that remained independent of a candidate and a candidate's campaign organization. Corporations and other political organizations were now free to use treasury funds for independent expenditures.

MISCONCEPTIONS OF *CITIZENS UNITED V. FEC*

In the aftermath of *Citizens United,* political observers and experts made numerous claims about the effects of the ruling. Some of these claims now look prescient, while others seem rooted in misconceptions about federal campaign finance law and the ruling in the case. A first set of claims famously came during President Obama's State of the Union Address in 2010. The president, as noted at the outset of this chapter, remarked that the *Citizens United* ruling "reversed a century of law" and that "foreign corporations" would be entitled to "spend without limit in our elections."[32] Justice Alito, who was in attendance at that State of the Union address, responded by mouthing the words, "not true."[33]

Obama's assertion that the ruling reversed a century of law appeared to reference the Tillman Act of 1907, which banned corporate contributions to federal candidates. However, the Court did not overturn, nor did it even address the Tillman Act, in *Citizens United.* Restrictions on campaign contributions for corporations, set forth in the Tillman Act, FECA, and upheld as constitutional in *Buckley v. Valeo*, remain federal law. The *Citizens United* decision, contrary to the claims of President Obama, did not reverse any laws pertaining to restrictions on corporate campaign *contributions*. Instead, the ruling addressed the more contentious issue of *expenditures*, which, dating back to the *Buckley* decision of 1976, has received different consideration and treatment by the Court than campaign contributions. The ruling ultimately overturned two earlier decisions, *Austin v. Michigan Chamber of Commerce* (1990) and a portion of *McConnell v. FEC* (2003). In other words, *Citizens United* rolled back two decades, not a century of law.

Obama's second claim that "foreign entities" might "bankroll" U.S. elections was a concern echoed in the dissenting opinion of Justice John Paul Stevens in *Citizens United.* Stevens warned that the decision "would appear to afford the same protection to multinational corporations controlled by foreigners as to individual Americans."[34] In 2015, Obama doubled-down on his claim, remarking that the *Citizens United* ruling "allowed big companies—including *foreign corporations*—to spend unlimited amounts of money to influence our elections" [italics added].[35]

Yet, the claim of foreign corporations playing a significant role in the U.S. electoral process as a result of the *Citizens United* ruling rests on dubious grounds and overlooks some important provisions in federal law. Notably, it is illegal for foreign nationals[36] to contribute in federal elections. Federal law further bars candidates from knowingly soliciting or receiving campaign contributions from foreign nationals or foreign entities. These prohibitions remain in effect even in the aftermath of the *Citizens United* ruling.

Federal law does allow a U.S. subsidiary of a foreign corporation to form a PAC, but only if the foreign parent corporation does not finance the cost of its establishment or administration. Individual foreign nationals cannot participate in the operation of the PAC or participate in the selection of persons who operate the PAC, serve as officers of the PAC, or make decisions regarding PAC contributions or expenditures. All of these requirements remain federal law, and campaign finance records show no evidence that the amounts spent by these foreign-connected PACs have increased since the *Citizens United* ruling.[37]

Of course, there are hypothetical scenarios that could potentially funnel foreign money into elections. Some political observers have raised the point that foreign entities can finance blogs, videos, and even advertise on non-U.S. websites.[38] While this is true, it is unlikely that the *Citizens United* ruling hastened this development. Others point out that foreign entities may hire American lobbyists, who, in turn, can legally contribute up to $2,700 per election to a federal candidate.[39] But given the high costs of campaigns for federal office, contributions of this amount cover only a small portion of the total amount raised during a typical campaign and fall well short of supporting any claim that foreign entities or foreign corporations "bankroll" U.S. elections.

Finally, some critics of the decision have pointed to the possibility of foreign "dark" money (money whose source has not been disclosed) finding its way into U.S. campaigns.[40] However, as noted above, there are strict laws that prohibit foreign funding of U.S. campaigns, and any effort to circumvent these laws would constitute illegal activity. While there may be the potential for foreign entities and corporations to exploit U.S. campaign finance laws, there have been no federal charges brought against anyone for such illegal activity since the *Citizens United* ruling, nor have there been any IRS investigations into such matters.[41]

WHAT *DID* CHANGE AS A RESULT
OF *CITIZENS UNITED V. FEC*

Other predictions regarding the effect of *Citizens United*, including those from President Obama in his 2010 State of the Union Address, rest on a stronger foundation. For example, the president's claim that the ruling would "open the floodgates for special interests . . . to spend without limit in our elections"[42] has ample evidence to support it. The nonpartisan Center for Responsive Politics shows that combined spending by outside groups in the 2012 and 2014 elections topped an astounding $1.6 billion.[43] By comparison, outside-group spending in the 2006 and 2008 elections, the two elections that preceded the *Citizens United* ruling, was approximately $263 million.[44]

While some increase could be attributed to inflation, the steep rise of more than $1.3 billion over just two election cycles is unprecedented.

Further evidence comes from the Brennan Center for Justice, which reported that in the ten most competitive U.S. Senate elections in 2014, outside groups accounted for the greatest share of spending of any source (47 percent), topping even the amounts spent by candidates (41 percent), who are typically the largest source of funds.[45] So-called "Super PACs," which formed in the aftermath of the *Citizens United* ruling and are allowed to accept unlimited donations because they only make independent expenditures, have spent more than $1 billion since the *Citizens United* decision.[46]

Obama raised additional concerns that the *Citizens United* decision would provide advantages to "America's most powerful interests."[47] Analysis from the Brennan Center supports this conclusion as well. Their research finds that of the $1 billion in Super PAC spending, "almost 60 percent of that money—more than $600 million" was given by only 195 individuals and their spouses.[48]

One can certainly debate whether these developments are detrimental to the democratic system. To some, the sharp increases in outside-group spending in the immediate aftermath of the *Citizens United* ruling lends support to the notion that too much money has entered the electoral process, reducing political campaigns to an auction in which the wealthy play the determining role of kingmaker in the electoral process. Indeed, a CBS News poll from May of 2014 indicated that 75 percent of Americans believe the wealthy have more of a chance to influence elections than do others.[49] Worse, many view the rise of "big money" as a return to the early days of the pre-reform era when big money corruption of the political process was rampant.[50] However, others see little wrong with these developments. To them, increased spending suggests greater amounts of speech, which in turn benefits the democratic process.[51] While honest debate exists about the normative implications of the Citizen United ruling, there is no debate whatever that huge increases in outside group spending resulted.

Finally, one of the most controversial aspects of the *Citizens United* ruling is the claim that it inadvertently weakened disclosure laws. The *Citizens United* decision actually upheld federal disclosure requirements as constitutional, but some political observers have noted that, as a consequence of the ruling, donors have found new avenues to funnel their money to various groups without disclosing their identities. For example, in 2015, President Obama asserted that the electoral process was "drowning in dark money."[52] This claim has some support. The amount of dark money in electoral politics has increased since the *Citizens United* ruling, although it is worth noting that amounts were increasing even before the decision.[53] The direct connection between dark money and the *Citizens United* ruling is therefore unclear.

Nonetheless, increases in dark money represent the further unraveling of the modern campaign finance system that many see as emblematic of the post-*Citizens United* environment.

CONCLUSION

The *Citizens United* decision provoked a range of reactions from political figures and commentators across the nation. This chapter's purpose was to provide background on our history of campaign finance laws in order to contextualize the *Citizens United* decision and then to assess claims about the effects of the ruling. With so much rhetoric surrounding the decision, there has been no shortage of misconceptions about the ruling.

In reviewing the various claims, it seems clear that several criticisms of the decision are simply false. The *Citizens United* decision did not reverse a century of law, but rather reversed two more recent decisions: *Austin v. Michigan Chamber of Commerce* (1990) and a portion of *McConnell v. FEC* (2003). There is also no direct evidence to support the claim that the *Citizens United* decision has led to a rise in foreign money into the U.S. electoral process.

However, the decision has not been without consequences. Spending from outside groups has surged in the aftermath of the ruling. If money is the equivalent of speech, as the Court has long argued, then *Citizens United* can certainly be credited with paving the way for more political speech. Yet, the evidence also shows that a very small number of very wealthy donors have helped to funnel these additional funds into the system.[54] The strong "upper-class accent" of these donors presents a serious concern to some who fear that moneyed interests are now well positioned in the aftermath of the *Citizens United* decision to dominate, and potentially corrupt, the electoral and political process. Whatever position one may take in this debate, this chapter has provided a clearer understanding of how the *Citizens United* ruling has and has not affected the modern campaign finance system.

NOTES

1. *Citizens United v. Federal Election Commission*, 558 U.S. 08-205 (2010). Justice Kennedy's quotation in *Citizens United v. Federal Election Commission* was accessed from http://www.law.cornell.edu/supct/html/08-205.ZO.html.

2. Fred Wertheimer, "Pro & Con: Is the Supreme Court's Ruling on Campaigns Bad for Democracy? Yes, Turning Clock Back 100 Years, Decision will Corrupt Government," *Atlanta Journal Constitution*, January 27, 2010, http://www.ajc.com/opinion/pro-s-ruling-on-285259.html.

3. Keith Olbermann, "Olbermann: U.S. Government for Sale," MSNBC, January 21, 2010, accessed from http://www.msnbc.msn.com/id/34981476/ns/msnbc_tv-count down_with_keith_olbermann/print/0/displaymode/1098/.

4. President Obama's remarks were accessed from a press release issued by the White House Office of the Press Secretary on January 27, 2010. The press release is available at https://www.whitehouse.gov/the-press-office/remarks-president-state-union-address.

5. Robert Costa, "First Amendment 451," *National Review Online*, January 29, 2010, http://www.nationalreview.com/article/229044/first-amendment-451-robert-costa.

6. Theodore B. Olson's quotation appears on the website for Citizens United, accessed from http://www.cuvfec.com.

7. Bradley A. Smith, *Unfree Speech: The Folly of Campaign Finance Reform* (Princeton: Princeton University Press, 2001), 22.

8. Nathan Miller, *Theodore Roosevelt: A Life* (New York: William Morrow and Company, 1992), 245.

9. Robert K. Goidel, Donald A. Gross, and Todd G. Shields, *Money Matters: Consequences of Campaign Finance Reform in U.S. House Elections* (Lanham, MD: Rowman & Littlefield, 1999), 21.

10. Anthony Corrado, "A History of Federal Campaign Finance Law," in *Campaign Finance Reform: A Sourcebook*, ed. Anthony Corrado, Thomas E. Mann, Daniel R. Ortiz, Trevor Potter, and Frank J. Sorauf (Washington, D.C.: Brookings, 1997), 27.

11. For more information, see Document 2.4, The Federal Corrupt Practices Act of 1925, in *Campaign Finance Reform: A Sourcebook*, ed. Anthony Corrado, Thomas E. Mann, Daniel R. Ortiz, Trevor Potter, and Frank J. Sorauf (Washington, DC: Brookings, 1997), 42–6.

12. For a good summary of various campaign reform efforts, see Robert E. Mutch, *Buying the Vote: A History of Campaign Finance Reform* (New York: Oxford University Press, 2014) and R. Sam Garrett, "Back to the Future? The Quest for Public Financing of Congressional Campaigns," in *Public Financing in American Elections*, ed. Costas Panagopoulos (Philadelphia: Temple University Press, 2011).

13. Federal law first prohibited corporate contributions under the Tillman Act of 1907 and union contributions under the Smith-Connally Act of 1943. These laws were strengthened under the Taft-Hartley Act of 1947.

14. Robert E. Mutch, *Buying the Vote: A History of Campaign Finance Reform* (New York: Oxford University Press, 2014). For more on the Watergate scandal, see Stanley I. Kutler, *The Wars of Watergate: The Last Crisis of Richard Nixon* (New York: W.W. Norton, 1990).

15. *Buckley v. Valeo*, 424 U.S. 1 (1976). The quotation in *Buckley v. Valeo* was accessed from http://www.law.cornell.edu/supct/html/historics/USSC_CR_0424_0001_ZO.html. For more information about the case, see Document 7.3, Buckley v. Valeo, 424 U.S. 1 (1976), in *Campaign Finance Reform: A Sourcebook*, ed. Anthony Corrado, Thomas E. Mann, Daniel R. Ortiz, Trevor Potter, and Frank J. Sorauf (Washington, DC: Brookings, 1997), 245–8.

16. David B. Magleby and Eric A. Smith, "Party Soft Money in the 2000 Congressional Elections," in *The Other Campaign: Soft Money and Issue Advocacy in the 2000 Congressional Elections*, ed. David B. Magleby (Lanham, MD: Rowman & Littlefield, 2003), 33.

17. For more information about the case, see Document 3.4, Colorado Republican Federal Campaign Committee v. Federal Election Commission, 116 S. Ct. 2309 (1996), in *Campaign Finance Reform: A Sourcebook*, ed. Anthony Corrado, Thomas E. Mann, Daniel R. Ortiz, Trevor Potter, and Frank J. Sorauf (Washington, DC: Brookings, 1997), 87–92.

18. Trevor Potter, "Issue Advocacy and Express Advocacy: Introduction," in *Campaign Finance Reform: A Sourcebook*, ed. Anthony Corrado, Thomas E. Mann, Daniel R. Ortiz, Trevor Potter, and Frank J. Sorauf (Washington, DC: Brookings, 1997), 233–4.

19. See for example, William Greider, "The Hard Fight Against Soft Money," Rolling Stone, June 26, 1997, http://www.rollingstone.com/politics/news/the-hard-fight-against-soft-money-19970626 and Alexander Keyssar, "The Right to Vote and Election 2000," in *The Unfinished Election of 2000*, ed. Jack N. Rakove (New York: Basic Books), 98.

20. Peter L. Francia, Wesley Y. Joe, and Clyde Wilcox, "Campaign Finance Reform: Present and Future," in *Campaigns on the Cutting Edge*, ed. Richard J. Semiatin (Washington, DC: CQ Press, 2008), 165.

21. Ted Nance, *Gangs of America: The Rise of Corporate Power and the Disabling of Democracy* (San Francisco: Berrett-Koehler, 2003), 150.

22. Specifically, any broadcast, cable, or satellite communication received by 50,000 or more people.

23. *McConnell v. Federal Election Commission*, 540 U.S. 93 (2003). Quotation in *McConnell v. Federal Election Commission* was accessed from http://www.law.cornell.edu/supct/html/02-1674.ZS.html.

24. Ibid.

25. *Federal Election Commission v. Wisconsin Right to Life, Inc.*, 551 U.S. 449 (2007).

26. Conor M. Dowling and Michael G. Miller, *Super PAC! Money, Elections, and Voters After Citizens United* (New York: Routledge, 2014), 11.

27. Robert Barnes, "'Hillary: The Movie' to Get Supreme Court Screening," *The Washington Post*, March 15, 2009, http://www.washingtonpost.com/wp-dyn/content/article/2009/03/14/AR2009031401603.html.

28. Likewise, in 1990, the U.S. Supreme Court ruled in *Austin v. Michigan Chamber of Commerce* that corporations could not use their general treasuries for independent expenditures in federal elections.

29. For a more detailed summary, see Conor M. Dowling and Michael G. Miller, *Super PAC! Money, Elections, and Voters After Citizens United* (New York: Routledge, 2014), 19.

30. These two exchanges in oral arguments were accessed from http://www.supremecourt.gov/oral_arguments/argument_transcripts/08-205.pdf.

31. *Citizens United v. Federal Election Commission*, 558 U.S. 08-205 (2010). Justice Kennedy's quotation in *Citizens United v. Federal Election Commission* was accessed from http://www.law.cornell.edu/supct/html/08-205.ZO.html.

32. President Obama's remarks were accessed from a press release issued by the White House Office of the Press Secretary on January 27, 2010. The press release is available at https://www.whitehouse.gov/the-press-office/remarks-president-state-union-address.

33. "Justice Mouths 'Not True' as Obama Slams Court," Fox News, January 28, 2010, http://www.foxnews.com/politics/2010/01/27/justice-mouths-true-obama-slams-court.

34. *Citizens United v. Federal Election Commission*, 558 U.S. 08-205 (2010). Justice Stevens' quotation in *Citizens United v. Federal Election Commission* was accessed from https://www.law.cornell.edu/supct/html/08-205.ZX.html.

35. Quoted in Philip Bump, "How Citizens United is—and isn't—to Blame for the Dark Money President Obama Hates So Much," *The Washington Post*, January 21, 2015, http://www.washingtonpost.com/blogs/the-fix/wp/2015/01/21/how-citizens-united-is-and-isnt-to-blame-for-the-dark-money-president-obama-hates-so-much.

36. Defined legally as any partnership, association, corporation, organizations, or other combination of persons under the laws of, or having its principal place of business in, a foreign country.

37. Peter L. Francia, "Back to the Future? The Effects of Citizens United v. FEC in the 2010 Election," *The John Marshall Law Review* 44 (2011): 595–618.

38. Zephyr R. Teachout, "Extraterritorial Electioneering and the Globalization of American Elections," *Berkeley Journal of International Law* 27 (2009): 162–91.

39. Dan Froomkin, "How Foreign Money Can Find Its Way Into Political Campaigns," *The Huffington Post*, July 18, 2011, http://www.huffingtonpost.com/2011/07/18/foreign-money-campaign-finance-lobbying_n_897189.html.

40. Andy Kroll, "How Secret Foreign Money Could Infiltrate US Elections," *Mother Jones*, August 8, 2012, http://www.motherjones.com/politics/2012/08/foreign-dark-money-2012-election-nonprofit.

41. For a good summary of this issues, see "10 Things They Won't Tell You About Money in Politics: Dollars from Doha, Dakar, and Dengzhou," Center for Responsive Politics, http://www.opensecrets.org/resources/10things/08.php.

42. President Obama's remarks were accessed from a press release issued by the White House Office of the Press Secretary on January 27, 2010. The press release is available at https://www.whitehouse.gov/the-press-office/remarks-president-state-union-address.

43. "Total Outside Spending by Election Cycle, Excluding Party Committees," Center for Responsive Politics, https://www.opensecrets.org/outsidespending/cycle_tots.php.

44. Ibid.

45. Ian Vandewalker and Eric Petry, "Election Spending 2014: Outside Spending in Senate Races Since 'Citizens United'," Brennan Center for Justice, January 13, 2015, https://www.brennancenter.org/publication/election-spending-2014-outside-spending-senate-races-citizens-united.

46. Vandewalker and Petry, "Election Spending 2014: Outside Spending in Senate Races Since 'Citizens United'."

47. President Obama's remarks were accessed from a press release issued by the White House Office of the Press Secretary on January 27, 2010. The press release is available at https://www.whitehouse.gov/the-press-office/remarks-president-state-union-address.

48. Vandewalker and Petry, "Election Spending 2014: Outside Spending in Senate Races Since 'Citizens United'."

49. Sarah Dutton, Jennifer De Pinto, Anthony Salvanto, and Fred Backus, "Americans' View of Congress: Throw 'em Out," CBS News, May 21, 2014, http://www.cbsnews.com/news/americans-view-of-congress-throw-em-out.

50. James Bennet, "The New Price of American Politics," *The Atlantic*, October 2012, http://www.theatlantic.com/magazine/archive/2012/10/the/309086.

51. "James Bopp: What Citizens United Means for Campaign Finance," Frontline, October 30, 2012, http://www.pbs.org/wgbh/pages/frontline/government-elections-politics/big-sky-big-money/james-bopp-what-citizens-united-means-for-campaign-finance and George Will, "The Judiciary and Free Speech," *The Washington Post*, October 30, 2013, http://www.washingtonpost.com/opinions/george-f-will-the-judiciary-and-free-speech/2013/10/30/1da4119c-40bb-11e3-9c8b-e8deeb3c755b_story.html.

52. Bump, "How Citizens United is—and isn't—to Blame for the Dark Money President Obama Hates So Much."

53. Ibid.

54. Ian Vandewalker, "Election Spending 2014: Outside Spending in Senate Races Since 'Citizens United'," Brennan Center for Justice, 2015, https://www.brennancenter.org/sites/default/files/analysis/Outside%20Spending%20Since%20Citizens%20United.pdf.

FOR MORE READING

Dowling, Conor M. and Michael G. Miller. *Super PAC! Money, Elections, and Voters After Citizens United*. New York: Routledge, 2014.

Mutch, Robert E. *Buying the Vote: A History of Campaign Finance Reform*. New York: Oxford University Press, 2014.

Smith, Bradley A. *Unfree Speech: The Folly of Campaign Finance Reform*. Princeton, NJ: Princeton University Press, 2001.

Chapter 6

The Veepstakes

Balancing the Ticket and Other Myths about the Significance of Vice Presidential Selection

Every four years, political observers, commentators, and experts, spill a great deal of ink predicting who the eventual winner of the presidential nomination will select as his or her vice presidential candidate. This exercise, known as the "veepstakes," has become one of the most entertaining sideshows of the presidential election season. In fact, it is so popular that speculation often starts a full year before the presidential nomination has been decided.[1] In June of 2008, one writer counted over 80 names that had been mentioned as vice presidential possibilities for either John McCain, Hillary Clinton, or Barack Obama in news articles, opinion pieces, and expert commentary—and this compilation ignored most blogs and other essays written by ordinary citizens.[2] However, one observer, noting the sheer volume of articles on the subject and their largely speculative nature has labeled the veepstakes a "largely fact free parlour game."[3]

To be fair, some veepstakes speculation is based on a fairly good understanding of the process of vice presidential selection. But much of this understanding, which constitutes the majority of the conventional wisdom on the subject, is rooted in a historical view of selecting a running mate. In fact, most of the conventional wisdom on this subject centers around the idea of balancing the presidential ticket. Historically this has meant selecting an individual from a larger state, in a different region of the country, and a different faction or ideological wing of the party (or both) from that of the presidential candidate.

In the past several decades, however, the conventional wisdom about what matters in the selection of a presidential running mate has been discarded by presidential candidates and their advisers in favor of a much more complex model. And, while many observers understand this, it is difficult to factor in all of the favorable characteristics of a running mate into a short news story or op-ed piece. This is likely why most accounts continue to focus mainly on balancing the ticket with the vice presidential pick.[4]

In the next section of this chapter, we discuss this historical model of vice presidential selection. Following that, we introduce the modern model. In each section, the focus is the same: the method of selecting presidential running mates and what types of individuals are selected. We will see that in the modern era, the process of making the choice is much more systematic, and the factors that presidential candidates seem to consider in making the choice are more numerous than in the historical era.

THE HISTORICAL ERA OF VICE PRESIDENTIAL SELECTION

Until fairly recently, the vice presidency was considered to be a consolation prize of sorts. The office had few formal or informal responsibilities, and as the result of this, few men aspired to the office. In fact, history is filled with examples of notable political leaders who refused the vice presidential nomination. In 1848, Daniel Webster declined to run on the Whig ticket with Zachary Taylor, saying "I do not propose to be buried until I am really dead and in my coffin."[5] The individuals who did run and serve as vice president in the nineteenth century were decidedly mediocre in terms of their qualifications.[6]

Because the office was considered to be a political dead end prior to the middle of the twentieth century, little energy or effort was expended in the process of selecting the individual who would round out the ticket. One observer noted, "very little pains are bestowed on the election of a vice-president."[7] After the selection of the presidential candidate was made by delegates at the party national convention, attention turned to the selection of his running mate. The convention's decision rarely took very long. Balloting for the vice presidential candidate hardly ever went more than one or two votes.

The overriding concern in the selection of a running mate during this period was how to best "balance" the ticket. Other factors, like the idea that a vice president should be somewhat compatible with the president, were not considered. In truth there have been any number of vice presidents who openly defied their presidents. John Calhoun, for example, actively worked in the Senate to oppose the policies of both of the presidents he served under (John Quincy Adams and Andrew Jackson), and George Clinton did not attend the inauguration of his president (James Madison). In fact, many vice presidents in the nineteenth century did not even live in Washington, and of those who did, many did not meet with their president more than a few times.[8]

The issue of competence was not considered during the selection process either. While vice presidents and vice presidential candidates in the historical era were not completely unqualified, they were generally not men of great stature or leadership caliber, at least when compared with other leaders of the time or with vice presidential candidates in the modern era.[9] One authoritative account from the time noted:

> The convention . . . usually [gave] the nomination to this post to a man in the second rank, sometimes as a consolation to a disappointed candidate for the presidential nomination, sometimes to a friend of such a disappointed candidate in order to "placate" his faction, sometimes to a person from whom large contributions to the campaign fund may be expected, sometimes as a compliment to an elderly leader who is personally popular.[10]

The overriding concern in the selection process during this period was political: How could the vice presidential selection help the ticket win? This is where the issue of balance came into play.

What was meant by "balancing" the presidential ticket? Although there was no precise formula, there were several considerations that were almost always followed, all of which were designed to broaden the appeal of the ticket as well as to unify the party. First, the vice presidential candidate typically represented a state that was from a different region of the country than the home state of the presidential candidate. From 1804 through 2008, only 11 of the major party presidential tickets have *not* been regionally balanced. The most recent of these was in 1992 when Bill Clinton of Arkansas selected Al Gore of Tennessee, another Southerner. This was done in part to broaden the appeal of the ticket in the South, a region that Democratic presidential candidates have had difficulty winning since 1968.[11]

American political parties have always been broad-based coalitions of a variety of interests. This is inevitable with a two-party system in a country as large and diverse as the United States. For example, the modern Republican Party is a loose coalition of Southern Evangelical Christians, fiscal conservatives, antigovernment individuals hailing from the mountain West, and foreign policy hawks. As such, balancing the ticket regionally was frequently an attempt to add factional balance as well. Beyond broadening the appeal of the ticket, this was done to unify the party. Because the presidential nomination could only go to a representative of one faction of the party, the vice presidential nomination was used to mollify other wings or sects within the party. This practice can be seen in the modern era as well, and is often reduced to insuring that the ticket has a certain ideological balance. The more liberal John Kennedy, for example, selected the more conservative Lyndon Johnson in 1960; Gerald Ford, a moderate, selected the more conservative Bob Dole in 1976.[12]

A final factor affecting the selection of a running mate revolved around other political considerations. Vice presidential candidates were usually selected from states that had a large share of Electoral College votes. This was done because it was assumed, or hoped, that the vice presidential candidate could help win the state for the ticket. For example, New York state, which commanded anywhere from eight to 15 percent of available Electoral College votes, fielded fourteen of the forty-eight vice presidential candidates from 1804 through 1896. Conversely, only two came from Maine: Hannibal Hamlin, Republican, in 1860 (2.6 percent of available Electoral College votes) and Arthur Sewall, Democrat, in 1896 (1.3 percent). Recent exceptions to this rule were the selection of the Republican Dick Cheney in 2000, and Republican Sarah Palin and Democrat Joe Biden in 2008, each of whose home states (Wyoming, Alaska, and Delaware, respectively) have approximately one-half of 1 percent of available Electoral College votes.[13] As an historical footnote, presidential tickets have only carried the vice presidential candidate's home state approximately 50 percent of the time.[14]

In short, the main objective of the vice presidential pick in the historical era was to unify the party and insure that the ticket had a broad appeal, in order to prevail in November. This translated into a desire to balance the ticket regionally and ideologically, and, to select a candidate from a state rich in Electoral College votes. When pundits attempt to forecast the vice presidential pick, these factors play heavily into their predictions. However, in the modern era, the process of selecting a running mate has become far more complex. We turn to a discussion of the modern system next.

THE MODERN ERA OF VICE PRESIDENTIAL SELECTION

Vice presidential selection has changed dramatically in the past 50 years. To begin with, while delegates at the party national convention still formally nominate and select the vice presidential candidate, this process only ratifies the choice that the presidential candidate has made. Second, the process by which presidential candidates make the selection is longer and more complicated. Finally, the qualities and characteristics of modern vice presidential candidates have changed as well. While the historical factors of balance and state size still matter, a number of other considerations, including experience in public office, enter into the decision-making process as well.

One of the reasons for this new focus on experience is the increased prominence of the office of the vice presidency. Starting in the middle part of the twentieth century, the vice president has become a more important player in the American system of government. This change occurred slowly, mainly as the result of concerns over presidential succession. These concerns began when Harry Truman assumed the presidency after the death of Franklin Roosevelt in 1945 without knowing an atomic bomb was close to completion. President Dwight Eisenhower had a heart attack in 1955 and other health problems, and John Kennedy was assassinated in 1963. In 1972, Democrat George McGovern asked his vice presidential nominee, Thomas Eagleton, to withdraw from the ticket after reports surfaced that he had undergone electric shock treatment. And, in 1973, Vice President Spiro Agnew resigned in the face of corruption charges, followed by Richard Nixon's resignation in 1974.[15] All of these events served as high-profile reminders that the vice president is only "one heartbeat away" from the presidency.[16]

In large part because of these increased concerns over presidential succession, vice presidents began playing a more important role in their presidents' administrations. Although the formal role of the vice president has not changed (he or she is the president of, and breaks tie votes in, the Senate, and assumes the presidency in the event of presidential vacancy), vice presidents, starting with Richard Nixon (1953–1961) began taking on a number of informal roles. These included traveling abroad to meet with foreign leaders, campaigning for his party's congressional candidates in the midterm elections, acting as presidential spokesperson, presidential adviser, and other, more specialized tasks. Al Gore, for example, was charged with the task of streamlining the federal bureaucracy with his "Reinventing Government" initiative; Dick Cheney was put in charge of crafting a new and comprehensive energy policy; Joe Biden was responsible for insuring that monies from the 2009 economic stimulus package were spent as intended.[17]

Changes in the vice presidential selection process began in 1960, when for the first time, the presidential candidates (John Kennedy and Richard Nixon) chose their own running mates. Previously, as noted, the convention made this choice, although there had been some movement toward giving presidential candidates a say in the matter beginning with Franklin Roosevelt. Of course, candidates consult with any number of advisers, party and interest group leaders, but the choice is now theirs.[18] The fact that the decision maker in the process has changed, should, by itself, suggest that the model for understanding candidate selection has changed as well.

The selection process underwent another dramatic change in the 1970s. As the result of the shift to the primary system of selecting presidential candidates, the presidential nomination is now decided long before the party convention begins. This gives the presumptive presidential nominee a great deal of time to examine the experience, personal background, and political ramifications of his or her possible choices. Jimmy Carter was the first presidential candidate to engage in this lengthy vetting process in 1976, using the five weeks between the end of the primary season and the start of the convention to first narrow a list of 400 possible candidates down to approximately

12 names. His chief pollster Pat Caddell "then tested the relative strengths of these names" and further narrowed the list of possibilities to seven. The campaign team then examined each of these extensively and Carter met with each to discover how compatible each would be with him, both in terms of policy and personality.[19]

If Carter's eventual choice, Walter Mondale, had been a poor vice president, this method of selecting a running mate may have become an historical footnote. In fact, Mondale is widely acknowledged to have been an excellent vice president, the first example of the new model of active vice presidents.[20] The Carter model of extensively vetting vice presidential possibles has become the new standard. What was formerly a hasty and haphazard process—at best—is now lengthy and fairly systematic. The vetting process is typically headed by someone who enjoys the complete trust of the presidential candidate. In 2000, for example, Warren Christopher, who had headed Bill Clinton's search in 1992, headed Al Gore's search, while Dick Cheney was in charge of the process for George W. Bush.[21] Barack Obama relied on Jim Johnson until he resigned over controversy surrounding his Washington insider status, while John McCain's search was headed by Senator Lamar Alexander of Tennessee.[22] In 2012, Mitt Romney asked long-time aide Beth Myers to head his search for a running mate.

Finally, in terms of changes in the modern era, the list of characteristics that modern vice presidential candidates consider has expanded well past the historical factors discussed earlier. In part, this is because of the increased visibility of the office. In addition, because presidential candidates are now the ones selecting their running mates, they can pay attention to more personal factors like compatibility. A lengthy vetting process allows more factors to be examined and considered. The selection itself occurs in context of a different social and political environment that forces presidential candidates to consider characteristics once not considered to be important. So what qualities are modern presidential candidates looking for in their selection of a running mate? We turn to that question in the following section.

VICE PRESIDENTIAL CANDIDATES IN THE MODERN ERA

Given the amount of attention paid to the veepstakes by political observers, it is difficult to believe that scholars have not extensively studied the characteristics of vice presidential candidates. They have not, perhaps because most observers are confident that the conventional wisdom about balancing the ticket is correct. Or, it might be the case that the poor reputation that the office and the men who occupied it enjoyed for so many years made the subject seem unimportant. In either case, it remains the case that the subject is relatively understudied. It has only been in the past decade or so that research has been published that systematically examines this question.[23]

It is important to note here that these few studies address not only the characteristics of vice presidential candidates, but also those who were being considered for the ticket but were not chosen, which typically includes about a half dozen people. The names of possible choices are usually leaked to the press at some point just prior to the announcement of the selection, and confirmed in accounts written after the campaign has concluded. Table 6.1 lists the eventual nominees, the year they ran, and their presidential running mates.

An examination of the characteristics of vice presidential nominees shows how complex this decision has become. Not every candidate possesses all of the qualities that statistical analyses suggest are important in the selection

Table 6.1 Vice Presidential Candidates and their Presidential Running Mates, 1960–2012

Year	Winning VP Candidate (Presidential Candidate, Party)	Losing VP Candidate (Presidential Candidate, Party)
1960	Lyndon B. Johnson (John F. Kennedy, Democrat)	Henry Cabot Lodge, Jr. (Richard M. Nixon, Republican)
1964	Hubert H. Humphrey, Jr. (Lyndon B. Johnson, Democrat)	William E. Miller (Barry M. Goldwater, Republican)
1968	Spiro T. Agnew (Richard M. Nixon, Republican)	Edmund S. Muskie (Hubert H. Humphrey, Jr., Democrat)
1972	Spiro T. Agnew (Richard M. Nixon, Republican)	R. Sargent Shriver (George S. McGovern, Democrat)
1976	Walter F. Mondale (James E. Carter, Jr., Democrat)	Robert J. Dole (Gerald R. Ford, Jr., Republican)
1980	George H. W. Bush (Ronald W. Reagan, Republican)	Walter F. Mondale (James E. Carter, Jr., Democrat)
1984	George H. W. Bush (Ronald W. Reagan, Republican)	Geraldine A. Ferraro (Walter F. Mondale, Democrat)
1988	J. Danforth Quayle (George H. W. Bush, Republican)	Lloyd M. Bentsen, Jr. (Michael S. Dukakis, Democrat)
1992	Albert A. Gore, Jr. (William J. Clinton, Democrat)	J. Danforth Quayle (George H. W. Bush, Republican)
1996	Albert A. Gore, Jr. (William J. Clinton, Democrat)	Jack F. Kemp (Robert J. Dole, Republican)
2000	Richard B. Cheney (George W. Bush, Republican)	Joseph I. Lieberman (Albert A. Gore, Jr., Democrat)
2004	Richard B. Cheney (George W. Bush, Republican)	John R. Edwards (John F. Kerry, Democrat)
2008	Joseph R. Biden, Jr. (Barack H. Obama, Jr., Democrat)	Sarah L. Palin (John S. McCain, III, Republican)
2012	Joseph R. Biden, Jr. (Barack H. Obama, Jr., Democrat)	Paul D. Ryan (Willard Mitt Romney, Republican)

process. This is due to the fact that statistics rely on probabilities, not certainties. In other words, the best that a statistical analysis can tell us with regard to this question is what qualities are likely to be important to presidential candidates in their decision making.

We begin with what these studies have found with respect to the historical factors. Research has confirmed the idea that presidential candidates seek to balance their ticket regionally.[24] It also suggests that in the modern era, ideological balance is no longer important in the ticket-balancing equation.[25] While measuring the ideological orientation of a politician is not a precise science, there have been many instances in the past few decades where the presidential and vice presidential candidates were from the same ideological wing of the party. For example, the elections of 2000, 2004, and 2008 all featured ideologically unbalanced tickets. In 2008, both Obama and Biden could fairly be classified as relatively liberal. Likewise, Democrats John Kerry and John Edwards in 2004 were liberals; Al Gore and Joe Lieberman in 2000, moderates; George W. Bush and Dick Cheney in 2000, conservatives.[26] In fact, a full 50 percent of the tickets since 1960 have not been ideologically balanced. Ideological balancing of the ticket still occurs (e.g., Republicans Bob Dole and Jack Kemp in 1996), but it is no longer as important as in years past, and, is not significant from a statistical standpoint.

Similarly, state size seems to matter less in the modern era as well. In 2008, for example, neither Joe Biden nor Sarah Palin offered more than three potential Electoral College votes to the ticket. A similar situation prevailed in 2000 with Dick Cheney, who registered in Wyoming (three votes). As it happens, the number of Electoral College votes in the candidate's home state is less important than how competitive the state is. While presidential tickets have carried the home state of the vice presidential candidate 14 of 20 times (70 percent) since 1960,[27] coming from either a safe state or a state the ticket has no chance of winning would seem to offer no electoral advantage. Selecting a running mate from a competitive state, however, might boost the ticket's chances of winning that state.[28] While there are different ways of determining which states are competitive, we can safely conclude that they are *not* states that the candidate is certain of winning or losing.

Having said this, not all vice presidential candidates come from competitive states. For example, the Obama campaign was probably not concerned about winning Biden's Delaware, a state that had gone Democratic since 1992. Similarly, the last time Palin's Alaska voted for a Democratic candidate was in 1964. Recent examples notwithstanding, statistical analysis confirms the idea that since 1960, the competitiveness of the vice presidential candidate's home state matters.[29] John Kerry's choice of John Edwards was in part made in an attempt to win North Carolina, even though at the time of the selection, the state had not voted for a Democratic candidate since 1976 (for

Jimmy Carter). And in 1992, Clinton's selection of Al Gore may have been a reflection of the fact that his home state of Tennessee was perceived to be competitive. In fact, the Democratic ticket carried Tennessee in both 1992 and 1996, reversing Republican wins in 1980, 1984, and 1988.

One of the more common misconceptions in the modern era is that the presidential candidate might select their main rival from the primary season for the nomination. This is rarely the case. In fact, the modern vice presidency is built around the premise that the vice president is the president's loyal lieutenant. Because of this, a bitter primary struggle that leaves hard feelings all but precludes the nominee from selecting his main opponent. This, perhaps more than anything, was why Hillary Clinton was reportedly not even considered among the finalists for Obama's eventual selection, or, why George W. Bush's main rival, John McCain, was never considered in 2000.[30]

If the nominee's main opponent either withdraws from the race soon after it becomes obvious they will not win the nomination, or, stays in the race but does not campaign too aggressively, there is some chance of being selected. In 2004, for example, after it became clear that John Kerry would win the Democratic primary, John Edwards withdrew and began campaigning for him. Similarly, although Ronald Reagan's main rival George H. W. Bush had criticized Reagan in the opening caucuses and primaries, he withdrew from the race at an early stage and backed away from earlier criticisms of him. Although Joe Biden was not Obama's main opponent in 2008, he withdrew after the first contest without making any harsh public comments about Obama. The point is that doing well in the presidential primaries is no guarantee that one can eventually secure the vice presidential nomination.[31]

Having served in some capacity in the military seems to be a significant factor in vice presidential selection since 1960, although this may be changing. Since 1960, only eight vice presidential candidates (of a total of 21) have not served in the military, but only two of these ran prior to 2000 (Hubert Humphrey in 1964 and Geraldine Ferraro in 1984). Since 2000, all six vice presidential candidates (Dick Cheney and Joe Lieberman, 2000; John Edwards, 2004; Sarah Palin and Joe Biden, 2008; Paul Ryan, 2012) had no military experience.[32]

In addition to military experience, youth seems to be a desirable factor in selecting a vice presidential candidate in the modern age. The average age of a vice presidential candidate since 1960 was 53 years. Joe Biden was older than this average at the time of his run in 2008 (66), but only 9 years older than the average age of those who Obama considered. Biden is the second oldest vice presidential candidate in the modern era, behind Lloyd Bentsen, who ran with Democrat Michael Dukakis in 1988. At 67, Bentsen was 12 years older than the average age of those under consideration by Dukakis. Sarah Palin, in contrast, was 44 years old, 12 years younger than McCain's other possible choices. Paul Ryan was 42 at the time Mitt Romney selected him in 2012. The youngest candidate during this time period was Dan Quayle (Republican, 1988), who at the age of 41 was 11 years younger than the average of all the candidates who George H. W. Bush considered as a possible running mate. Al Gore was 43 at the time he ran with Bill Clinton in 1992, also 11 years younger than the group average. In all, almost half of the candidates from this period were younger than the average of the group under consideration.[33]

There are two other important factors in the vice presidential selection process that have emerged in the modern era. The first is political experience. Despite the recent example of McCain selecting the relatively inexperienced Palin, the trend in this regard is to draw from a more experienced pool of individuals. For example, of the twenty-one (nonincumbent) vice presidential candidates since 1960, eleven have come from the U.S. Senate. Only three have come from the House of Representatives: William Miller, who ran with Republican Barry Goldwater in 1964; Geraldine Ferraro, Democrat Walter Mondale's running mate in 1984; and Paul Ryan, Mitt Romney's vice presidential candidate in 2012. Others have brought other high-level experience to the ticket (e.g., Dick Cheney was Secretary of Defense under George H. W. Bush).[34] Just two candidates had *only* subnational government experience (Spiro Agnew and Sarah Palin) before their run for vice president.

The point here is that unlike vice presidential selection in the historical era, political experience has become an important factor in the selection process. The good news here is that political experience may translate into competence or fitness to assume the presidency in the event of a presidential vacancy. If nothing else, modern vice presidential candidates are probably more qualified than their premodern counterparts. This is ironic. The original, pre-Twelfth Amendment system for selecting a vice president was to take the second-place winner in presidential balloting. This almost guaranteed that the vice president was of presidential caliber. The Twelfth Amendment relegated one candidate on the ticket to the second spot, all but insuring that great leaders would not seek the position.[35]

The average candidate for vice presidential office in the modern era brought 19 years of governmental experience to the ticket, of which only five were spent in subnational (local and or state government) office. A few were exceedingly qualified. In 1960, Lyndon Johnson had 25 years of experience in national government, 23 in Congress; his opponent, Henry Cabot Lodge, brought 23 years of experience to the Republican ticket. Similarly, in 1964 the Democrat Hubert Humphrey boasted 21 years of experience; his opponent William Miller, 18 years. In 2000, Dick Cheney could claim 21 years of public service, while his Democratic opponent Joe Lieberman had 25 years. The candidate with the most experience in the modern era was Joe Biden, who had 38 years of experience in government, 36 of which were in the U.S. Senate.

Of course, there are exceptions to this trend toward selecting more experienced running mates. In 1968, Richard Nixon selected the moderately well-known governor of Maryland, Spiro Agnew, as his running mate. Agnew had a total of nine years of government experience. Like the campaign against Sarah Palin in 2008, Democrats blatantly exploited his inexperience throughout the campaign. After Thomas Eagleton withdrew from the Democratic ticket in 1972, George McGovern selected Sargent Shriver, who had seven years appointive experience in various national government agencies. In 1980, Ronald Reagan selected George H. W. Bush, who only had nine years of experience in government. In 1984, Walter Mondale selected little-known, three-term House member Geraldine Ferraro, who had a total of ten years of government experience. George H. W. Bush's choice in 1988 was Dan Quayle, who had served two relatively undistinguished terms in the U.S. Senate. John Kerry's choice in 2004 was John Edwards, a first-term U.S. Senator with no other political experience. And in 2008, John McCain selected Sarah Palin, who, before becoming Alaska's governor, had served on the city council and as the mayor of the small town of Wasilla, Alaska (pop. 8,600). To many observers, Palin's experience was insufficient for national office, and she was widely perceived as underqualified.[36]

The point is that there is now a great deal of pressure to select a running mate capable of assuming the presidency. Presidential tickets that ignore this pay a heavy political price, as was the case with Nixon–Agnew in 1968, Bush–Quayle in 1988, and McCain–Palin in 2008. While it is true that Agnew and Quayle became vice presidents, the campaign worked overtime to counter claims they were not qualified.

A final factor that has emerged as significant in the selection process is attention from, or exposure in, the national media. This has become especially important in the Carter model of vice presidential selection, since presidential candidates must do extensive vetting of their possible choices. Allowing the media to do this, wittingly or otherwise, makes good sense. As one account summarizes:

> No presidential candidate has the resources to fully research every aspect of a potential vice president's background . . . [presidential] nominees have increasingly in recent years turned to . . . people who not only have been fully investigated but also have extensive experience dealing with the national media.[37]

Few candidates want a surprise similar to the one McGovern received in 1972 about Thomas Eagleton's psychiatric history. It has been argued that one of the reasons Dan Quayle had the reputation for being less intelligent than some is the fact that the Bush campaign surprised the media by select-ing a relative unknown. Quayle also mishandled some early appearances.[38] The same seems true for Sarah Palin, who was not only a surprise choice, but also was unknown to most of the media elite. Conversely, Joe Biden (2008), John Edwards (2004), Dick Cheney and Joe Lieberman (2000), Jack Kemp (1996), and Al Gore (1992) were all fairly well known by media elite, and had extensive experience with and exposure in the national media. This has become the norm.[39]

Table 6.2 summarizes the characteristics of the 21 nonincumbent vice presidential candidates since 1960. In the next section, we summarize our discussion, rating several of the most recent choices according to the discus-sion presented here.

RATING RECENT VICE PRESIDENTIAL CANDIDATES

Analyses of vice presidential selections since 1960 demonstrate that the old model of understanding the process no longer suffices. While regional bal-ance is still important, ideological balance is not. Moreover, state size is less important than the perception of the vice president's home state as being competitive. Youth, military service, political experience, and exposure in the national media are also important in the modern age. As a side note, various demographic factors such as gender, race and ethnicity, and religion, while often discussed in terms of balancing the ticket, are not significant factors in the selection process. This is likely because the eventual selections are no more or no less diverse than the ones who are not chosen.

So what of recent selections? How well do they fit this model? Bill Clin-ton's selection of Al Gore in 1992 flew in the face of both geographic con-siderations in that both were Southerners, and Gore's Tennessee was not an extremely competitive state for the Democrats (in spite of this, the Democrats did carry the state). Gore was younger, had military experience, only slightly less than average political experience, and enjoyed an average amount of exposure in the national media. Bob Dole's selection of Jack Kemp in 1996 brought regional balance to the ticket, and Kemp came from New York, at the time a fairly competitive state. While slightly older, he also had military experience, a higher than average number of years in government, and expo-sure in the national media.

In 2000, both Dick Cheney and Joe Lieberman brought regional balance to their respective tickets. Both men were slightly older and lacked military experience, but had above average years of political experience. Of the two, Cheney had a great deal of exposure in the national media, while Lieberman had an average amount. John Edwards in 2004 provided the Democratic

Table 6.2 Characteristics of (nonincumbent) Vice Presidential Candidates, 1960–2012

Year	Candidate	State (E.C. Votes)	Regional Balance?	Ideological Balance?	Competitive State?*	Age	Military Service	Years (Govt. Experience Subational, National)	Media Exposure**
1960	Lyndon Johnson (D)	TX (24)‡	Yes	Yes	Yes	52	Yes	25 (0, 25)	High
	Henry Cabot Lodge (R)	MA (16)	Yes	Yes	No	58	Yes	23 (3, 20)	High
1964	Hubert Humphrey (D)	MN (10)‡	Yes	Yes	Yes	53	No	21 (3, 18)	High
	William Miller (R)	NY (43)	Yes	No	Yes	50	Yes	18 (4, 14)	Low
1968	Spiro Agnew (R)	MD (10)	Yes	No	Yes	50	Yes	9 (9, 0)	Low
	Edmund Muskie (D)	ME (4)‡	Yes	Yes	Yes	54	Yes	25 (15, 10)	Low
1972	Sargent Shriver (D)	MD (10)	Yes	Yes	No	57	Yes	7 (0, 7)	High
1976	Walter Mondale (D)	MN (10)‡	Yes	Yes	No	48	Yes	20 (4, 16)	Low
	Bob Dole (R)	KS (7)‡	No	Yes	No	53	Yes	25 (10, 15)	High
1980	George H. W. Bush (R)	TX (26)‡	Yes	Yes	Yes	56	Yes	9 (0, 9)	High
1984	Geraldine Ferraro (D)	NY (36)	Yes	No	Yes	49	No	10 (4, 6)	Low
1988	Dan Quayle (R)	IN (12)‡	Yes	Yes	No	41	Yes	12 (0, 12)	Average
	Lloyd Bentsen (D)	TX (29)	Yes	No	No	67	Yes	26 (2, 24)	High
1992	Al Gore (D)	TN (11)‡	No	No	No	43	Yes	16 (0, 16)	Average
1996	Jack Kemp (R)	NY (33)	Yes	Yes	Yes	61	Yes	23 (1, 22)	High
2000	Dick Cheney (R)	WY (3)‡	Yes	No	No	59	No	21 (0, 21)	High
	Joe Lieberman (D)	CT (8)‡	Yes	No	Yes	58	No	25 (13, 12)	Average
2004	John Edwards (D)	NC (15)	Yes	No	Yes	51	No	5 (0, 5)	High
2008	Joe Biden (D)	DE (3)‡	Yes	No	No	66	No	38 (2, 36)	High
	Sarah Palin (R)	AK (3)‡	Yes	No	No	44	No	12 (12, 0)	Low
2012	Paul Ryan (R)	WI (10)	Yes	Yes	Yes	42	No	14 (0, 14)	Average

Incumbent candidates are not listed. In 1972 Sargent Shriver is listed as the choice, having run on the Democratic ticket after McGovern's first selection, Thomas Eagleton, withdrew.

*"Competitive" is when the average margin of victory from the previous three presidential elections was less than 10 percent.

**Based primarily on author calculations of number of stories that named candidates in *Time* magazine and the *New York Times* in the 18 months prior to the selection of the vice presidential candidate.

‡Ticket won the vice presidential candidate's home state.

ticket with regional balance. North Carolina was also somewhat competitive, although the ticket did not carry the state. Edwards was young, but boasted no military service and little political experience. He did, however, have a higher than average level of exposure in the national media.

In 2008, Barack Obama selected Joe Biden, which balanced the ticket regionally, but with a noncompetitive state that the ticket would surely have won otherwise. Biden was older and lacked military experience. However, he brought a wealth of experience to the Democratic ticket, as well as a relatively high profile in the media. The selection of Sarah Palin by John McCain also added regional balance to the ticket, but with a state that was similarly noncompetitive. She was young at the time of her selection, but like Biden lacked military experience. However, unlike Biden, she had a relative lack of political experience, and, virtually no exposure in the national media. So why did McCain select Palin, especially given the controversy that the choice generated? First, it was unconventional (to state it mildly), emphasizing his reputation as a "maverick." Beyond this, it helped mobilize support from the previously lukewarm Republican base of evangelical Christians. Whether it was a strategically sound move by McCain is open to interpretation.

Finally, in 2012, Paul Ryan brought several qualities to the Republican ticket. First, one hope for Republicans was that his youth might help counter the perception that Romney was out of touch, especially with a younger generation that Obama had connected with so well. Second, his home state of Wisconsin, with ten Electoral College votes, was (too optimistically, it turns out) thought to be somewhat competitive in 2012. The belief was that adding Ryan to the ticket may have helped the Republicans carry the state. Ryan was also known as a fiscal conservative, which brought some conservative credentials to a ticket that was somewhat lacking in that department. Finally, Ryan's reputation in the House was built primarily on his focus on economic issues. As Chairman of the House Ways and Means Committee, he had also been a member of the 2010 bipartisan National Commission on Fiscal Responsibility and Reform (Bowles–Simpson Commission), responsible for producing a plan to reduce the federal deficit. Ryan, who had long been a proponent of fiscal responsibility, was opposed to the final report of the commission on the grounds that it did not go far enough. In short, Ryan's policy focus on economic issue complemented Romney's focus on the still-recovering economy in 2012.

CONCLUSION: DOES IT MATTER?

One of the reasons why predicting the vice presidential choice will never be a perfect science is that presidential candidates select their running mate in order to emphasize or deemphasize a particular aspect of their own candidacy. The notion of regional and ideological ticket balancing with a selection from a large state is a good way to understand vice presidential selection in a previous era, but no longer suffices. Vice presidential selection is now a complex process, dependent on a number of factors.

But does the choice really matter? Does it have any real impact? On the one hand, the vice president is the constitutional successor to the president in the event of a presidential vacancy (death, disability, resignation, or impeachment). As one account summarizes:

> From 1841 to 1975 more than one-third of all U.S. presidents either died in office or quit, paving the way for the vice president to occupy the White House. Eight vice presidents became president as a result of the death of a sitting president (John Tyler, Millard Fillmore, Andrew Johnson, Chester Arthur, Theodore Roosevelt, Calvin Coolidge, Harry Truman, and Lyndon Johnson) and one, Gerald Ford, became president as the result of presidential resignation.[40]

Therefore the question of how qualified the vice president is to assume the presidency is extremely important.

But for all of the attention paid to the veepstakes by political pundits and observers, does the selection of a running mate have any effect on the outcome of the election? Some suggested that in 1992, George H.W. Bush may have been able to secure as much as eight percentage points extra without Quayle as his running mate.[41] Others were quick to suggest that McCain's loss in 2008 was in part attributable to his selection of Palin.[42] To be fair, there is no question that both of these individuals were a public relations drag on their respective tickets. But did they cost their tickets actual votes? Research on this question is notoriously difficult because it is "virtually impossible to disentangle presidential and vice presidential preferences in our system of presidential elections."[43] While a handful of studies suggest that Palin may have cost McCain some support,[44] the predominance of the evidence points in a clear direction: "the vice presidential candidate has—at most—a marginal effect on voters' choices."[45]

It is true that vice presidents and vice presidential candidates are in the spotlight more than in earlier eras. It is also true that vice presidents are an integral part of their president's team, again, unlike in earlier times. However, people cast their vote for the presidential ticket based on party preference and the presidential candidate—not the vice presidential candidate.

Richard Nixon once remarked that a vice president "can't help you . . . he can only hurt you."[46] According to this Nixon doctrine, which virtually all presidential scholars agree with, vice presidential candidates can hurt, but not help the ticket. So while the question of whether an individual is qualified to assume the presidency in the event of a presidential vacancy is clearly an important one, the selection of a vice presidential candidate has almost no impact on the outcome of the election.

NOTES

1. Herman Cain, "Let the Veepstakes Begin," TownHall.com, February 26, 2007, www.townhall.com/columnists/HermanCain/2007/02/26/let_the_veepstakes_begin; Rick Klein, "Never Too Early for the Veepstakes Race," ABC News Online, June 12, 2007, abcnews.go.com/Politics/story?id=3270446&page=1; Matt Mackowiak, "Veepstakes: The Contenders," PoliticalInsider.com, February 5, 2007, politicalinsider.com/2007/02/veepstakes_the_contenders.html; Larry Sabato, "The Outrage of Early Vice Presidential Speculation," *Sabato's Crystal Ball*. Volume V, Issue 9, March 29, 2007, www.centerforpolitics.org/crystalball/article.php?id=LJS2007032901.

2. Jody C Baumgartner, "The Veepstakes: Forecasting Vice Presidential Selection in 2008," *PS: Politics and Political Science*, 41 (October 2000): 765–72.

3. James Harding, "Voters Weigh up Kerry by the Company He Keeps: Speculation on the Democrat's Likely Running Mate Is Rife," *Financial Times*, May 20, 2004, search.ft.com/nonFtArticle?id=040520000684.

4. For a recent example of the "ticket balance" claim, see John Feehery, "Picking a Vice President," *The Hill*, March 12, 2012, http://thehill.com/opinion/columnists/john-feehery/215591-picking-a-vice-president.

5. Jody C Baumgartner, *The American Vice Presidency Reconsidered* (Westport Conn., Preager, 2006), 1.

6. Jody C Baumgartner, "The Second Best Choice? Vice Presidential Candidate Qualifications in the Traditional and Modern Eras," *White House Studies*, 6 (2006): 179–95.

7. James Bryce, *The American Commonwealth*, Volume II (New York: Macmillan, 1893), 46.

8. Baumgartner, *The Modern Vice Presidency Reconsidered*, 21–2.

9. Baumgartner, "The Second Best Choice?"

10. Bryce, *The American Commonwealth*.

11. Baumgartner, *The Modern Vice Presidency Reconsidered*, 18–19.

12. Ibid.

13. Ibid.

14. Robert L. Dudley and Ronald B. Rapoport, "Vice Presidential Candidates and the Home State Advantage: Playing Second Banana at Home and on the Road," *American Journal of Political Science* 33 (1989): 537–40.

15. Baumgartner, *The Modern Vice Presidency Reconsidered*, 55–6.

16. Birch Bayh, *One Heartbeat Away: Presidential Disability And Succession* (Indianapolis, IN: Bobbs-Merrill, 1968); Michael Nelson, *A Heartbeat Away* (New York: Twentieth Century Fund, 1988).

17. Joel K. Goldstein, *The Modern American Vice Presidency: The Transformation of a Political Institution* (Princeton, NJ: Princeton University, 1982); Paul C. Light,

Vice-Presidential Power: Advice and Influence in the White House (Baltimore: Johns Hopkins University, 1984); Baumgartner, *The Modern Vice Presidency Reconsidered*.

18. Baumgartner, "The Veepstakes."

19. Baumgartner, *The Modern Vice Presidency Reconsidered*, 62–3.

20. Light, *Vice-Presidential Power*.

21. Baumgartner, *The Modern Vice Presidency Reconsidered*, 59.

22. Tom Hamburger, "Obama Advisor Jim Johnson Resigns Amid Criticism," *Los Angeles Times*, June 12, 2008, articles.latimes.com/2008/jun/12/nation/na-johnson12; J. Taylor Rushing, "McCain Picks Former Reagan Official To Head VP Search," The Hill, May 23, 2008, thehill.com/campaign-2008/mccain-selects-former-reagan-official-to-head-vp-search-2008-05-23.html.

23. See, for example, Lee Sigelman and Paul J. Wahlbeck, "The 'Veepstakes': Strategic Choice in Presidential Running Mate Selection," *American Political Science Review* 91 (1997): 855–64; Robert P. Watson and Richard M. Yon, "Vice Presidential Selection in the Modern Era," *White House Studies* 6 (2006): 163–78; Baumgartner, "The Second Best Choice"; Mark Hiller and Douglas Kriner, "Institutional Change and the Dynamics of Vice Presidential Selection," *Presidential Studies Quarterly* 38 (2008): 401–21; Jody C Baumgartner, "The Post-Palin Calculus: The 2012 Republican Veepstakes," PS: Politics and Political Science 45 (2012): 605–9; this discussion draws heavily on Baumgartner, "The Veepstakes."

24. Jody C Baumgartner, "Vice Presidential Selection in the Convention Era: Experience or Electoral Advantage?" Congress and the Presidency 39 (2012): 297–315.

25. Baumgartner, "The Veepstakes."

26. Baumgartner, *The American Vice Presidency Reconsidered*, 78.

27. Jody C Baumgartner, *The Vice Presidency: From the Shadow to the Spotlight* (Lanham, MD: Rowman & Littlefield, 2015), 107.

28. Baumgartner, "The Veepstakes," 765–6.

29. Ibid.

30. Ibid.

31. Ibid.

32. Ibid.

33. Ibid.

34. Ibid.

35. Baumgartner, "The Second Best Choice?"

36. Baumgartner, *The American Vice Presidency Reconsidered*.

37. Nelson W. Polsby and Aaron Wildavsky, *Presidential Elections: Strategies and Structures in American Politics*. Eleventh Edition (Lanham, MD: Rowman & Littlefield, 2004), 132.

38. David S. Broder and Bob Woodward, *The Man Who Would Be President: Dan Quayle* (New York: Simon & Schuster, 1992).

39. Baumgartner, *The American Vice Presidency Reconsidered*.

40. Baumgartner, *The Vice Presidency*, 2.

41. Nelson, "The Election," 68.

42. See for example, Matthew Continetti, "Five Myths About Sarah Palin," *The Washington Post*, October 17, 2010 http://www.washingtonpost.com/wp-dyn/content/article/2010/10/14/AR2010101404794.html.

43. Baumgartner, *The Vice Presidency*, 115.

44. For a summary of these studies, see Jonathan Chait, "Did Palin Hurt McCain?" *New Republic*, October 15, 2010, http://www.newrepublic.com/blog/jonathan-chait/78407/did-palin-hurt-mccain.

45. From Baumgartner, *The Vice Presidency*, 115; see Danny M. Atkinson, "The Electoral Significance of the Vice Presidency," *Presidential Studies Quarterly* 12(3) (1992): 330–36; David W. Romero, "Requiem for a Lightweight: Vice Presidential Candidate Evaluations and the Presidential Vote," *Presidential Studies Quarterly* 31(3) (2001):454–63; Thomas M. Holbrook, "The Behavioral Consequences of Vice Presidential Debates: Does the Undercard Have Any Punch?"; Brian J. Brox and Madison L Cassels, "The Contemporary Effects of Vice-Presidential Nominees: Sarah Palin and the 2008 Presidential Campaign," *Journal of Political Marketing* 8 (2009): 349–63; Erward M. Burmilla and Josh M. Ryan, "Reconsidering the 'Palin Effect' in the 2008 Presidential Election," *Political Research Quarterly* 66 (2013): 952–9; Jonathan Knuckey, "Comments on Reconsidering the "Palin Effect"," *Political Research Quarterly* 66 (2013): 960–3; and Jonathan Knuckey, "The 'Palin Effect' in the 2008 U.S. Presidential Election," *Political Research Quarterly* 20 (2008): 1–15.

46. Natoli, *American Prince, American Pauper*, 43.

FOR MORE READING

Baumgartner, Jody C "The Post-Palin Calculus: The 2012 Republican Veepstakes." *PS: Politics and Political Science*. 45(2012): 605–9.

Baumgartner, Jody C *The Vice Presidency: From the Shadow to the Spotlight*. Lanham, MD: Rowman & Littlefield, 2015.

Goldstein, Joel K. *The Modern American Vice Presidency*. Princeton, NJ: Princeton University Press, 1982.

Light, Paul C. *Vice-Presidential Power: Advice and Influence in the White House*. Baltimore: Johns Hopkins University, 1984.

Mayer, William G. "A Brief History of Vice Presidential Selection," in William G. Mayer, ed., *In Pursuit of the White House 2000: How We Choose Our Presidential Nominees*. Chatham, NJ: Chatham House, 2000.

Chapter 7

Myth or Reality? Presidential Campaigns Have Become Nastier

In almost every election, political observers comment on the declining quality of political campaigns. One of the most frequently made charges is that negative campaigning has grown worse over the years. In 2012, for example, one analyst asked—presumably rhetorically—"is this the nastiest election ever?"[1] Another lamented that while "past campaigns have featured their fair share of punches . . . 2012 is setting an unprecedented tone. . . . Both campaigns have also released a slew of . . . attack ads."[2] Obama supporters, for example, went so far as to blame Romney for the death of the wife of a laid-off steel worker from cancer.[3] Many suggested that, "negative presidential campaign ads [are] going to new extremes."[4]

This apocalyptic view of the state of political advertising is not new. In fact, we were treated to similar analyses in 2008. One political observer characterized the 2008 presidential election as history's "longest, meanest and most expensive."[5] Opinion pieces flashed headlines with titles such as, "McCain Campaign is the Ugliest Ever."[6] Others involved in the campaign made accusations about the shrill content of their opponents' campaign attacks. Cindy McCain, the wife of John McCain, commented to a newspaper in Tennessee that the Obama campaign had "waged the dirtiest campaign in American history."[7] Obama's running mate, Joe Biden, countered that the McCain campaign was "running the most scurrilous campaign in modern history."[8]

This reaction was due, at least in part, to some controversial attacks that surrounded the 2008 presidential election. Critics of the McCain campaign cited its efforts to label Obama as a socialist, a traitor, and as someone who "pals around with terrorists" as a desperate and even dangerous tactic that was "sowing the seeds of hatred and division."[9] Others suggested that McCain's ads, such as those connecting Obama with 1960s radical Bill

Ayers, had contributed to a hostile environment best illustrated by a McCain supporter who screamed "Kill him!" (in reference to Obama) during a rally led by McCain's running mate, Sarah Palin.[10] Republicans countered by claiming that the Obama campaign used "coded language" about McCain's age and health (McCain was 72 years old).[11] Conservatives were especially upset with the some of the harsh attacks by Obama supporters comparing Sarah Palin "to a Nazi sympathizer" and those that attacked her family.[12]

While few would dispute the fact that recent presidential elections are replete with egregious examples of political attacks, it is highly debatable that any of the recent contests were the "dirtiest" ever. Indeed, negative campaign tactics have always played a pervasive role in American presidential elections. Opponents of Thomas Jefferson suggested that his victory would lead to the rise of atheism and the burning of the Bible.[13] Andrew Jackson had to endure attacks by his political opponents that his deceased mother was a prostitute.[14] These and other examples illustrate that the mean-spirited, personal attacks in American campaigns are hardly new to the political landscape.

Our goal in this chapter is to demonstrate that personal attacks during political campaigns have long been a part of American politics. Our focus is on presidential elections. This is because while state and local elections can also be very negative, presidential races are the "Super Bowl" of campaigns. As such, perceptions of American elections are most heavily shaped by these contests. In the next section, we briefly review what it means to "go negative." We then turn to an examination of three presidential campaigns from the nineteenth century that stand out as particularly negative. These historical examples cast considerable doubt on the repeated claims that "today's campaigns are the most negative ever." Following this, we examine some recent campaigns, illustrating that even the worst of these have been no more negative than campaigns in earlier times.

"GOING NEGATIVE" AND NEGATIVE CAMPAIGNS IN THE NINETEENTH CENTURY

Evaluating how negative a campaign is to some degree a subjective endeavor. Indeed, there are slightly different definitions in the literature about what exactly constitutes negativity in a campaign. There is some agreement that it typically involves discrediting, criticizing, or publicizing the deficiencies of the opponent.[15] A truly balanced examination would allow for the fact that ads which compare and contrast some aspect of both candidates' record or background should more properly be thought of as comparative, or contrast ads. Although critical of the opponent, these ads present information that the voting public should know before they make their decision about who will best serve their interests if elected.[16] There is justification for the idea that these ads serve the public. Some mention of the opponent's background, experience, and public record should probably be part of the campaign discourse.

Some political scientists suggest that negative campaigning has had a deleterious effect on American democracy. Their research finds that negative advertisements heighten political cynicism, depress voter turnout, and reduce political efficacy.[17] Others argue that negative advertisements provide important information to voters, help draw clearer distinctions between candidates, and improve voters' recall of information and memory of the ad.[18] Our central purpose in this chapter, however, is not to weigh into the debate about the effects of negative advertising. Rather, it is to counter the ever-present claim that the present campaign is the "dirtiest ever." With an understanding of what "negative" campaigns really are, we now turn to various historical cases which illustrate that vicious negative campaigning is nearly as old as the republic.

In his book, *Mudslingers*, the scholar Kerwin Swint examined the 25 dirtiest political campaigns in history. According to Swint, four of the five dirtiest campaigns occurred in the nineteenth century. Here we will review three of these four: the presidential elections of 1800, 1828, and 1864.

The Election of 1800

The election of 1800 pitted the Federalist President John Adams against his Democratic–Republican Vice President Thomas Jefferson. Besides the election precipitating the passage of the Twelfth Amendment, the election was significant in that it set a rather high standard for negativity and viciousness.[19] While there were legitimate differences separating the two on many issues, supporters often focused their efforts on negative personal attacks.

Adams' supporters spread stories that Jefferson had "cheated his British creditors, obtained property by fraud, robbed a widow of an estate worth ten thousand pounds, and behaved in a cowardly fashion as Governor of Virginia during the Revolution."[20] Another attack claimed Jefferson was "mean-spirited" and the "son of a half-breed Indian squaw, sired by a Virginia mulatto father."[21] One newspaper opined that a victory for Jefferson in 1800 would result in the teaching and practice of "murder, robbery, rape, adultery, and incest" and added that the "air will be rent with cries of the distressed, the soil will be soaked with blood, and the nation black with crimes."[22] The president of Yale University believed that Jefferson's election would result in "the Bible [being] cast into a bonfire . . . our wives and daughters [becoming] the victims of legal prostitution."[23] Others attacked him as a dangerous rebel "who writes against the truths of God's word . . . without so much as a decent external respect for the faith and worship of Christians."[24]

Jefferson's supporters attacked Adams as a "fool, hypocrite, criminal, and tyrant."[25] Jeffersonians also planted a rumor that Adams had intended to arrange a marriage between one of his sons and one of the daughters of King George III in a plot to reunite the United States and Great Britain. Another rumor suggested that Adams had sent his running mate, General Charles Pinckney, to England on a trip to secure four mistresses, two for each of them. To these charges, Adams famously retorted, "If this be true, [then] General Pinckney has kept them all for himself and cheated me out of two."[26]

While negativity swirled in both directions, the political environment favored Jefferson in 1800. Adams would garner just 39 percent of the popular vote compared to 61 percent for Jefferson. In the Electoral College vote, however, Jefferson received seventy-three of the necessary seventy Electoral College votes to win the presidency, while Adams received sixty-five. However, because the Electoral College at the time did not distinguish between votes for president and vice president, Jefferson's running mate, Aaron Burr, also received seventy-three Electoral College votes, creating a tie and moving the election to the House of Representatives. There, Jefferson was finally elected president on the thirty-sixth ballot.[27]

The Twelfth Amendment eventually altered the chaotic process that ensued following the tie between Jefferson and Burr, giving the election of 1800 special historical significance. However it was also significant in that many credit it as the first seriously contested presidential election campaign. The campaign certainly set a standard for negativity that would generate notice even by today's standards.[28]

The Election of 1828

The election of 1828 matched incumbent President John Quincy Adams (the son of former President John Adams) of the Whig Party against challenger Andrew Jackson, a Democrat and former army general who led American troops to a decisive victory over the British in the Battle of New Orleans during the War of 1812. The election was a rematch of sorts of the previous election, which had ended in bitter controversy.

In 1824, Jackson faced Adams, as well as William Crawford and Henry Clay. Jackson garnered 41 percent of the popular vote, ten percentage points more than that of Adams. Yet, all four received votes in the Electoral College: Jackson (99), Adams (84), Crawford (41), and Clay (37). Because no candidate received a majority of Electoral College votes, the election was thrust into the House of Representatives.[29] In the House, Clay was disqualified for finishing fourth (the Twelfth Amendment stipulates that the House may consider only the top three finishers). However, as the Speaker of the House, Clay wielded considerable influence, and because he deeply disliked Jackson[30] he threw his support to Adams. The Adams win infuriated Jackson supporters because their candidate received the most popular and the most Electoral College votes. To add to the outrage, Adams named Clay his secretary of state, prompting critics to suggest that the two had struck a "corrupt bargain."[31] This set the stage for the bitter 1828 rematch.

Jackson supporters attacked Adams for his excesses, suggesting "King John the Second" lived in "kingly pomp and splendor."[32] The charge centered on Adams' purchase of a billiards table, which Jacksonians falsely claimed was purchased at taxpayer expense. Jacksonians also questioned Adams' religious sincerity, claiming he sometimes traveled on Sundays and had "premarital relations" with his wife. These attacks came despite the fact that Adams was a Puritan and, by all reasonable accounts, a devout Christian. Most outrageous was the Jacksonian claim that, while serving as the minister to Russia, Adams handed over a young American girl to Czar Alexander I.[33]

The Adams campaign played equally dirty in attacking Jackson. A pro-Adams political handbook claimed Jackson was "wholly unqualified by education, habit and temper for the station of President,"[34] but this was tame compared to other accusations. Adams' supporters attacked Jackson with an endless barrage of charges that included adultery, bigamy, gambling, drunkenness, theft, and even murder. The murder charge involved Jackson's approval to execute six militiamen for desertion during the Creek War in 1813. A pro-Adams editor described the event as "the Bloody Deeds of General Jackson," cold-blooded murder in which Jackson sanctioned killing innocent soldiers.[35]

Attacks against Jackson even extended to his family. One newspaper story was particularly vicious, attacking Jackson's mother as a prostitute. According to the account, "General Jackson's mother was a COMMON PROSTITUTE, brought to this country by the British soldiers. She afterward married a MULATO MAN, with whom she had several children, of which GENERAL JACKSON IS ONE!!!"[36] Jackson also had to endure attacks against his wife. Adams' supporters spread misleading stories that Jackson's wife, Rachel, was an adulterer and a bigamist. The story underlying the charge, however, was more complicated. Jackson's wife had been married previously and believed she had lawfully divorced her first husband, when she began her relationship with Jackson. This, however, was not the case. By the time Jackson and Rachel became aware of this, the two had already married.[37]

In the end, Jackson defeated Adams in the 1828 election, winning 56 percent of the popular vote and 178 of the 261 Electoral College votes. However, the victory came at a deep personal cost to Jackson. His wife, Rachel, died a month after the election in December 1828. Jackson blamed Adams' supporters for their relentless attacks against his wife, referring to them as "murderers" and vowing never to forgive them. At her funeral, Jackson declared, "May God Almighty forgive her murderers, as I know she forgave them. I never can."[38]

The 1828 election certainly rises to the highest levels of negativity in American campaigns. Indeed, many scholars consider the election of 1828 to be one of dirtiest presidential contests in American history.[39] As negative as modern campaigns can sometimes become, it seems difficult to argue that the 2012 election contained anything that surpassed the attacks of the 1828 election.

The Election of 1864

The two principle candidates in the 1864 presidential election were President Abraham Lincoln (Republican) and challenger General George McClellan (Democrat) of New Jersey. While Lincoln is revered today as one of the greatest presidents in American history, he was not nearly as popular in 1864. The Civil War was responsible for rising death tolls and mounting financial costs, which critics suggested were Lincoln's fault. His opponents in the Democratic Party believed that this presented them with an opportunity to win the White House.

During the campaign, Lincoln's opponents labeled him ignorant, incompetent, and corrupt. Others went further, referring to him as "Ignoramus Abe." Additional pejorative descriptions of Lincoln included ape, gorilla, Old Scoundrel, despot, liar, perjurer, thief, swindler, robber, buffoon, monster, fiend, and butcher.[40] One critic claimed the "idea that such a man as he should be president of such a country is a very ridiculous joke."[41] Another attack involved a false story that Lincoln demanded one of his officers sing him a song while passing the bodies of dead Union solders after the Battle of Antietam.[42]

Other anti-Lincoln groups relied on overtly racist appeals in their attempts to discredit Lincoln. One pamphlet labeled Lincoln as "Abraham Africanus the First" for his opposition to slavery (see Figure 7.1). Another was titled "Miscegenation: The Theory of the Bending of the Races, Applied to the American White Man and Negro," and claimed that Lincoln favored "race mixing" and actively encouraged and supported the "intermarriage" between whites and blacks. Many anti-Lincoln newspapers aggressively publicized the pamphlet.[43] Another claimed his election with the "Black Republican Ticket" would "bring on NEGRO EQUALITY, more DEBT, HARDER TIMES . . . Universal Anarchy, and Ultimate RUIN! (see Figure 7.2). Yet a third, labeled "The Lincoln Catechism," outlined the "despotism" and horrors another Lincoln term would bring (Figure 7.3).

Lincoln supporters attacked McClellan personally as well, labeling him a "coward" and criticizing his "defeatism" and "lack of patriotism."[44] Some even suggested that Democratic opposition to the war constituted treason.

Figure 7.1 Attack Ads, circa 1864. *Source*: Answers.com, at http://www.answers.com/topic/united-states-presidential-election-1864.

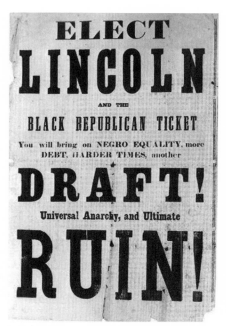

Figure 7.2 Attack Ads, circa 1864. *Source*: Illinois Periodicals Online, at http://www.lib.niu.edu/2001/iht820144.html.

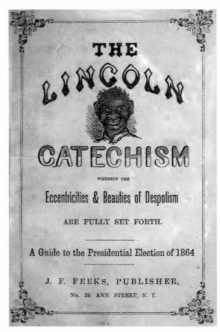

Figure 7.3 Attack Ads, circa 1864. *Source*: Communities Digital News, at http://
www.commdiginews.com/politics-2/the-lincoln-catechism-and-president-barack-
obama-31745/.

Republicans ridiculed McClellan as "Little Mac," and attacked his military
credentials as a general, noting that he had "nothing to offer but a tradition of
defeat."[45] In Pennsylvania, Republicans warned in one poster that a McClellan victory would lead to anarchy, despotism, and the end of civilization.

The election concluded with a clear victory for Lincoln and had significant implications for American history. Lincoln's presidency would also be
remembered for its high ideals. However, even "Honest Abe" could not avoid
negative campaigning in the election of 1864.

MODERN "NEGATIVE" CAMPAIGNS

Extreme examples of negative campaigning exist in the modern era as well.
Similar to the nineteenth century, modern campaigns have continued the
practice of ruthlessly attacking the opposition. However, unlike the nineteenth
century, modern campaigns could package negative messages into 30-second
(or less) television advertisements capable of reaching millions of citizens.
Television also provides a "perfect medium" for tapping into voters' "surface

feelings."[46] The emotional appeals of television can have the effect of mobilizing citizens to vote and participate in the political process.[47] In the television era, two campaigns stand out as particularly negative: the presidential elections of 1964 and 1988.[48]

The Election of 1964

The presidential election of 1964 was a contest between two candidates with sharply different views about the proper role of government. The political ideologies of the incumbent president, Democrat Lyndon Johnson of Texas, and his Republican challenger, Senator Barry Goldwater of Arizona, could not have been more different. Johnson believed in an active role for government to combat poverty, racism, and other social ills, whereas Goldwater campaigned on a conservative platform, claiming that smaller government was essential to expanding individual freedom and liberty. Indeed, Goldwater himself promised voters a "choice rather than an echo."[49]

As the incumbent president, Johnson faced little serious opposition for the Democratic nomination. However, Goldwater's nomination divided the Republican Party. Moderates, led by Governors Nelson Rockefeller of New York and George Romney of Michigan, refused to support or campaign on Goldwater's behalf. Goldwater alienated Dwight Eisenhower as well, referring to his presidential administration as a "dime store New Deal."[50] When asked about the presidential prospects of Eisenhower's brother, Milton Eisenhower, Goldwater told *Time Magazine*, "One Eisenhower in a generation is enough."[51] Goldwater also exacerbated tensions with moderate Republicans in his acceptance speech at the Republican convention in San Francisco, famously remarking that "extremism in the defense of liberty is no vice . . . [and] that moderation in the pursuit of justice is no virtue."[52] Reacting to the speech, Senator Kenneth Keating of New York and others from the New York delegation walked out on the convention in protest.

Goldwater faced not only divisions within his own party, but also was up against his own tendency to provide colorful, but highly controversial public statements, which the Johnson campaign ultimately exploited. In particular, the Johnson campaign made use of several Goldwater statements in its advertisements to paint him as a dangerous, prowar candidate. In one short, 20-second television ad, viewers see a nuclear explosion as an announcer recites: "On October 24, 1963, Barry Goldwater said of the nuclear bomb, 'Merely another weapon'. Merely another weapon? Vote for President Johnson. The stakes are too high for you to stay home."[53]

The aforementioned advertisement, however, is less well-known than the so-called "Daisy girl commercial," which one scholar dubbed, "the Mother of all televised attack ads."[54] In this ad, a young girl plucks the petals of a

WiscAds
"DAISY GIRL"
Lyndon Johnson, 1964

[Girl]: One...two...

three...four...five

seven...six...six

eight...nine...nine
[General (fade over)]: Ten...

nine...eight...seven...six...five

four...three...two...one

zero! **[sounds of explosion]**

[Lyndon Johnson]: These are
the stakes, to make a world in
which all of God's children

can live, or to go into the dark.

We must either love each other,
or we must die.

[Narrator]: Vote for President
Johnson on November Third

The stakes are too high for you
to stay home.

Figure 7.4 The 1964 "Daisy Girl" Ad. *Source*: University of Wisconsin Advertising
Project, at http://wiscadproject.wisc.edu/historic-ads/daisygirl.php.

daisy while the ad transitions into a nuclear countdown that ends in an atomic explosion. Although the ad never mentions Goldwater by name, it clearly makes a less than subtle suggestion that a Goldwater victory would lead the nation into nuclear war (see Figure 7.4). Interestingly, while the "Daisy girl" ad would go on to become one of the most controversial commercials in presidential election history, it was only aired once (on CBS' *Monday Night at the Movies*, September 7, 1964). However, because the ad generated near-instant controversy, all three networks replayed it the following day. The Goldwater campaign reacted in outrage at the ad and filed a complaint with the Fair Campaign Practices Committee. The attention that the ad generated helped more people see the ad and likely increased its effects.

Perhaps equally vicious was a Johnson spot that attacked Goldwater's opposition to a treaty banning atmospheric testing of nuclear weapons. The so-called "Ice Cream" ad suggests that Goldwater's opposition to a nuclear test ban treaty could led to the poisoning—and even death—of innocent children. The 60-second advertisement features a young girl licking an ice-cream cone, while a female announcer warns of Strontium 90 and Cesium 137 (present in nuclear fallout) and the potential dangers of electing Goldwater (see Box 7.1).

The Johnson campaign also went after Goldwater for his opposition to the 1964 Civil Rights Act. One ad goes so far as to tie Goldwater to the Ku Klux

Box 7.1 Transcript of "Ice Cream" Ad

Female Announcer: Do you know what people used to do? They used to explode atomic bombs in the air. Now children should have lots of Vitamin A and calcium, but they shouldn't have any Strontium 90 or Cesium 137. These things come from atomic bombs and they're radioactive. They can make you die. Do you know what people finally did? They got together and signed a nuclear test ban treaty, and then the radioactive poisons started to go away.

But now, there's a man who wants to be President of the United States and he doesn't like this treaty—he fought against it. He even voted against it. He wants to go on testing more bombs. His name is Barry Goldwater. And if he's elected, they might start testing all over again.

Male Announcer: Vote for President Johnson on November 3. The stakes are too high for you to stay home.

Source: The Living Room Candidate, http://www.livingroomcandidate.org/commercials/1964.

Klan. As a cross burns in the background surrounded by Klan members, a narrator quotes Robert Creel, the leader of the Alabama Ku Klux Klan, who offers his support for Goldwater, stating: "I like Barry Goldwater. He needs our help."[55] Other Johnson spots suggested that Goldwater would destroy Social Security and that he harbored animosity toward Americans living on the east coast with one ad quoting Goldwater as saying, "sometimes I think this country would be better off if we could just saw off the Eastern Seaboard and let it float out to sea."[56] The Johnson campaign added to the assault by altering Goldwater's slogan of "In your heart, you know he's right," to "In your guts, you know he's nuts."[57]

The Goldwater campaign hit back at the Johnson campaign. Goldwater ran advertisements suggesting that Johnson was corrupt and was morally deficient, noting his connections to disgraced figures such as Billy Sol Estes who was involved in a scam to swindle the Department of Agriculture out of millions of dollars. In one ad, Goldwater accuses Johnson directly of "running a country" by "buying and bludgeoning votes."[58] Goldwater also used his advertisements to make dire predictions. In an ad entitled, "Moral Responsibility," Goldwater himself tells the audience that the Johnson administration was "not far from the kind of moral decay that has brought on the fall of other nations and people. The philosophy of something for nothing . . . is an insidious cancer that will destroy us as a people unless we recognize it and root it out now."[59]

Like Johnson, Goldwater was also willing to use children in his ads. In one ad, a boy rides a bicycle as an announcer tells the audience, "Don't look now young man, but somebody has his hand in your pocket. It's the hand of big government. It's taking away about four months pay from what your daddy earns every year—one dollar out of every three in his paycheck. And it's taking security out of your grandmother's Social Security."[60]

Despite Goldwater's counterattacks, Johnson went on to win the election easily. Johnson won 44 states, amassing 486 Electoral College votes to 52 for Goldwater. Johnson also won 61 percent of the popular vote, marking one of the largest landslide victories in presidential election history. However, Johnson's victory was only part of the story. Ultimately, the presidential election of 1964 marked what one scholar claimed was the "moment when the negative TV ad was born."[61] This pioneering election set a negative tone that few campaigns have since matched.

The Election of 1988

Vice President George H.W. Bush faced Massachusetts Governor Michael Dukakis in the presidential election of 1988. The election followed the two-term presidency of Republican Ronald Reagan. Bush assumed the role as Reagan's heir apparent and pledged to continue the "Reagan Revolution" of lower taxes, famously proclaiming at the Republican convention, "Read my lips, no new taxes." In contrast, Dukakis campaigned on a platform to balance the federal budget, after the deficit increased significantly under Reagan, and to cut military spending for increased spending on education, health care, and other social programs.

In the early stages of the election, Dukakis led in most polls.[62] However, with the assistance of political consultant, Lee Atwater, the Bush campaign went on the attack, calling into question Dukakis's patriotism, ability to lead the military, environmental record, and his commitment to fighting crime. The Bush attacks effectively cut into the Dukakis lead and ultimately propelled Bush to frontrunner status in the late stages of the election.

Perhaps the most memorable negative advertisements against Dukakis was the infamous "Willie Horton" spot, which suggested that Dukakis was ineffective in fighting violent crime during his time as governor of Massachusetts. The ad featured the picture of a convicted murderer, Willie Horton, who raped a Maryland woman during a weekend furlough from a Massachusetts prison. An announcer tells viewers, "Dukakis not only opposes the death penalty, he allowed first-degree murderers to have weekend passes from prison."[63] The final screen read simply, "Weekend Prison Passes: Dukakis on Crime." Significant controversy followed. Critics charged that the ad was racist because it featured an African American, which some claimed was an attempt to exploit "racist fears" about crime.[64] A similarly themed ad, "Revolving Door," also attacked Dukakis's record on crime, although without the image of Willie Horton. The ad, nevertheless, suggests that a Dukakis victory was a "risk" for the nation (see Box 7.2).

Box 7.2   Transcript of "Revolving Door" Ad

Male Announcer: As Governor Michael Dukakis vetoed mandatory sentences for drug dealers. He vetoed the death penalty. His revolving door prison policy gave weekend furloughs to first degree murders not eligible for parole.

[Text appears on screen: "268 Escaped"]

Male Announcer: While out, many committed other crimes like kidnapping and rape and many are still at large.

[Text appears on screen: "Many are still at large"]

Male Announcer: Now Michael Dukakis says he wants to do for America what he's done for Massachusetts. America can't afford that risk.

Source: The Living Room Candidate, http://www.livingroomcandidate.org/commercials/1988/.

   The Bush campaign attempted to paint Dukakis as not only weak on crime, but also weak on military and defense issues. Dukakis had attempted to address this perceived problem by visiting the General Dynamics plant in Michigan and then riding in an M1 Abrams tank for a campaign photo op. While riding in the tank, Dukakis wore a large helmet and grinned awkwardly. Instead of failing to dispel the attack against him as unfit to be commander-in-chief, the so-called "Dukakis in the tank" footage became synonymous with public relations disasters. Dukakis was pretending to be something he was not. The implied message was that he could not be trusted with the job of commander-in-chief. The Bush campaign used this footage to reinforce its attacks that Dukakis was not a credible military leader (see Figure 7.5, Box 7.3).

Figure 7.5   Dukakis "Tank" Ad, 1988.

Box 7.3   Transcript of "Tank Ride" Ad

Male Announcer: Michael Dukakis has opposed virtually every defense system we developed.

Male Announcer and Text: He opposed new aircraft carriers. He opposed anti-satellite weapons. He opposed four missile systems, including the Pershing II missile deployment. Dukakis opposed the stealth bomber, a ground emergency warning system against nuclear testing. He even criticized our rescue mission to Grenada and our strike on Libya. And now he wants to be our commander-in-chief. America can't afford that risk.

Source: The Living Room Candidate, http://www.livingroomcandidate.org/commercials/1988/.

Box 7.4   Transcript of "Harbor" Ad

[Text appears on screen: "Harbor"]

Male Announcer: As a candidate, Michael Dukakis called Boston Harbor an open sewer. As Governor, he had the opportunity to do something about it but chose not to. The Environmental Protection Agency called his lack of action the most expensive public policy mistake in the history of New England. Now Boston Harbor is the dirtiest harbor in America. It cost residents six billion dollars to clean.

And Michael Dukakis promises to do for America what he's done for Massachusetts.

Source: The Living Room Candidate, http://www.livingroomcandidate.org/commercials/1988/.

The attacks against Dukakis extended to other areas as well. The Bush campaign skewered Dukakis for his record on environmental pollution, citing problems with Boston Harbor (see Box 7.4). There were also false rumors spread during the campaign that Dukakis received treatment for mental illness and that his wife, Kitty, burned an American flag in protest of the Vietnam War.

The Dukakis campaign was slow in responding to the attacks, which some believe contributed to his sharp decline in the polls as the campaign progressed. Dukakis ultimately fought back by questioning Bush's honesty and claiming in one ad that the Bush had taken a "furlough from the truth."[65] Other ads attacked Bush for his record in the war on drugs, blamed the Republicans for increasing the federal deficit, and poked fun at the selection of Bush's running mate, Senator Dan Quayle of Indiana, who was perceived by some as too young and inexperienced to be president. There were also rumors spread by a member of the Dukakis staff that Bush had an affair with his secretary, Jennifer Fitzgerald. Dukakis, however, failed to regain his early lead and won just 111 Electoral College votes compared to 426 for Bush.

CONCLUSION

As noted at the outset of this chapter, the 2012 presidential election campaign had its fair share of negative attacks. Yet, while there were numerous examples of nasty personal attacks, it was probably not "the dirtiest" presidential election in American history. Nor, for that matter, were the campaigns of 2008, 2004, 2000, and so on, nastier than previous campaigns. As the examples presented in this chapter make clear, vicious personal attacks and negative campaigning have been present for centuries. Negative campaigning has been and continues to be a part of presidential elections, and each future election will undoubtedly bring about the familiar claim that it is the "most negative ever." Such lines certainly make for flashy headlines and provocative quotations. However, as the historical record rather plainly suggests, these claims come much closer to hyperbole than they do to reality.

NOTES

1. Peter Manseau, "'Is This the Nastiest Election Ever?' 'Campaign Stops'," *The New York Times*, September 27, 2012. Available at http://campaignstops.blogs. nytimes.com/2012/09/27/is-this-the-nastiest-election-ever/?_r=0.

2. Nicole Greenstein, "Negative Ads: A Shift in Tone for the 2012 Campaign," *Time*, July 17, 2012. Available at http://swampland.time.com/2012/07/17/negative-ads-a-shift-in-tone-for-the-2012-campaign/.

3. Olivier Knox, "Obama Camp Denies Knowledge of Cancer Tale it Told in May," Yahoo News, "The Ticket," August 8, 2012. Available at http://news.yahoo.com/blogs/the-ticket/obama-camp-denies-knowledge-cancer-tale-told-may-195237581.html.

4. Nancy Cordes, "Negative Presidential Campaign Ads Going to New Extremes," CBS News, August 10, 2012. Available at http://www.cbsnews.com/news/negative-presidential-campaign-ads-going-to-new-extremes/.

5. Craig Crawford, "Memorable Moments 2008," *Huffington Post*, November 3, 2008, www.huffingtonpost.com/craig-crawford/memorable-moments-2008_b_140442.html.

6. Michael Musto, "The McCain Campaign is the Ugliest Ever," *The Village Voice*, October 24, 2008, blogs.villagevoice.com/dailymusto/archives/2008/10/the_mccain_camp.php.

7. "Cindy McCain: Obama Has 'Waged the Dirtiest Campaign in American History'," ABC News, October 7, 2008, blogs.abcnews.com/politicalpunch/2008/10/cindy-mccain-ob.html.

8. "Most Scurrilous Campaign in History?" MSNBC, October 15, 2008, firstread. msnbc.msn.com/archive/2008/10/15/1548251.aspx.

9. "Congressman says McCain 'Sowing Seeds of Hatred'," Fox News, October 11, 2008, www.foxnews.com/wires/2008Oct11/0,4670,McCainLewis,00.html.

10. Julian E. Zelizer, "Worst Campaign Ever?" *Newsweek*, November 5, 2008, www.newsweek.com/id/167561.

11. Russell Goldman, "'Dirtiest Campaign', Really, Cindy?" ABC News, October 10, 2008, abcnews.go.com/Politics/Vote2008/story?id=6005513.

12. Ibid.

13. Kathleen Hall Jamieson, *Dirty Politics: Deception, Distraction, and Democracy* (New York: Oxford University Press, 1992), 43.

14. Jamieson, *Dirty Politics*, 43.

15. See, for example, Stephen Ansolabehere, Shanto Iyengar, Adam Simon, and Nicholas Valentino, "Does Attack Advertising Demobilize the Electorate?" *American Political Science Review* 88 (1994): 829–38; William G. Mayer, "In Defense of Negative Campaigning," *Political Science Quarterly* 111 (1996): 437–55; Richard R. Lau and Gerald M. Pomper, *Negative Campaigning: An Analysis of U.S. Senate Elections* (Lanham, MD: Rowman & Littlefield, 2004); David Mark, *Going Dirty: The Art of Negative Campaigning* (Lanham, MD: Rowman & Littlefield, 2006).

16. Mark, *Going Dirty*, chap. 1.

17. Ansolabehere et al., "Does Attack Advertising Demobilize the Electorate?"; Stephen Ansolabehere and Shanto Iyengar, *Going Negative* (New York: Free Press, 1995); Stephen Ansolabehere, Shanto Iyengar, and Adam Simon, "The Case of Negative Advertising and Turnout," *American Political Science Review* 93 (1999): 901–33.

18. Gina M. Garramone, Charles T. Atkin, Bruce E. Pinkleton, and Richard T. Cole, "Effects of Negative Political Advertising on the Political Process," *Journal of Broadcasting and Electronic Media* 34 (1990): 299–311; Craig L. Brians and Martin P. Wattenberg, "Campaign Issue Knowledge and Salience: Comparing Reception from TV Commercials, TV News, and Newspapers," *American Journal of Political Science* 40 (1996): 172–93; Mayer, "In Defense of Negative Campaigning"; Steven E. Finkel and John Geer, "A Spot Check: Casting Doubt on the Demobilizing Effect of Attack Advertising," *American Journal of Political Science* 42 (1998): 573–95; Kim Fridkin Kahn and Patrick J. Kenney, "Do Negative Campaigns Mobilize or Suppress Turnout? Clarifying the Relationship between Negativity and Participation," *American Political Science Review* 93 (1999): 877–89.

19. Aaron Burr, who became the Vice President after the election of 1800, later shot and killed Alexander Hamilton in a duel, at least in part because of the political attacks and opposition he endured from Hamilton. See Buckner F. Melton Jr., *Aaron Burr: Conspiracy to Treason* (New York: John Wiley & Sons, 2002), 23–4.

20. Paul F. Boller Jr., *Presidential Campaigns: From George Washington to George W. Bush* (New York: Oxford University Press, 2004), 11. See also Charles O. Lerche Jr., "Jefferson and the Election of 1800: A Case Study in the Political Smear," *The William and Mary Quarterly* 5 (1948): 467–91.

21. Victor Kamber, *Poison Politics: Are Negative Campaigns Destroying Democracy?* (New York: Basic Books, 1997), 15.

22. Boller, *Presidential Campaigns*, 12.

23. Jamieson, *Dirty Politics*, 31.

24. Boller, *Presidential Campaigns*, 12.

25. Kerwin C. Swint, *Mudslingers: The Top 25 Negative Political Campaigns of All Time* (Westport, Conn.: Praeger, 2006), 184.

26. Swint, *Mudslingers*, 185.

27. For more information about the election of 1800, see Susan Dunn, *Jefferson's Second Revolution: The Election Crisis of 1800 and the Triumph of Republicanism* (New York: Houghton Mifflin, 2004). For more information about election results and totals for the election of 1800 and others covered in this chapter, see Jerrold G. Rusk, *A Statistical History of the American Electorate* (Washington, DC: CQ Press, 2001).

28. According to Kerwin Swint, in *Mudslingers*, the election of 1800 ranks as the fourth dirtiest campaign in U.S. history.

29. Totals from Rusk, Statistical History of the American Electorate.

30. Swint, *Mudslingers*, 213.

31. Jeffrey A. Jenkins and Brian R. Sala, "The Spatial Theory of Voting and the Presidential Election of 1824," *American Journal of Political Science* 42 (1998): 1157–79.

32. Boller, *Presidential Campaigns*, 44.

33. Ibid.

34. Swint, *Mudslingers*, 217.

35. Norma Basch, "Marriage, Morals, and Politics in the Election of 1828," *The Journal of American History* 80 (1993): 890–918. See also Boller, *Presidential Campaigns*, 45.

36. Boller, *Presidential Campaigns*, 46.

37. Basch, "Marriage, Morals, and Politics in the Election of 1828."

38. Boller, *Presidential Campaigns*, 46.

39. In *Mudslingers*, Kerwin Swint labeled the 1828 election as the most negative presidential campaign in history and the second most negative of all time (with only the George Wallace–Albert Brewer election for governor of Alabama in 1970 coming in higher).

40. Swint, *Mudslingers*, 194.

41. Boller, *Presidential Campaigns*, 118–19.

42. Ward Hill Lamon, *Recollections of Abraham Lincoln, 1847–1865* (Chicago: A.C. McClurg, 1895), 143–8; Boller, *Presidential Campaigns*, 120.

43. Boller, *Presidential Campaigns*, 121–2.

44. Ibid.

45. John C. Waugh, *Reelecting Lincoln: The Battle of the 1864 Presidency* (New York: Perseus Books, 2001).

46. Swint, *Mudslingers*, 32.

47. Paul Freedman and Ken Goldstein, "Measuring Media Exposure and the Effects of Negative Campaign Ads," *American Journal of Political Science* 43 (1999): 1189–208; Paul Fredman, Michael Franz, and Kenneth Goldstein, "Campaign Advertising and Democratic Citizenship," *American Journal of Political Science* 48 (2004): 723–41.

48. In *Mudslingers*, Kerwin Swint placed the 1964 and 1988 presidential elections as among the most negative campaigns in history.

49. Emmett H. Buell Jr. and Lee Sigelman, *Attack Politics: Negativity in Presidential Campaigns since 1960* (Lawrence, KS: University Press of Kansas, 2008), 29.

50. Goldwater quoted in Adam Cohen, *Nothing to Fear: FDR's Inner Circle and the Hundred Days that Created Modern America* (New York: Penguin Books, 2009), 317.

51. Goldwater quoted in Gerald Garner, *Campaign Comedy: Political Humor from Clinton to Kennedy* (Detroit: Wayne State University Press, 1994), 260.

52. Goldwater quoted in Robert Andrews, *The Columbia Dictionary of Quotations* (New York: Columbia University Press, 1993), 303.

53. The Living Room Candidate, www.livingroomcandidate.org/commercials/1964.

54. Swint, *Mudslingers*, 31.

55. The Living Room Candidate, www.livingroomcandidate.org/commercials/1964.

56. Ibid.

57. Kathleen Hall Jamison, *Packaging the Presidency: A History and Criticism of Presidential Campaign Advertising* (New York: Oxford University Press, 1996), 220.

58. The Living Room Candidate, www.livingroomcandidate.org/commercials/1964.

59. Ibid.

60. Ibid.

61. Swint, *Mudslingers,* 272.

62. E. J. Dionne Jr. "Poll Shows Dukakis Leads Bush; Many Reagan Backers Shift Sides," The *New York Times*, May 17, 1988, A1.

63. CNN ad archive, www.cnn.com/ALLPOLITICS/1996/candidates/ad.archive/horton.mov.

64. Jamieson, *Dirty Politics*, 17.

65. The Living Room Candidate, www.livingroomcandidate.org/commercials/1999.

FOR MORE READING

Boller, Paul F., Jr. *Presidential Campaigns: From George Washington to George W. Bush.* New York: Oxford University Press, 2004.

Buell, Emmett H., Jr. and Lee Sigelman. *Attack Politics: Negativity in Presidential Campaigns since 1960.* Lawrence, KS: University Press of Kansas, 2008.

Geer, John G. *In Defense of Negativity: Attack Ads in Presidential Campaigns.* Chicago: University of Chicago Press, 2006.

Mark, David. *Going Dirty: The Art of Negative Campaigning.* Lanham, MD: Rowman & Littlefield, 2006.

On the Web: "The Living Room Candidate: Presidential Campaign Commercials, 1952–2008." Available at: http://www.livingroomcandidate.org/.

Chapter 8

Ratings, Ratings, Ratings

Common Misconceptions about Media Bias

Many Americans believe there is a bias, either liberal or conservative, in the mass media's coverage of politics. According to a recent survey, a majority (53 percent) of people "believe that news organizations are politically biased, while just 29 percent say they are careful to remove bias from their reports."[1] In another poll, 67 percent agreed with the following statement: "In dealing with political and social issues, news organizations tend to favor one side."[2] Yet another report found that "78 percent of adults agree with the assessment that there is bias in the news media,"[3] while another one showed that almost two-thirds (64 percent) disagreed with the idea that "the news media try to report the news without bias."[4] Most Americans (51 percent) describe news organizations as "liberal," while a smaller segment of the public perceives the press as "conservative" (26 percent). An even smaller group believes the press is neither liberal nor conservative (14 percent).[5] Still, in one poll, 46 percent of respondents viewed their newspaper as more liberal than they are, while 36 percent perceived their newspaper to be more conservative than they are.[6] In short, healthy percentages of Americans see bias in the news.

Does the perception that the news media are biased match reality? More interesting for our purposes, does news coverage of campaigns favor one candidate or the other? How objective has reporting been in recent elections? In this chapter, we explore these questions. First, we briefly review the legal environment within which the press operates in the United States, and the emergence of objective journalism as a professional norm, highlighting the idea that for the first one hundred years or so of the republic it was accepted that news carried with it a partisan slant. Next, we examine the forms, or possible sources of bias in news coverage of campaigns, as well as what researchers have found with respect to charges of partisan bias in the media.

In the end, we focus on the idea that bias in the media is primarily commercial in nature, reflecting the fact that news organizations are for-profit enterprises that must consider the "bottom line" (i.e., making money) in their campaign coverage. We discuss several ways that this commercial bias manifests itself during election seasons. This commercial bias includes a relatively recent development in the modern media environment that many point to when discussing media bias. Cable news outlets, in particular, MSNBC and Fox News, can be thought of as partisan political media outlets. However, strictly speaking, most of what we see on these two channels is not biased *news*, but rather *opinion*. Moreover, even if their news reporting reflects bias, both fit the model of commercial bias in the news inasmuch as they fill a niche in marketplace. In other words, MSNBC, Fox News, and other media outlets, much like a variety of websites, deliver partisan news and opinion to people who are seeking it.

THE EMERGENCE OF OBJECTIVE JOURNALISM
AS A PROFESSIONAL NORM

The First Amendment states that "Congress shall make no law . . . abridging the freedom of speech, or of the press." This provision has powerful implications for the organization of the media. In particular, it states that government cannot control the media, which applies to issues of censorship and by extension, to ownership of media outlets as well. As the old adage goes, "He who pays the piper calls the tune." If government owned and operated the media, it could control the news we receive. This is why the media environment in the United States is mainly characterized by private ownership. In most constitutional democracies, there is both private and public (government) ownership of media outlets, especially broadcast (radio and television) media.[7] There are very few government-owned or government-sponsored media outlets in this country. Partial exceptions exist, but these are restricted mainly to foreign broadcast services (e.g., the Voice of America), which cannot air in the United States. So-called public broadcasting (National Public Radio and the Public Broadcasting System) are actually joint ventures funded by federal, state, and local governments, universities, private sponsors and foundations, and individual citizens.[8]

Unlike publicly (or government) owned media outlets, private media outlets are continually under pressure to make money. In the case of newspapers and magazines, this translates into selling copy; for television and radio, it means selling airtime to advertisers. The greater number of viewers or listeners a television or radio station or network has, the more it can charge for its advertising time. In the end, television and radio stations attempt to attract viewers, much in the same way that newspapers and magazines try to sell copy. All media outlets are thus under pressure to make money by orienting their product toward what consumers (viewers, listeners, readers) want. Commercial considerations, inevitable products of the First Amendment, are never far from the minds of those responsible for news production in the United States.

The Constitution does not prohibit the press from presenting the news in a biased fashion. In fact, in colonial times, the expectation of journalistic objectivity did not exist. Printing shops produced the earliest newspapers. These small businesses were interested in selling papers, and therefore attempted to maintain editorial neutrality in order to avoid controversy. Printed "news" was mainly foreign news, less controversial because of its distance from local affairs. But as the conflict with the British intensified, this began to change. News had a pro-independence slant, which became a pro-government slant after independence. This was mainly because Federalist sympathizers controlled most newspapers. Most editors and printers did not subscribe to the idea of press objectivity or neutrality.[9]

Well into the nineteenth century, most newspapers had an identifiable partisan bias. For example, the *Albany Argus* was the newspaper of the nation's first political machine, the Albany Regency (the Democratic Party machine).[10] While the *Argus* prided itself in the accuracy of its reporting, coverage of political campaigns remained selective at best. This was true of many other newspapers during the Golden Age of political parties, when party machines were highly influential, at least at the local level.[11]

The demise of the partisan press began with improvements in printing technology, which made it possible to mass produce newspapers at a low price. New urban centers provided potential markets for these "penny papers" and many thrived, attracting major advertising dollars. By the late 1800s, owners and editors began to understand that partisan presentation of news effectively cut them off from half of their potential market. Republicans, for example, would not buy a Democrat-leaning newspaper, and vice versa. In other words, the notion of presenting objective, impartial news was not a high-minded ideal but rather a response to commercial considerations.

As the century progressed, newspapers began to feature more local news stories in a further attempt to increase sales.[12] This focus on local stories meant that newspapers began to employ more reporters. For example, one report suggests that by 1895 Joseph Pulitzer's *New York World* employed 1,200 people, scores of whom were reporters. It was perhaps natural that as the number of reporters increased, journalism grew "as an occupational culture." Reporters began frequenting the same clubs, restaurants, and taverns. The Missouri School of Journalism, the world's first, opened in 1908. The Columbia University School of Journalism, where classes started in 1913, was endowed by Joseph Pulitzer for the purpose of raising "journalism to the rank of a learned profession." Within a few decades, other schools had begun programs as well. Importantly, these programs began to inculcate in their students a "self-conscious ethic of objectivity."[13] By the 1920s, journalists and others began to articulate this ethic as a professional norm. The American Society of News Editors, formed in 1922, adopted the "Cannons of Journalism," one of which was impartiality. Other newly formed professional associations (e.g., the Newspaper Guild, formed in 1933) followed.[14]

The norm of objectivity thus emerged originally in response to the commercial nature of news production. As newspaper production technology improved, supply increased and prices dropped, while at the same time demand and competition grew. Part of the increased demand included a desire on the part of readers for more local news, rather than stories about foreign affairs previously printed in London or elsewhere. The desire for local news created a need for more reporters, who, as they increased in numbers, began to see themselves as professionals with their own code of ethics. This code of ethics included the notion that journalists report their stories fully and accurately, devoid of value judgments.

Further driving a move toward impartiality was the emergence of, and reliance by newspapers on, the national wire services. Following the same commercial logic that drove local papers away from partisan presentation of the news, the Associated Press and United Press International understood that neutrality in reporting was necessary for them to sell stories.[15] In short, the development of news as an industry and as big business helped drive the emergence and acceptance of objectivity as a journalistic norm.

BIAS

Before proceeding in our discussion of bias in the news, we should be clear about what we mean by the word bias. As it relates to news, bias refers to the idea that the selection and presentation of a particular story explicitly or implicitly reflects the political views of some person or persons involved in the news production process. In other words, bias in the news results in a presentation that does not adequately or completely reflect reality.

When we refer to bias in campaign news, we are typically referring to unequal coverage or treatment of one or the other candidate or party. The notion that election news should be impartial is based on the idea that voting should be an informed choice; and the only way for citizens to make an informed choice is to have facts, not value judgments or opinions, at their disposal. Therefore, the standard that news organizations adhere to and that citizens use to evaluate them is one of objectivity.

There are many possible sources of bias in the news. Many, for example, point to the political leanings of those responsible for news production, such as editors, producers, reporters, and so on. Studies conducted in the past two decades show that newspaper reporters are more liberal than the average citizen. Similar studies (surveys of reporters) also show that reporters tend to vote for Democrats.[16] Other research has demonstrated that the owners of media organizations tend to be more conservative and vote Republican.[17]

Do these tendencies manifest themselves into an ideological or partisan slant in the news? Looking for bias in the news—or in campaign coverage— may not be as straightforward a task as it may seem. If there was bias in news coverage of presidential campaigns, what form would it take? The following list outlines several possibilities:

- One of the candidates might be the subject of more news stories than the other, resulting in a greater amount of coverage;
- Alternatively, stories about one of the candidate's campaign effort might consistently be longer or shorter than the others, also resulting in an unequal amount of coverage;
- Regardless of the amount of coverage a candidate receives, one or the other candidate might consistently be cast in a more positive or negative (e.g., a focus on a scandal of some sort) light;
- Stories about one of the candidate's campaign effort might consistently be placed more prominently (e.g., on the front page of the newspaper, or the lead story in a news broadcast) than those of the other;
- The focus of the story or stories of one of the candidates might be consistently accompanied by pictures or video casting the candidate in either a positive (cheering crowds in the background) or negative (worried or harried look on his or her face) light.

Can these, or any other patterns, be detected in news coverage of presidential campaigns? Is news coverage of presidential campaigns biased, or less than adequate or complete? Fortunately, there is an abundance of research informing us on this subject. Most scholars have concluded that there is no convincing evidence of media bias in either a liberal or a conservative direction. One recent and comprehensive study found no ideological or partisan bias in newspapers, and a slight, but statistically insignificant effect of Republican bias in news magazines and Democratic bias on television.[18] In fact, some suggest that because reporters tend to be more liberal they overcompensate to some extent in their treatment of political candidates, slightly favoring Republicans.[19]

The reality is that numerous studies over the years suggest that there is no systematic ideological or partisan bias—either liberal or conservative—in the news. How then do we explain the fact that the perception of bias persists in many peoples' minds? The short answer is that ideological bias may be in the eye of the beholder. There is strong evidence, in other words, that liberals see a conservative bias, while conservatives see a liberal bias. Communication scholars refer to this as the "hostile media effect."[20] Experimental research demonstrates that when a group of people are presented with a neutral news story, those who lean left will perceive the story as having a conservative or no bias, while those on the right will see a liberal bias. Partisans, in other words, see bias, even when it may not exist.

Public opinion polls reinforce these findings. In 2011, Gallup found that:

> Partisans . . . perceive the media very differently. Seventy-five percent of Republicans and conservatives say the media are too liberal. Democrats and liberals lean more toward saying the media are "just about right," at 57% and 42%, respectively. Moderates and independents diverge, however, with 50% of independents saying the media are too liberal and 50% of moderates saying they are just about right.[21]

Other polls show that Democrats and liberals are less trusting of news that comes from sources that many consider to be on the right (e.g., Fox News), while Republicans and conservatives treat news that comes from media outlets perceived to be on the left (e.g., MSNBC) with greater skepticism.[22] In fact, there is considerable evidence that many, if not most people are selective in which media outlets they acquire their news from, based on their ideological or partisan leanings. Conservatives, in other words, watch Fox News, while liberals tune into MSNBC.[23] Communication scholars explain this selective consumption of media by way of what is known as the "uses and gratification" theory.[24] People use the media that best fits with their views.

Does the fact that there is no discernible ideological or partisan bias in the news mean that we always get the complete story? The short answer is, decidedly not. In the next section, we illustrate that the true bias in news coverage of campaigns is of a commercial nature.

COMMERCIAL BIAS IN CAMPAIGN COVERAGE

"News" is the product of a series of decisions made by owners, editors, producers, reporters, and journalists. While the masthead of the *New York Times* claims the paper presents "all the news that's fit to print," in actuality there are any number of newsworthy events that occur in a given day that go unreported or underreported. The individuals working in news organizations decide what stories are worthy of attention and how to present them. Commercial factors also balance these considerations. Editors, for example, are more likely to choose stories that will capture the average news consumer's attention. This explains why there is so much celebrity news, or why scandal and sex are often prominently featured in news coverage.

The need to make a profit naturally puts pressure on news organizations to keep costs down and sales up. This results in national coverage of political campaigns which displays a distinct commercial bias.[25] Campaign news, in other words, is biased in favor of stories that hold a commercial appeal, that news producers believe people will want to read, listen to, or watch. This type of coverage may be very different from an objective overview of what is actually happening on the campaign trail. Below, we discuss some of the ways that this commercial bias is evident in national news coverage of presidential campaigns.

Horse race Coverage

Most campaign coverage falls into the category of what political scientist and media scholar Thomas Patterson labels "horse race" coverage.[26] Most stories focus on, or are framed around, the competitive or strategic aspect of the campaign: who is leading, who fell behind, and why. This type of coverage dominates news about the campaign from the pre-primary season through Election Day.[27] According to authoritative sources, approximately two-thirds of all coverage throughout the campaign was comprised of stories focused on the horse race in 2008.[28] Conversely, substantive (issue-oriented) stories accounted for only 18 percent of the coverage on the three major television networks (ABC, CBS, and NBC) in 2004. This was down from 22 percent in 2000 and compares with an overall average of 26 percent from 1988 to 2004.[29]

The reason horse race coverage dominates campaign news is rather straightforward: it makes for a more exciting story, and all other things being equal, more exciting stories sell better. Of course, news organizations can only present a certain number of stories in any given day. Therefore, horse race coverage pushes out other types of stories, including an examination of issues, policy positions of the candidates and parties, qualifications, and so on. This horse race coverage, as we will show, affects campaign coverage in other ways as well.

The Press as King Maker or Winnower

The decisions that news organizations make about the deployment of their resources and the stories that they run often have a profound impact on who will eventually win the party nomination. In part, this is because most people do not know much, if anything, about many of the aspirants for their party's nomination. This is especially true in years when there are many candidates vying for the nomination. In the year preceding the election, media organizations make decisions about which candidates they will and will not cover. These decisions translate directly into the amount of coverage a given candidate receives in print or on television. Here, the rule of thumb is that better-known candidates are more likely to be the subject of a story than their lesser-known opponents.

This is mainly due to simple economics. Media organizations must make decisions about how to deploy scarce resources to cover a crowded field of aspirants. In 2015, for example, there were almost two dozen names that media outlets mentioned as Republican hopefuls for the presidential nomination. News organizations simply cannot assign a reporter to cover every candidate and every campaign event. In 2004, the cable television network MSNBC assigned an "embedded" journalist to travel with and cover each of the nine Democratic hopefuls, but this was an exception to the rule.[30] Generally, news organizations focus primarily on candidates who are leading in early, prepri-mary polls (those taken during the year prior to the Iowa caucuses). This, of course, means that candidates who are not doing well in public opinion polls receive less attention in the news, thus making it more difficult for them to raise their public profile, attract campaign contributions, and ultimately, do well. To overstate the case somewhat, many of the hidden decisions made by news organizations about who to cover become self-fulfilling prophecies.[31]

For example, four of the twelve Republican aspirants in 2012 received the lion's share of the coverage. Mitt Romney, Rick Santorum, Newt Gingrich, and Ron Paul were the subjects of the overwhelming amount of the cover-age throughout the spring.[32] Of course, these four were the frontrunners, but there is evidence that to some extent "news coverage drove [their] surges."[33] In 2008, the candidates leading in the polls as 2007 drew to a close included Democrats Barack Obama, Hillary Clinton, and John Edwards, and, Repub-licans John McCain, Mitt Romney, Rudy Giuliani, and Mike Huckabee. Not surprisingly, these individuals captured most of the press attention and cover-age throughout the primary season.[34] In 2003, Howard Dean, Wesley Clark, John Kerry, and Joseph Lieberman were the focus of most of the television news stories about the Democrat hopefuls. They were also, not coincidently, leading in the preprimary polls throughout the year.[35] After January 1, the pat-tern of coverage shifted to account for John Edwards's increased popularity and Joseph Lieberman's decreased popularity (as well as the fact that he did not compete in Iowa).[36]

Winnowing also occurs in the substance of the coverage. For example, one analysis of articles by several leading political pundits in early 2004 suggests that Democratic candidates Carol Moseley Braun, Dennis Kucinich, and Al Sharpton were all but dismissed in analyses by these writers.[37] Few were as blunt as Ted Koppel, the host of ABC's Nightline, who hosted a Democratic debate in Durham, New Hampshire, on December 9, 2003. In preparation before the debate, Koppel asked staffers,

How did Dennis Kucinich and Al Sharpton and Carol Moseley Braun get into this thing—the debate? Nobody seems to know. Some candidates who are perceived as serious are gasping for air, and what little oxygen there is on the stage will be taken up by one-third of the people who do not have a snowball's chance in hell of winning the nomination.[38]

During the debate, Koppel asked provocative questions of each of these three candidates and, at one point, asked directly whether they would eventually "drop out" or continue their "vanity" candidacies. Koppel's apparent resentment of the minor candidates and their dismissal by others relates to the fact that news organizations have limited resources with which to cover the campaign. Moreover, likely losers usually do not make for good stories.

The amount and substance of news coverage toward presumed front-runners has the effect of forcing lesser-known candidates to withdraw from the race earlier than they otherwise might. It is highly unlikely that Herman Cain, Michelle Bachman, or Jon Hunstman could have captured the Republican presidential nomination in 2012 under most any circumstances. The same applies to Democrats Joe Biden, Chris Dodd, Bill Richardson, Mike Gravel, or Republicans Sam Brownback, Duncan Hunter, Ron Paul, or Tommy Thompson in 2008. However, each was a recognized candidate whose inclusion in the race added something to the democratic process. Whether intentional or not, bias in the form of noncoverage or less-than-favorable coverage contributed, at least slightly, to their early withdrawal, and thus detracted from the campaign.

The Expectations Game

In addition to helping winnow the field of primary candidates early by way of devoting less coverage to those who are doing poorly in the polls, the press handicaps the primaries. The expectations game actually starts long before the primaries begin, escalating during the fall of the year prior to the Iowa caucuses. Pundits regularly report on who is leading in the polls, who is raising how much money, who is endorsing which candidate, and more. Based on this, they typically anoint a front-runner who is therefore expected to win either the Iowa caucuses, the New Hampshire primary, or both. If the presumed front-runner loses either, the media typically frame the resulting story line in terms of the uphill battle faced by the candidate in upcoming contests. Interestingly, however, if the front-runner wins, but does worse than expected, the media frame the story in terms of a loss or setback.

In 1992, for example, media accounts declared George H. W. Bush, who most experts expected to win in New Hampshire by a large margin, the loser after placing first, "only" sixteen percentage points ahead of Pat Buchanan. This was the result of Bush falling short of expectations and Buchanan exceeding them. A similar situation occurred in that year's Democratic primary in New Hampshire when Bill Clinton finished a surprising second in the aftermath of accusations from Gennifer Flowers that she had engaged with Clinton in a romantic affair. In 1996, the Republican nominee Bob Dole lost a few early primaries, including one to Steve Forbes in Arizona, that threw the race into "turmoil."[39] In 2000, Al Gore defeated his Democratic rival Bill Bradley in New Hampshire in what one source called an "uncomfortably tight race."[40] While Gore's victory was indeed newsworthy, few observers believed that given his financial and organizational resources Bradley could actually secure the nomination. In 2008, John Edwards, who had spent much of the previous four years campaigning in Iowa, was expected by many to win the Iowa caucuses. After essentially tying for second place with Hillary Clinton behind Barack Obama, his candidacy never recovered.

In addition, because the primary season begins early, the media often pays a disproportionate amount of positive attention to the underdog, or candidate trailing in the race. For example, John McCain was the media favorite throughout the 2000 Republican primary season, in part because he was trailing Bush. However, while McCain won important primaries and caucuses, Bush's grip on the nomination was never in serious doubt. During the latter part of 2003, when Howard Dean was the front-runner for the Democratic nomination, he was the recipient of much negative press. Shortly after his loss in Iowa, however, coverage became more favorable.[41] And long after it was apparent that John McCain would secure the Republican nomination in 2008, the press paid a great deal of attention, most of it positive, to the candidacy of rival Mike Huckabee.[42] The reason for this focus on the underdog is simply that it makes for a more exciting and compelling story.

A Focus on the Negative

Similar to its ability to anoint a winner, the press can also help drive candidates from the field with a focus on mistakes, scandals, and gaffes. This is especially true during the primary season. In 1988, Democratic candidate Senator Joseph Biden was charged with plagiarizing parts of his speeches. He withdrew from the primary race after a flurry of negative media attention. That same year, Democrat Gary Hart dropped out of the race after a widely publicized sex scandal.

George H. W. Bush delivered a campaign speech in 1988 in which he mistakenly referred to September 7 as the anniversary of the attack on Pearl Harbor (the actual date is December 7). His audience caught the mistake, and based on their reaction, he quickly corrected himself. While the audience seemed to pay no further attention to the incident, all three television networks featured a story about it that evening. Their coverage was less than flattering. Dan Rather of CBS News, for example, told viewers that "Bush's talk to audiences in Louisville was overshadowed by a strange happening."[43]

In addition to simple gaffes, the media often focus on more salacious stories. An inordinate amount of coverage in 1992 centered on charges that Bill Clinton had been unfaithful to his wife, had experimented with marijuana, was a draft dodger, and had burned an American flag while a student in England.[44] Of course, Clinton was able to overcome this focus on the negative and secure the Democratic nomination. This negative focus on simple mistakes, scandals, and so forth, is part of a pattern in American journalism referred to by Larry Sabato as "attack journalism." Sabato uses the metaphor of "feeding frenzy" to describe how the press is drawn to, highlights, and repeats negative news from the campaign trail.[45]

Often the focus on the negative is not scandal related but simply mistakes made on the campaign trail. In 2000, for example, days of coverage were devoted to an alleged subliminal message (rats) found in a George Bush campaign ad or the fact that Bush, thinking his microphone was off, referred to long-time reporter Adam Clymer as a "major league—hole."[46] In 2004, media organizations ran numerous stories about John Kerry's testimony to the Senate after his service in Vietnam, whether President Bush had lied about his National Guard service, the fact that Kerry mentioned Vice President Dick Cheney's gay daughter Lynn during the final presidential debate, and more. Similarly, in 2008, an inordinate amount of attention was paid to the fact that Obama stopped wearing his American flag lapel pin or to a comment Michelle Obama made about her husband's candidacy being the first time as an adult she was proud of her country.[47]

According to one study, there was only one instance in 1968 where a television network newscast took notice of a "minor incident unrelated to the content of the campaign."[48] The reason for the change is best summarized by the "orchestra pit" theory of politics coined by former Republican media consultant and current president of Fox News, Roger Ailes. As Ailes explained, "If you have two guys on stage and one says, 'I have a solution to the Middle East problem', and the other guy falls into the orchestra pit, who do you think is going to be on the evening news?"[49]

Pack Journalism

Exacerbating the commercial patterns of campaign coverage noted above is a phenomenon known by many as "pack journalism." A term originally coined by Timothy Crouse in his 1973 account of the Nixon campaign,[50] pack journalism refers to the fact that much of what appears in the news media is remarkably homogenous. Crouse argued this was because reporters who spend a great deal of time together (on the campaign trail) end up with similar ideas. But the homogeneity of news coverage has other sources as well. For example, the competitive pressure of knowing another network or newspaper is running a particular story exerts pressure on producers and editors to do the same.[51]

The pressure to meet deadlines also contributes to uniformity in the news, as reporters have less time to explore a story. Smaller media organizations tend to take their cues from more prestigious outlets (*New York Times, Washington Post*) and, in many cases, subscribe to the same wire service stories (Associated Press, Reuters). The result is uniformity in campaign coverage. If the aforementioned commercial biases were not operative, this might not be problematic. However, pack journalism only multiplies these biases as each story repeats itself.

Other Commercial Biases

There are several other patterns evident in the news coverage of presidential primaries that reflect a commercial bias in the media. One is a focus on attractive personalities. In particular, there is a tendency for the media to give attractive personalities more positive press, especially during the primary season. This particular bias was apparent in 2004. The highly telegenic and upbeat John Edwards received the best press of any major candidate since 1988. A full 96 percent of the coverage of Edwards by the three major television networks (ABC, CBS, and NBC) from January 1 through March 1, 2004, was positive.[52] Barack Obama probably benefitted from this focus on attractive personalities in 2008 as well (see below).

Another pattern, evident during both the primary and general election season, is an anti-incumbency bias. This is because sitting presidents (or vice presidents in the case of George H. W. Bush in 1988 and Al Gore in 2000) are not fresh "news." Challengers add something new to the race, thus making it more attractive to news consumers. While Bill Clinton received more favorable coverage than challenger Bob Dole in 1996, virtually all incumbents since Jimmy Carter in 1980 have been the recipients of negative press during their reelection campaign. This also holds true for the incumbent vice presidents George H. W. Bush in 1988 and Al Gore in 2000. In 2004, coverage of the incumbent George W. Bush on the three broadcast networks from September through November was only 37 percent positive, as compared with John Kerry's 59 percent.[53]

Cable News and the Internet: A New Partisan Press?

The cable news market—as well as the Internet—has now segmented into distinct partisan camps, perhaps reminiscent of the nineteenth century era of the partisan press. Fox News began in 1996 in response to a perceived need by conservative Americans for a counterbalance to the dominant liberal media establishment. Programming on Fox is generally acknowledged to be more conservative in nature, in spite of their claim to be "fair and balanced."

MSNBC, also launched in 1996, took a sharp turn to the left in 2007, in order to capture more of a share of the cable news market. In addition, by the early 2000s, there were any number of websites catering to the tastes of both liberals (e.g., the *Huffington Post*, the *Daily Kos*) and conservatives (e.g., *Town-Hall*, the *Drudge Report*).

Many believe that the success and prominence of these organizations is evidence of bias in the news. Indeed, it might even seem as if this development in the media environment heralds a return to the days of a partisan press. These arguments ignore two important points. First, much of what we see on MSNBC and Fox News is opinion. Two of the biggest personalities on the cable news networks, Bill O'Reilly of Fox News and Chris Matthews of MSNBC, are not news reporters, but rather are news commentators—cable news' functional equivalent of the editorial and opinion pages of the newspapers. The commentators and hosts that appear on these cable news programs are doing what they are being paid to do, namely, voice their opinion. This in itself is not evidence of bias in the news. Moreover, even these two partial exceptions demonstrate that profit motives drive news coverage in that both are supplying a product to a "niche" market.[54]

CONCLUSION

Criticizing the media has become something of a national pastime. However, in a media environment dominated by private ownership, news organizations must attract viewers or readers. This makes commercial bias inevitable. Of course, this is a welcome trade-off to government ownership of the media, which is anathema to the First Amendment and to a free and independent press.

By way of a postscript, it should be mentioned that there is some consensus and considerable evidence to suggest that in 2008, Barack Obama was the clear favorite of news organizations, and that this favoritism was reflected in biased reporting. Obama, for example, was the recipient of positive press in 75 percent of the stories about his candidacy throughout the primary season, while others received more even coverage. During the fall campaign season, he received 68 percent more coverage than McCain, and, the ratio of positive to negative coverage was 2:1, while McCain's was 2:1 negative.[55] Nonetheless, this is the exception rather than the rule.

Because of the need to attract viewers, attack journalism has become a norm in newsrooms. The sharp and sometimes unfair criticisms of political candidates frequently bring about charges of ideological bias in the media. Yet despite a good deal of research on the subject, there is no clear consensus to support those charges. Generally speaking, campaign coverage during a presidential election campaign is fairly objective in terms of its partisan or ideological orientation. Instead, the pressure for profit, rather than some broad left-wing or right-wing conspiracy, is what predominantly shapes media coverage of American elections and campaigns.

NOTES

1. "Strong Opposition to Media Cross-Ownership Emerges," Pew Research Center for the People and the Press, July 13, 2003, people-press.org/reports/print. php3?PageID=719.

2. "Fewer Favor Media Scrutiny of Political Leaders," Pew Research Center for the People and the Press, March 21, 1997, people-press.org/reports/print.php3? PageID=530.

3. "Journalism Credibility Project, 1998, the Findings in Brief," *American Society of Newspaper Editors*, August 4, 1999, www.asne.org/kiosk/reports/99reports/1999ex aminingourcredibility/p5-6_findings.html.

4. Rachel Smolkin, "A Source of Encouragement," *American Journalism Review* (August/September 2005), www.ajr.org/article_printable.asp?id=3909. See also David Niven, *Tilt? The Search for Media Bias* (Westport, Conn.: Praeger, 2002), chap. 2.

5. "Strong Opposition to Media Cross-Ownership Emerges," Pew Research Center for the People and the Press.

6. "Journalism Credibility Project, 1998, the Findings in Brief," *American Society of Newspaper Editors*.

7. Peter Humphreys, *Mass Media and Media Policy in Western Europe* (Manchester, UK: Manchester University Press, 1996).

8. Doris Graber, *Mass Media and American Politics*, 7th ed. (Washington, DC: CQ Press, 2006).

9. Michael Schudson, "The Objectivity Norm in American Journalism," *Journalism* 2 (2001): 149–70. See also Michael Emery, Edwin Emery, and Nancy L. Roberts, *The Press and America: An Interpretive History of the Mass Media*, 9th ed. (Boston: Allyn & Bacon, 1999).

10. Jody Baumgartner, "Hunker Democrats (1848)," in *Encyclopedia of American Third Parties*, ed. Ronald Hayduk, Immanuel Ness, and James Ciment (Armonk, NY: M. E. Sharpe, 2000).

11. Baumgartner, *Modern Presidential Electioneering*, chap. 2.

12. Schudson, "The Objectivity Norm in American Journalism."

13. Ibid., 156, 158, 163.

14. "Newspaper Guild," Wikipedia, en.wikipedia.org/wiki/Newspaper_Guild.

15. Wayne, *Road to the White House*, 226.

16. "Bottom-Line Pressures Now Hurting Coverage, Say Journalists," Pew Research Center for the People and the Press, May 23, 2004, people-press.org/reports/ display.php3?PageID=825; "The Newspaper Journalists of the '90s," *American Society of Newspaper Editors*, October 31, 1997, www.asne.org/index.cfm?ID=2480; Niven, Tilt? 13–14.

17. S. Robert Lichter, Stanley Rothman, and Linda S. Lichter, *The Media Elite* (Bethesda, MD: Adler & Adler, 1986).

18. Dave D'Alessio and Mike Allen, "Media Bias in Presidential Elections: A Meta-Analysis," *Journal of Communication* 50 (2000): 133–56. See also Niven, *Tilt?* especially chap. 1.

19. Eric Alterman, *What Liberal Media? The Truth About Bias and the News* (New York: Basic Books, 2008); Timothy Crouse, *Boys on the Bus* (New York: Ballantine Books, 1973), 355–6.

20. Robert P. Vallone, Lee Ross, and Mark R. Lepper, "The Hostile Media Phenomenon: Biased Perception and Perceptions of Media Bias in Coverage of the 'Beirut Massacre'," *Journal of Personality and Social Psychology* 49 (1985): 577–85.

21. Lymari Morales, 2011. "Majority in U.S. Continues to Distrust the Media, Perceive Bias," Gallup, September 22, 2011. Available at http://www.gallup.com/poll/149624/majority-continue-distrust-media-perceive-bias.aspx.

22. Pew Research Center, 2012. "Further Decline in Credibility Ratings for Most News Organizations." Available at http://www.people-press.org/2012/08/16/further-decline-in-credibility-ratings-for-most-news-organizations/.

23. Shanto Iyengar and Kyu S. Hahn, 2009. "Red Media, Blue Media: Evidence of Ideological Selectivity in Media Use," *Journal of Communication* 59: 19–39.

24. Jay G. Blumler and Elihu Katz eds. *The Uses of Mass Communications: Current Perspectives on Gratifications Research* (Beverly Hills, CA: Sage, 1974); Tomas Ruggiero, "Uses and Gratifications Theory in the 21st Century," *Mass Communication & Society* 3 (1) (2000): 3–37.

25. Robert W. McChesney, Rich Media, *Poor Democracy: Communication Politics in Dubious Times* (New York: The New Press, 2000).

26. Thomas E. Patterson, *The Mass Media Election: How Americans Choose Their President* (New York: Praeger, 1980).

27. Thomas E. Patterson, *Out of Order: An Incisive and Boldly Original Critique of the News Media's Domination of America's Political Process* (New York: Vintage, 1994).

28. Katharine Q. Seelye, "2008 Coverage Focuses on Horse Race," *New York Times*, October 29, 2007, thecaucus.blogs.nytimes.com/.../2008-coverage-focuses-on-the-horse-race/; Center for Media and Public Affairs, "Election Watch: Campaign 2008 Final," *Media Monitor* 23 (Winter 2009), www.cmpa.com/pdf/media_monitor_jan_2009.pdf.

29. Center for Media and Public Affairs, "Campaign 2004-The Primaries," *Media Monitor* 18 (March/April 2004), www.cmpa.com/mediaMonitor/documents/marapr04.pdf.

30. Howard Kurtz, "Embedded Reporters See What Makes Candidates Tick," *Milwaukee Journal Sentinel*, January 21, 2004.

31. Graber, *Mass Media and American Politics*, 221–2.

32. Tom Rosenstiel, Mark Jurkowitz, and Tricia Sartor, 2012. "How the Media Covered the 2012 Primary Campaign," Pew research Center, April 23, 2012. Available at http://www.journalism.org/2012/04/23/romney-report/.

33. John Sides, 2013. "Media Coverage of the 2012 Election was Fair and Balanced After All," Washington Post, October 14, 2013. Available at http://www.

washingtonpost.com/blogs/monkey-cage/wp/2013/10/14/media-coverage-of-the-2012-election-was-fair-and-balanced-after-all/.

34. Center for Media and Public Affairs, "Election Watch '08: The Primaries," *Media Monitor* 22 (March/April 2008), www.cmpa.com/studies_election_08.htm.

35. Graber, *Mass Media and American Politics*, 221.

36. Center for Media and Public Affairs, "Campaign 2004-The Primaries."

37. Jacqueline Bacon, "Weeding the field: The lowest circle," Extra! (September/October 2003), www.fair.org/index.php?page=1153.

38. Howard Kurtz, "Ted Koppel, Anchor Provocateur," *Washington Post*, December 10, 2003, C1.

39. "Forbes Wins Ariz, Stunner, Dole Captures the Dakotas," *Baltimore Sun*, February 28, 1996, http://articles.baltimoresun.com/1996-02-28/news/1996059030_1_buchanan-arizona-primary-dole.

40. Ian Christopher McCaleb, "Gore, McCain Tops in Nation's First Election 2000 Primary," CNN, February 2, 2000, archives.cnn.com/2000/ALLPOLITICS/stories/02/01/nh.primary.

41. Graber, *Mass Media and American Politics*, 222.

42. Center for Media and Public Affairs, "Election Watch '08: The Primaries," *Media Monitor* 22 (March/April 2008), www.cmpa.com/studies_election_08.htm.

43. Kiku Adatto, "The Incredible Shrinking Soundbite," *New Republic*, May 28, 1990.

44. Graber, *Mass Media and American Politics*, 222.

45. Larry J. Sabato, *Feeding Frenzy* (New York: Free Press, 1993).

46. "Bush Not Apologizing for Obscenity," ABC News, September 5, 2000, http://abcnews.go.com/Politics/story?id=122985.

47. David Wright and Sunlen Miller, "Obama Dropped Flag Pin in War Statement," ABC News, October 4, 2007, abcnews.go.com/Politics/story?id=3690000&page=1; Jennifer Parker, "Michelle Obama Defends Patriotism, Jokes of 'Girl Fight' on 'View'," ABC News, June 18, 2008, abcnews.go.com/Politics/Vote2008/story?id=5193627&page=1.

48. Adatto, "The Incredible Shrinking Soundbite," 22.

49. David R. Runkel, ed., *Campaign for President: The Managers Look at '88* (Dover, MA: Auburn House, 1989), 136.

50. Timothy Crouse, *The Boys on the Bus* (New York: Random House, 1973).

51. W. Lance Bennett, *News: The Politics of Illusion*, 7th ed. (New York: Longman, 2007), 171–3.

52. Center for Media and Public Affairs, "Campaign 2004-The Primaries."

53. Wayne, Road to the White House, 230; "Campaign 2000 Final," *Media Monitor* 14 (November/December 2000).

54. Brian Stelter, "Seeking More Viewers, MSNBC Turns Left," *New York Times*, August 21, 2008, www.nytimes.com/2008/08/22/business/media/22adco.html; Project for Excellence in Journalism, "The Color Of News: How Different Media Have Covered The General Election," October 29, 2008, www.journalism.org/node/13436.

55. Center for Media and Public Affairs, "Election Watch '08: The Primaries"; Center for Media and Public Affairs, "Election Watch: Campaign 2008 Final."

FOR MORE READING

Bennett, W. Lance. *News: The Politics of Illusion*. 7th ed. New York: Longman, 2007.

Bennett, Stephen Earl, Staci L. Rhine, Richard S. Flickinger, and Linda L. M. Bennett. "Video Malaise Revisited: Public Trust in the Media and Government." *Harvard International Journal of Press/Politics* 4 (4) (1999): 8–23.

Fallows, James. *Breaking the News*. New York: Vintage, 1996.

Graber, Doris. *Mass Media and American Politics*. 7th ed. Washington, DC: CQ Press, 2006.

Jamieson, Kathleen Hall and Paul T. Waldman. *The Press Effect: Politicians, Journalists, and the Stories That Shape the Political World*. New York: Oxford University Press, 2002.

Patterson, Thomas E. *Out of Order*. New York: Vintage Books, 1994.

Chapter 9

Game Changer? Misconceptions about the Significance of Presidential Debates

Every four years presidential elections dominate American politics. As Election Day approaches, the most talked-about events of the campaign season—what some political observers call the "Super Bowl of American democracy"[1]—are the presidential debates that pit the two major-party nominees against one another. Media outlets hype each debate like a heavyweight championship fight, with commentators breathlessly discussing the strengths and weaknesses of each candidate, analyzing what each needs to do to "score points" or land the "knockout blow" in the debate. Political pundits and others often claim that any "big punch" landed by a candidate in the debate could be the moment that serves as the "game changer" of the election. As one political strategist recently proclaimed, "Debates are always game changers. If you kick somebody's butt in a debate, that matters a lot. It changes votes."[2]

The 2012 campaign was no exception when it came to making "game-changing" predictions. Governor Chris Christie of New Jersey predicted that his party's nominee, Republican Mitt Romney, would get the better of President Barack Obama in their first debate. In an interview just days before the debate Christie commented, "We [Republicans] have a candidate [in Romney] who is going to do extraordinarily well on Wednesday night."[3] He then added, with the flare common before many presidential debates, "this whole race is going to turn upside down come Thursday morning."[4]

Predictions of such game-changing moments are rooted in presidential debate lore going all the way back to 1960 when Richard Nixon and John Kennedy became the first major-party presidential nominees to debate on television. But, do presidential debates really change votes? Are they the "game-changers" that many political observers often suggest? As this chapter will demonstrate, the empirical evidence simply does not support the case that presidential debates have much significance in influencing voting behavior or in affecting election outcomes. What presidential debates can do, as the evidence shows, is positively affect voters' knowledge of issues. Beyond this, there are other debate effects that may add to the larger democratic process as well. They may not be game changers, but they do not have to be.

GAME CHANGERS?

Political historians and observers have identified several presidential debate moments as having been potentially decisive in determining the outcome of the election. The debates of 1960, 1976, 1980, 1988, and 2000 have drawn particular attention. These five have helped to foster the notion that presidential debates are "game changers."

1960: Kennedy Versus Nixon

Perhaps the most widely discussed "game changer" in presidential debate history goes back to 1960. Senator John Kennedy and Vice President Richard Nixon were locked in a tight contest for the presidency. Polls from the Gallup Organization showed the contest nearly tied among registered voters before the debates began.[5] When the debates were over, Kennedy had built a small lead over Nixon, which he carried to one of the narrowest victories in presidential election history. According to many accounts of the 1960 election, the debates, particularly the first, were pivotal to Kennedy's success. As a *Time* magazine article recently declared, "It's now common knowledge that without the nation's first televised debate . . . Kennedy would never have been elected president."[6] Another account, making a similar claim, concluded that the Kennedy–Nixon debates "had a major impact on the election's outcome."[7]

Kennedy's success in the debates, according to many, was due to his telegenic appearance. The younger, handsome, and sun-tanned Kennedy answered his debate questions by looking directly into the television camera. The paler looking Nixon, sporting a five o'clock shadow, looked off to the side of his podium to make eye contact with the reporters asking the questions. Nixon's shifting gaze, combined with his less attractive appearance, sent the wrong visual cues to television viewers.[8] A poll from Albert Sindlinger's research firm showed that Kennedy won over the television audience, whereas Nixon won over those who listened to the debate on the radio.[9] Overall, a Gallup poll showed Kennedy moving ahead of Nixon by four points after the debates had concluded.[10] Kennedy beat Nixon by only the narrowest of margins, 49.7 to 49.6 percent of the popular vote. Narrow victories for Kennedy in Texas and Illinois were decisive: if Kennedy had lost those states it would have given Nixon the necessary majority of Electoral College votes. This added to the widespread perception of the debate's significance.

1976: Ford Versus Carter

There were no presidential debates for the next three elections (1964, 1968, and 1972), but debates returned in 1976. In an election in which the popular vote separated the two candidates by just two percentage points, Democrat Jimmy Carter won the presidency over incumbent Republican President Gerald Ford. Looking back on the election to explain Carter's narrow victory, some political observers point to a critical moment in one of the debates, a moment many claim may have been the biggest gaffe in presidential debate history.

In the second debate, Max Frankel of the *New York Times* asked Ford about the rise of communism throughout the world, specifically questioning whether U.S. influence was still on equal footing with the Soviet Union in Europe. After a somewhat lengthy answer, Ford concluded with a perplexing assertion, declaring that "there is no Soviet domination of Eastern Europe and there never will be under a Ford administration."[11] Frankel, visibly surprised by Ford's answer, followed up by asking Ford to clarify his comments. Ford repeated his assertion, stating at the outset of his reply, "I don't believe, Mr. Frankel, that the Yugoslavians consider themselves dominated by the Soviet Union. I don't believe that the Romanians consider themselves dominated by the Soviet Union. I don't believe that the Poles consider themselves dominated by the Soviet Union."[12] In the midst of the Cold War, this was not the case.

Post-debate analysis and media coverage focused heavily on Ford's controversial comment. Years later, in an interview with journalist Jim Lehrer, Carter remarked, "This was a very serious mistake that [Ford] made . . . . Certainly it cost him some votes, and as you know, the election was quite close."[13] Another account offered an even stronger assessment, "Why did Gerald Ford lose to Jimmy Carter? . . . President Ford lost because he committed a colossal blunder [of asserting "no Soviet domination of Eastern Europe"] in the second Ford–Carter debate in San Francisco, October 6, 1976. . . . Ford's debate performance lost the election."[14]

1980: Carter Versus Reagan

The 1980 presidential campaign entered the third week of October with President Carter holding a narrow three-point lead (45 to 42 percent) in a Gallup Poll of registered voters against former California Governor Ronald Reagan.[15] Carter and Reagan would debate only once on October 28, 1980. In an otherwise engaging debate, Carter closed his comments by attempting to humanize the serious issue of nuclear proliferation by discussing what his twelve-year old daughter, Amy, thought about the issue. Carter told a national audience, "I had a discussion with my daughter, Amy, the other day, before I came here, to ask her what the most important issue was. She said she thought nuclear weaponry—and the control of nuclear arms."[16]

After the debate ended, pundits labeled the comment as "bizarre" and late-night television hosts ridiculed Carter for seeming to depend on the advice of a daughter who had yet to reach her teenage years.[17] Reagan, by comparison, more eloquently summarized the case for his candidacy in his closing comments with a simple but memorable line: "Are you better off than you were four years ago?"[18] Carter's small lead evaporated and Reagan would go on to win in a landslide, capturing a ten-point victory in the popular vote and a 489-49 victory in the Electoral College. One account surmised that the debate "all but finished Carter."[19] Another asserted that, "absent the debate . . . Carter would have won re-election."[20]

1988: Bush Versus Dukakis

The 1988 presidential debates between Democratic nominee, Governor Michael Dukakis of Massachusetts, and Republican nominee, Vice President George H.W. Bush, included one of the most memorable of all debate moments. After a competitive performance from Dukakis in the first debate, followed by a strong showing from Dukakis' running mate Lloyd Bentsen against Republican Dan Quayle, the second Bush–Dukakis debate opened with a memorable question. Panelist Bernard Shaw of CNN asked Dukakis, "Governor, if Kitty Dukakis [the candidate's wife] were raped and murdered, would you favor an irrevocable death penalty for the killer?"[21] Dukakis answered simply and matter-of-factly that he opposed the death penalty and would not apply it even to someone who raped and murdered his wife.

While the substance of Dukakis' response was standard fare for a candidate who opposed the death penalty, Dukakis was criticized for his cold response to the question. To many political observers, Dukakis appeared emotionless in answering a question that many thought should have evoked passion. *Time* magazine later described it as "Dukakis' deadly response."[22] One summary described Dukakis as "in robot-mode" when he responded to Shaw and concluded that this debate was one that "contributed decisively to the outcome of [the] election."[23] Dukakis never recovered and ultimately lost the election in a landslide, losing the popular vote by seven points, 53 to 46 percent and the Electoral College vote, 426-111.

2000: Bush Versus Gore

The 2000 presidential election between Democratic nominee, Al Gore, and Republican nominee, George W. Bush, is best remembered for its historically close finish and controversial outcome. In an election that was ultimately decided by Florida's Electoral College votes, Bush narrowly defeated Gore by a mere 537 votes (out of more than 6 million votes cast), a margin of victory that was certified only after the U.S. Supreme Court intervened and ordered the state of Florida to end its recount of ballots. Gore's extremely narrow loss led many political pundits to point to various reasons to explain the defeat. This included his performance in the presidential debates.

According to Gallup, Gore took an eight-point lead into the debates with Bush. By the end of three debates, Gore trailed Bush by four points.[24] With such a significant swing before and after the debate period, several political observers cited Gore's performance in his first debate with Bush as the "game-changing" moment.[25] Specifically, Gore was criticized for sighing audibly into his microphone during Bush's debate responses. A number of media analysts described Gore's sighs and general demeanor during the debate as "condescending."[26] Just days after the debate, Gallup showed Gore's eight-point lead was gone.

Gore's numbers continued to decline over the next two debates, moving him from front-runner status before the debates to underdog status after the debates. This shift prompted some political observers to conclude that Gore "gave away" the election and that his debate performances were one of the major causes.[27] As one account summarized, "Once the television cameras caught that sighing, that constant look on [Gore's] face where he seemed annoyed by the whole idea of having to be there with Bush, it seemed to underscore, as somebody said, [the impression of him] as a teacher's pet who knew all the answers but was annoying and irritating . . . . Then people began to project onto Gore a personality trait of just annoyance and irritation of people in general and it became devastating for him to live that down."[28] Lydia Saad, writing for Gallup, added that "Gore won the popular vote, but he might also have won the Electoral College vote had his 8-point pre-debate-period lead not slipped away in the last few weeks of the campaign."[29]

Other Memorable Debate Moments

Although the 1960, 1976, 1980, 1988, and 2000 presidential debates stand out as the ones most frequently mentioned for their "game-changing" moments, a few other examples deserve honorable mention. In 1984, Ronald Reagan sought reelection and faced former Vice President Walter Mondale. Battling charges that his advanced age of 73 could potentially impair his decision-making capability, Reagan was asked directly in the second debate about his age. In response, he humorously commented that he was not "going to exploit, for political purposes, [his] opponent's youth and inexperience."[30] Reagan would go on to win 49 of the 50 states against Mondale in one of the most lopsided landslide victories in presidential history, making it difficult to assign any particular debate moment to Reagan's easy reelection win. Still, at least one set of reporters concluded that after Reagan's punch line about his age, "for all practical purposes, the presidential election was over."[31]

In 1992, President George H.W. Bush lost his reelection bid to Democrat Bill Clinton. In a relatively competitive contest that included a serious third-party candidate, Texas billionaire Ross Perot, Bush drew some negative media attention when he glanced at his watch during a town hall debate. In the words of one account, Bush "looked like he was bored, that he didn't care about the debate and that underscored the feeling that he wasn't connected to the problems of the people and the country."[32] The town hall format also played well to Clinton's strengths as he more comfortably engaged and connected with members in the audience. While not credited as a game-changing moment, Bush's glance at his watch is still often listed as a notable mistake in the history of presidential debates.[33]

THE EVIDENCE ON PRESIDENTIAL DEBATES AND VOTING BEHAVIOR

While there are numerous examples of political pundits and political operatives claiming that a specific debate or a particular moment in a debate was the decisive factor in determining the outcome of an election, the overwhelming body of political science research indicates that these claims are dubious. The Gallup Organization has done extensive polling on presidential debates since 1960. Based on data from their daily tracking polls, Gallup identified only two elections, 1960 and 2000, as potentially having had a "meaningful impact on the structure of the presidential races."[34] In other words, in only these two cases did the eventual winner of the election go from a deficit position to front-runner as the result of the debates. As noted earlier, Kennedy went from trailing Nixon by one point in the preelection period to leading by four points after their last debate in 1960. However, Kennedy's eventual margin over Nixon in the popular vote, an advantage of less than one-quarter of one percent, suggests that the debates may not have had a lasting impact.

In 2000, George W. Bush's pre-debate to post-debate surge in the polls seems, on the surface, the most likely evidence of debates playing a critical factor in an election outcome. Yet Gallup polls also reveal that voters thought Al Gore was the winner in two of the three of the presidential debates. This includes the first debate, where 48 to 41 percent of registered voters gave Gore the edge, in spite of his heavy sighing into the microphone.[35]

Other campaigns with "game-changing" debate moments also fail to survive scrutiny when examining public opinion data. In 1976, Gerald Ford's much publicized gaffe about "no Soviet domination of Eastern Europe" made headlines, but polls showed no appreciable decline for Ford in polls immediately afterward. In fact the opposite occurred: Ford's polling numbers improved dramatically during the debate period. According to Gallup, Ford entered the pre-debate period down 15 points to Carter, but was positioned only five points down to his challenger in the post-debate period.[36]

In 1980, President Carter's "Amy speech" and Ronald Reagan's strong performance in their debate resulted in voters judging Reagan as the winner. Reagan's ability to turn an otherwise close election into a landslide shortly after the debate provided ample fuel to the argument that the debate was a "game changer." However, a careful look at polling data reveals a more complex story. An average of all available polls showed Reagan with a two-point lead immediately before the debate.[37] By the day of the debate, Reagan's numbers had inched up a bit more, suggesting that his campaign was already beginning to generate upward movement in the polls.[38] A number of other events were taking place that may have been more damaging to Carter than the debate, notably the October release of economic data showing a rise in inflation and Carter's continued inability to negotiate the release of hostages in Iran. The debate seems at best to have merely reinforced the growing momentum in Reagan's favor.[39]

Four years later, Reagan's joke about his age in the second debate with Mondale made headlines—and certainly made people laugh—but it did little to change the dynamics of the race. Reagan entered the second debate with a solid lead and left the second debate with a solid lead. In their first debate, political observers universally agreed that Mondale got the better of Reagan, with some reports describing Reagan's performance as "confused" and most agreeing it was unsteady.[40] Still, Mondale's strong showing failed to revitalize his campaign, prompting one political scientist to conclude that voters, "don't easily change their views about who they want to run the country simply on the basis of debating skills."[41]

When examining other more recent and memorable debate moments (Dukakis' failure to show emotion, Bush peering at his watch, Gore's audible sighs) poll numbers again show little to no impact on voter preferences. In fact an analysis from one political scientist shows only a minimal effect, an average of a roughly one percent absolute change across 16 presidential debates from 1988 through 2008 (see Table 9.1). Another expert on public opinion claimed, "there is no case where we can trace a substantial shift [in public opinion] to the debates."[42] Yet another research team reached a similar conclusion after examining every available poll during presidential election cycles between 1952 and 2008.[43] In fact, the only election they identified as evidencing a shift during the debate period was in 1976, where evidence shows Ford gaining ground on Carter in spite of his gaffe.[44]

Table 9.1 Incumbent Party Candidates' Poll Standing During Debate Periods

Year	Debate	Pre-Debate	Post-Debate	"Bump"	Total Change During Debate Period
1988	First	52.9%	53.2%	0.3%	
	Second	53.7	55.3	1.60	2.4%
1992	First	41.6	41.7	0.2	
	Second	42.8	40.7	−2.0	
	Third	41.7	42.1	0.4	0.6
1996	First	60.3	58.8	−1.5	
	Second	58.6	58.8	0.2	−1.4
2000	First	51.1	50.1	−1.0	
	Second	49.7	48.5	−1.2	
	Third	48.9	47.6	−1.4	−3.5
2004	First	52.8	50.5	−2.3	
	Second	50.1	51.0	0.9	
	Third	50.6	50.9	0.3	−2.0
2008	First	48.1	46.8	−1.4	
	Second	46.7	45.7	−.9	
	Third	45.9	46.2	0.3	−1.9

Note: Percentages are standardized to reflect the two-party vote. The numbers reported for the pre-debate period are based on the polling averages over the six days prior to the debate and the day of the debate. The numbers reported for the post-debate period are based on the polling averages over the seven days following the debate.

Source: Thomas Holbrook, "Debate Expectations," Politics by the Numbers, October 1, 2012, http://politics-by-the-numbers.blogspot.com/2012/10/debate-expectations.html.

Even in the most decisive debate victory for any presidential candidate ever, a 72 to 20 percent advantage for Mitt Romney over Barack Obama in their first debate[45] in 2012, the effects proved only temporary. Obama's initial five-point advantage in the pre-debate period was washed away in the immediate aftermath of Romney's strong showing in the first debate. However, Obama regained his advantage as he went on to capture a four-point victory in the popular vote on Election Day (see Table 9.2). While it is possible that Obama's rebound may have been due to his stronger performances in the second and third debates, research suggests that debate effects appear to have only a short-term impact. Voters ultimately "come home" and return to initial pre-debate candidate preferences.[46]

In short, there is little evidence to support the contention that presidential debates have a meaningful impact on how voters cast their ballots. Even the rare instance of a major gaffe or memorable one liner during a debate will be highly unlikely to transform a presidential election. As one political observer notes, "Super Bowl moments don't happen in debates. If you are looking for a single, magical, transformative moment, you might be let down."[47]

Instead, there is overwhelming evidence to suggest that a myriad of other factors, notably a voter's party affiliation, socioeconomic status, and the state of the economy, play dominant roles in influencing individual voting

Table 9.2 Voter Preferences in 2012 Before and After the First Obama–Romney Debate

	Obama	Romney	Gap
*Pre-debate (September 30–October 2)	50%	45%	Obama +5
*Post-debate #1 (October 4–October 6)	47%	47%	Even
Popular Vote (Election Day)	51%	47%	Obama +4

*Source: Jeffrey M. Jones, "Romney Narrows Vote Gap After Historic Debate Win," Gallup, October 8, 2012, http://www.gallup.com/poll/157907/romney-narrows-vote-gap-historic-debate-win.aspx.

behavior. The rare voter may change his or her vote based on how a candidate performs in a presidential debate, but it is unlikely that these voters constitute a large enough bloc to affect an election outcome. As one political scientist explains, "When it comes to shifting enough votes to decide the outcome of the election, presidential debates have rarely, if ever, mattered."[48]

WHY PRESIDENTIAL DEBATES RARELY AFFECT VOTING BEHAVIOR

Presidential debates rarely affect voting behavior and election outcomes for a number of reasons. Perhaps the most straightforward explanation is that debates occur in the final weeks of the election cycle, when most Americans have already formed strong opinions about the candidates. This is especially true when there is an incumbent president running for reelection. In 2012, for instance, voters had a full four years to form an opinion about President Obama. His challenger, Mitt Romney, had begun campaigning for the Republican nomination as early as 2011. With Romney in the public spotlight for many months before his first debate with Obama, most voters had formed strong opinions about him as well. Voters' preexisting views about the candidates often prove difficult to change, even after a commanding debate performance in which one candidate clearly outshines the other. In fact, debates may actually come too late to change a voter's mind in some states because of early voting laws, which allow citizens to cast absentee ballots through the mail or at a designated polling place several weeks before Election Day.

Rather than swaying voters' minds, presidential debates tend to reinforce voters' preexisting views.[49] The debates in 2012 make this point clear. As Table 9.3 illustrates, Republicans overwhelmingly favored Romney over Obama in all three debates, and by margins considerably wider than by independents and Democrats. Likewise, Democrats were more likely than independents and Republicans to see Obama as the winner in each of the debates. As one political scientist summarizes, "By [debate] time voters have pretty much picked their candidates. . . . People who are political and have

Table 9.3   Perceived Winner of the Obama–Romney Debates by Party Affiliation

	Obama	Romney	Both/Neither/ No Opinion
First Debate			
All debate watchers	20%	72%	9%
Republicans	2	97	1
Independents	19	70	11
Democrats	39	49	12
Second Debate			
All debate watchers	51%	38%	11%
Republicans	9	78	13
Independents	54	33	13
Democrats	88	4	8
Third Debate			
All debate watchers	56%	33%	11%
Republicans	16	70	15
Independents	56	27	17
Democrats	95	4	2

Sources: Jeffrey M. Jones, "Romney Narrows Vote Gap After Historic Debate Win," Gallup, October 8, 2012, http://www.gallup.com/poll/157907/romney-narrows-vote-gap-historic-debate-win.aspx. Jeffrey M. Jones, "Obama Judged Winner of Second Debate" Gallup, October 19, 2012, http://www.gallup.com/poll/158237/obama-judged-winner-second-debate.aspx. Jeffrey M. Jones, "Viewers Deem Obama Winner of Third Debate, 56% to 33%," Gallup, October 25, 2012, http://www.gallup.com/poll/158393/viewers-deem-obama-winner-third-debate.aspx.

a party affiliation are hard to dislodge by the debates. And those rooting for their favorite candidate, even if he is doing poorly, aren't necessarily going to change their mind."[50]

Of course, there is a segment of the electorate without fully formed opinions about the candidates when the presidential debate period begins. These persuadable and undecided voters, however, tend to pay the least attention to politics and are thus the least likely to be watching the debates.[51] Of the persuadable and undecided voters who do happen to watch the debates, there is only a small chance that they will view something of significant consequence. A serious gaffe or a highly memorable and one-sided performance by a candidate is the exception rather than the rule in presidential debates.[52]

Finally, it is worth remembering that presidential debates do not occur in a vacuum. It is almost impossible for a voter to avoid exposure to additional information outside of the debates. Voters are likely to see television campaign advertisements, hear radio messages, read campaign materials dropped at their door, or visit a website that offers information about the candidates. Candidates also give speeches on the campaign trail, give interviews to reporters, and generally attract almost nonstop news coverage during the final weeks of the campaign. With so much attention focused on the candidates, there is always the possibility of a gaffe or misstep on the campaign trail that could potentially affect the dynamics of the election. Even without a major mistake by a candidate, the sheer volume of information that most voters are exposed to, particularly in the final weeks of the election when the debates occur, makes it difficult to isolate and disentangle the effects a debate may have on public opinion and voting behavior. Any movement in the polls from the pre- to post-debate period is thereby likely the product of more than just the debates themselves.

Yet, while the evidence is rather clear that presidential debates rarely, if ever, have a major effect on voting behavior and presidential election outcomes, it would be wrong to dismiss presidential debates as entirely irrelevant. Indeed, research shows presidential debates fulfill an important function in the electoral process. As the next section will discuss, presidential debates can improve voters' knowledge of the candidates and the major issues of the election, as well as improve voters' deliberation, all conditions that most agree are important to a healthy democracy.

THE RELEVANCE OF PRESIDENTIAL DEBATES

One of the unique features of a presidential debate is that it allows voters to compare candidates side by side in an unrehearsed setting. Candidates have to address the same questions and issues in a high-pressure environment, making debates an ideal forum for voters to compare and contrast candidates' issue positions. As two political communication scholars explain, "where in stump speeches candidates tend to indict their opponents, in debate the threat of imminent rebuttal invites a response to charges pending against one's candidacy."[53] The result is that debates are able "to produce a clarity and specificity otherwise absent in campaign discourse."[54] This dynamic makes presidential debates a unique source of political information.

Presidential debates take on added significance because they attract an extremely large audience. According to a poll from the Gallup Organization, more than two-thirds of Americans reported that they watched the first debate between Barack Obama and Mitt Romney in 2012.[55] The numbers jumped to 76 percent for the second debate, before leveling off slightly at 69 percent for the third debate.[56] The high percentages in 2012 were not an exception. Debates in previous presidential election years produced comparable rates of viewership and listenership.[57] Given that almost any type of learning requires exposure to information, the large audiences that presidential debates attract is no small matter.

Presidential debates not only attract large audiences, but also force candidates to simplify complicated political issues and communicate solutions that everyday people can easily understand. This is important because exposure

Chapter 9

to information alone is not sufficient for voters to gain knowledge. Voters also must be able to comprehend the information they receive for learning to occur.[58]

Polling data reveal that large majorities of voters typically report that presidential debates help them make more informed decisions when casting their vote. Survey results from the Pew Research Center, shown in Figure 9.1, indicate that in only one election (1996) over a twenty-year period from 1992 through 2012 did fewer than three-fifths of voters report presidential debates as helpful in their voting decision. Political commercials, by comparison, rated considerably lower, reaching a high of only 38 percent in 1992 and a low of 24 percent in 2012. Results from the Pew Research Center also noted that there were no significant partisan differences in how voters perceive the helpfulness of the presidential debates. In 2012, 69 percent of both Republican and Democratic voters and 61 percent of independent voters reported the debates as helpful in their voting decision.[59] Presidential debates thereby offer two critical prerequisites for learning: (1) exposure to political information and (2) information with substance that voters can easily process and understand.

Research confirms that individuals not only watch the debates to help them learn more about the candidates and the issues, but that learning indeed occurs.[60] With only few exceptions, studies show an improved ability among voters to answer questions correctly about the candidates and their issue positions, as well as improve their issue awareness and issue knowledge, after

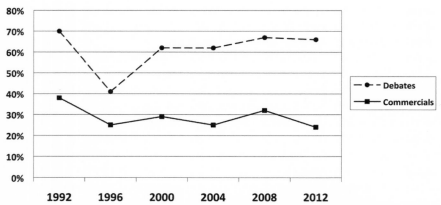

Figure 9.1. Public Perceptions of How Helpful Debates and Political Advertisements are to Vote Choice. *Note*: Percentages reflect those who reported that debates or commercials were "fairly" to "very" helpful in deciding for whom to vote. *Source*: The Pew Research Center, "Low Marks for the 2012 Election," November 15, 2012, http://www.people-press.org/2012/11/15/section-1-campaign-report-card.

viewing or listening to a presidential debate.[61] They also were better able to retain political information.[62]

As one would expect, information acquisition is most pronounced among undecided voters who typically have less knowledge about the candidates and issues prior to the debates.[63] In particular, the first debate, when many voters typically have the least amount of information, tends to have the strongest learning effects.[64] Research shows that even those who do not watch or listen to the debates experience a gain in issue awareness, primarily through exposure to media reports and from conversations with friends and family that are common after a presidential debate.[65]

In addition to improving voters' political knowledge, debates can heighten interest in the election.[66] Heightened interest can help bring more voters to the polls.[67] Likewise, partisan voters often have their political views and convictions reinforced after a presidential debate, which can further boost their level of excitement, and their likelihood of voting and becoming otherwise involved.[68]

From the perspective of campaign operatives, presidential debates can play an important role in reinforcing a particular narrative. In 1988, for example, the campaign of George H. W. Bush made efforts to portray Michael Dukakis as an emotionless, technocratic leader. When Dukakis later gave his dry answer to moderator Bernard Shaw's death penalty question during the debate, he strengthened the image of himself as emotionless that the Bush campaign had been pushing throughout the election.[69] Likewise, when George H. W. Bush looked at his watch in a town hall meeting in 1992, it reinforced the Clinton campaign's characterization of Bush as someone out of touch and uninterested in the plight of everyday Americans.[70] In this sense, debates can become important in the battle campaigns wage over trying to control the public's perceptions of the competing candidates.

Similarly, campaigns attempt to control the issue agenda in a way that is favorable to their candidate, and debates can reinforce these efforts as well. In fact, there is evidence to suggest that voters often perceive topics covered in a debate as more important than they did before the debate. In one study of the Carter–Ford presidential debate, scholars found that viewers ranked economic and foreign policy issues consistently high. However, after viewing one of the Carter–Ford debates focused entirely on domestic issues, foreign policy issues decreased in importance.[71]

Finally, debates can have significant effects on voters in primary elections. In one study, researchers found that debates held during the 1996 Arizona Republican presidential primary influenced respondents' assessments of the candidates' electability and even changed some voters' preferences.[72] Primary debates, like those that take place during the fall campaign, can also increase issue knowledge.[73]

Taken together, research on presidential debates reveals that they have some important effects. Debates can improve voters' knowledge of the candidates and issues, increase public interest in the election, serve to reinforce a candidate's image and shape the issue agenda, and can even affect voting behavior in primary elections. While presidential debates do not affect general election outcomes and fall short of being the proverbial "game changers" that they are sometimes touted to be, they most assuredly have an impact on voters and presidential campaigns.

CONCLUSION

Every four years, political pundits trot out the myth that presidential debates can be game-changing events in the upcoming November election. Yet evidence produced from public opinion polling data overwhelmingly suggest otherwise. Presidential debates rarely affect voting behavior in the November election, and almost never to the extent that they can alter the outcome.

Instead, presidential debates carry out a largely educative role in the electoral process, helping voters with information acquisition. Millions of Americans watch and listen to presidential debates, and they do so for reasons beyond the mere entertainment and spectacle aspect of these events. The public tunes in to presidential debates to learn more about the candidates, and research suggests that this is what occurs. Presidential debates can help voters' deliberation by improving their knowledge of the candidates and issues. They further aid the democratic process by increasing public interest in the election. This increased interest can spur political participation. Presidential debates can also shape the issue agenda, and may even affect voting behavior in presidential primaries. All of this suggests that presidential debates are an important part of American democracy—even if they are not ultimately the "game changers" that political operatives, pundits, and politicians often make them out to be.

NOTES

1. See "Presidential Debates and Their Effects," Journalist's Resource, October 16, 2012 http://journalistsresource.org/studies/politics/elections/presidential-debates-effects-research-roundup.

2. Quoted in Alexander Bolton, "Ten Game Changers That Could Decide the Race Between Obama and Romney," *The Hill*, June 3, 2012, http://thehill.com/homenews/campaign/230583-ten-game-changers-that-could-decide-the-presidency.

3. Quoted in Robert Schlesinger, "Sorry, Romney, Presidential Debates Are Rarely Game-Changers," *U.S. News & World Report*, October 3, 2012,

http://www.usnews.com/opinion/articles/2012/10/03/sorry-romney-presidential-debates-are-rarely-game-changers.

4. Schlesinger, "Sorry, Romney, Presidential Debates Are Rarely Game-Changers."

5. Lydia Saad, "Presidential Debates Rarely Game-Changers," Gallup, September 25, 2008, http://www.gallup.com/poll/110674/presidential-debates-rarely-gamechangers.aspx.

6. Kayla Webley, "How the Nixon-Kennedy Debate Changed the World," *Time*, September 23, 2010, http://content.time.com/time/nation/article/0,8599,2021078,00.html.

7. History.com Staff, "The Kennedy-Nixon Debates," History.com, 2010, http://www.history.com/topics/us-presidents/kennedy-nixon-debates.

8. See the various accounts in Sidney Kraus, ed., *The Great Debates: Kennedy vs. Nixon, 1960* (Bloomington, IN: Indiana University Press, 1977) and History.com Staff, "The Kennedy-Nixon Debates."

9. There is some debate about accounts that suggest Kennedy bested Nixon because he looked better on television. For a good summary of this, see David Greenberg, "Rewinding the Kennedy-Nixon Debates: Did JFK Really Win Because He Looked Better on Television?" Slate, September 24, 2010, http://www.slate.com/articles/news_and_politics/history_lesson/2010/09/rewinding_the_kennedynixon_debates.2.html. However, some credible evidence supports the notion that Kennedy's superior appearance had an impact. See James N. Druckman, "The Power of Television Images: The First Kennedy-Nixon Debate Revisited," *Journal of Politics* 65 (2003): 559–71.

10. Saad, "Presidential Debates Rarely Game-Changers."

11. See the Commission on Presidential Debates, Debate Transcripts, accessed from http://www.debates.org/index.php?page=debate-transcripts.

12. Ibid.

13. "Debating Our Destiny: The Ford/Carter Debates," PBS, September 24, 2000, http://www.pbs.org/newshour/spc/debatingourdestiny/doc1976.html.

14. Michael Reagan with Jim Denney, *The New Reagan Revolution: How Ronald Regan's Principles Can Restore America's Greatness Today* (New York: St. Martin's Press, 2010), 46.

15. Saad, "Presidential Debates Rarely Game-Changers."

16. See the Commission on Presidential Debates, Debate Transcripts, accessed from http://www.debates.org/index.php?page=debate-transcripts.

17. Quote from "1980 Presidential Debates," CNN, 1996, http://www.cnn.com/ALLPOLITICS/1996/debates/history/1980/index.shtml. For further information about the impact of the "Amy speech," see Paul F. Boller, Jr. *Presidential Campaigns: From George Washington to George W. Bush* (New York: Oxford University Press), 367.

18. See the Commission on Presidential Debates, Debate Transcripts, accessed from http://www.debates.org/index.php?page=debate-transcripts.

19. "American President: A Reference Resource," Miller Center, University of Virginia, http://millercenter.org/president/carter/essays/biography/3.

20. Quoted in Marc A. Thiessen, "Like Reagan, Romney Can Still Win," *The Washington Post*, October 1, 2012, http://www.washingtonpost.com/

opinions/like-reagan-romney-can-still-win/2012/10/01/01776f94-0bcb-11e2-bb5e-492c0d30bff6_story.html.

21. See the Commission on Presidential Debates, Debate Transcripts, accessed from http://www.debates.org/index.php?page=debate-transcripts.

22. M. J. Stephey, "Top Ten Memorable Debate Moments," *Time*, September 26, 2008, http://content.time.com/time/specials/packages/article/0,28804,1844704_1844706_1844712,00.html.

23. Rick Shenkman, "History Proves that Presidential Debates Matter," History News Network, September 22, 2004, http://historynewsnetwork.org/article/7478.

24. Saad, "Presidential Debates Rarely Game-Changers."

25. Bill Plante, "Game-Changing Presidential Debates Remembered," CBS News, October 2, 2012, http://www.cbsnews.com/news/game-changing-presidential-debates-remembered and "Game-Changing Debate Moments," NPR, February 29, 2012, http://www.npr.org/2012/02/29/147654737/game-changing-debate-moments.

26. See for example, Sean Sullivan, "The 10 Most Memorable Moments in Presidential Debates," *The Washington Post*, October 2, 2012, http://www.washingtonpost.com/blogs/the-fix/wp/2012/10/02/the-10-most-memorable-moments-in-presidential-debates.

27. Quoted in Nelson W. Polsby, Aaron Wildavsky, Steven E. Schier, and David A. Hopkins, *Presidential Elections: Strategies and Structures of American Politics*, 13th ed. (Lanham, MD: Rowman & Littlefield, 2012), 193.

28. Quoted in CNN Political Unit, "10 Debate Moments That Mattered," CNN, October 3, 2012 http://www.cnn.com/2012/10/02/politics/debate-moments-that-mattered.

29. Saad, "Presidential Debates Rarely Game-Changers."

30. See the Commission on Presidential Debates, Debate Transcripts, accessed from http://www.debates.org/index.php?page=debate-transcripts.

31. Jack Germond and Jules Witcover, *Wake Us When It's Over: Presidential Politics in 1984* (New York: Macmillan, 1985), 9.

32. CNN Political Unit, "10 Debate Moments That Mattered."

33. Ibid.

34. Saad, "Presidential Debates Rarely Game-Changers."

35. Frank Newport, "What History Tells Us About Second and Third Debates," Gallup, October 7, 2004, http://www.gallup.com/poll/13525/what-history-tells-about-second-third-debates.aspx.

36. Saad, "Presidential Debates Rarely Game-Changers."

37. John Sides, "What Really Happened in the 1980 Presidential Campaign," The Monkey Cage, August 9, 2012, http://themonkeycage.org/2012/08/09/what-really-happened-in-the-1980-presidential-campaign.

For further information, see Robert S. Erikson and Christopher Wlezien, *The Timeline of Presidential Elections: How Campaigns Do (And Do Not) Matter* (Chicago: University of Chicago Press, 2012).

38. Sides, "What Really Happened in the 1980 Presidential Campaign" and Erikson and Wlezien, *The Timeline of Presidential Elections: How Campaigns Do (And Do Not) Matter*.

39. Ibid.

40. Germond and Witcover, *Wake Us When It's Over: Presidential Politics in 1984*. Also discussed in "Romney's Debate Performance Was Presidential Game Changer, Analysts Say," *Star-Ledger*, October 5, 2012, http://www.nj.com/politics/index.ssf/2012/10/romneys_debate_performance_was.html.

41. Samuel L. Popkin, *The Reasoning Voter: Communication and Persuasion in Presidential Campaigns*, 2nd ed. (Chicago, IL: University of Chicago Press, 1994), 233.

42. Quote from James Stimson in John Sides, "Do Presidential Debates Really Matter?" *Washington Monthly* September/October 2012, http://www.washington-monthly.com/magazine/septemberoctober_2012/ten_miles_square/do_presidential_debates_really039413.php.

43. Erikson and Wlezien, *The Timeline of Presidential Elections: How Campaigns Do (And Do Not) Matter*. For a helpful summary, see also Sides, "Do Presidential Debates Really Matter?"

44. Ibid.

45. Jeffrey M. Jones, "Romney Narrows Vote Gap After Historic Debate Win," Gallup, October 8, 2012, http://www.gallup.com/poll/157907/romney-narrows-vote-gap-historic-debate-win.aspx.

46. John G. Geer, "The Effects of Presidential Debates on the Electorate's Preferences for Candidates," *American Politics Quarterly* 16 (1988): 486–501 and Erikson and Wlezien, *The Timeline of Presidential Elections: How Campaigns Do (And Do Not) Matter*.

47. Quoted in Karen E. Crummy, "Obama, Romney Engage in University of Denver Presidential Debate," *The Denver Post*, October 3, 2012, http://www.denverpost.com/ci_21691794/obama-romney-prepare-take-stage-first-debate.

48. Sides, "Do Presidential Debates Really Matter?"

49. David O. Sears and Steven H. Chafee, "Uses and Effects of the 1976 Debates: An Overview of Empirical Studies," in *The Great Debates*, ed. Sidney Kraus (Bloomington, IN: Indiana University Press, 1979). For more recent research, see Geer, "The Effects of Presidential Debates on the Electorate's Preferences for Candidates" and Erikson and Wlezien, *The Timeline of Presidential Elections: How Campaigns Do (And Do Not) Matter*.

50. Quoted in Miranda Green, "Presidential Debates Rarely Have Much Effect on Election Outcomes," *The Daily Beast*, September 29, 2012, http://www.thedailybeast.com/articles/2012/09/29/presidential-debates-rarely-have-much-effect-on-election-outcomes.html.

51. Stanley Kelley Jr., "Campaign Debates: Some Facts and Issues," *Public Opinion Quarterly* 26 (1962): 351–66.

52. Sides, "Do Presidential Debates Really Matter?"

53. Kathleen Hall Jamieson and David S. Birdsell, *Presidential Debates: The Challenge of Creating An Informed Electorate* (New York: Oxford University Press, 1988): 131–2.

54. Jamieson and Birdsell, *Presidential Debates: The Challenge of Creating An Informed Electorate*.

55. Frank Newport, "Viewers Deem Obama Winner of Third Debate, 56% to 33%," Gallup, October 25, 2012 http://www.gallup.com/poll/158393/viewers-deem-obama-winner-third-debate.aspx.

56. Newport, "Viewers Deem Obama Winner of Third Debate, 56% to 33%."

57. Frank Newport, "Debate Watchers Give Obama Edge Over McCain," Gallup, September 28, 2008, http://www.gallup.com/poll/110779/debate-watchers-give-obama-edge-over-mccain.aspx and Newport, "What History Tells Us About Second and Third Debates."

58. John Zaller, *The Nature and Origins of Mass Opinion* (Cambridge: Cambridge University Press, 1992).

59. The Pew Research Center, "Low Marks for the 2012 Election," November 15, 2012, http://www.people-press.org/2012/11/15/section-1-campaign-report-card.

60. Thomas M. Holbrook, "Political Learning From Presidential Debates," *Political Behavior* 21 (1999): 67–89.

61. Thomas M. Holbrook, "Political Learning From Presidential Debates." See also Alan I. Abramowitz, "The Impact of a Presidential Debate on Voter Rationality," *American Journal of Political Science* (1978) 22: 680–90, and Lee Becker, Idowu Sobowale, Robin Cobbey, and Chaim Eyal, "Debates' Effects on Voters' Understanding of Candidates and Issues," in *The Presidential Debates*, ed. George Bishop, Robert Meadow, and Marilyn Jackson-Meadow (New York: Praeger, 1978).

62. David J. Lanoue, "The 'Turning Point': Viewers' Reactions to the Second 1988 Presidential Debate," *American Politics Quarterly* 19 (1991): 80–95.

63. Steven H. Chaffee, "Presidential Debates—Are They Helpful to Voters?" *Communication Monographs* 45 (1978): 330–46, and Micahel Pfau, "Intraparty Political Debates and Social Learning," *Journal of Applied Communication Research* 16 (1988): 99–112.

64. Thomas M. Holbrook, "Political Learning From Presidential Debates" and Sears and Chafee, "Uses and Effects of the 1976 Debates: An Overview of Empirical Studies."

65. Abramowitz, "The Impact of a Presidential Debate on Voter Rationality."

66. Robert E. Denton and Gary C. Woodward, *Political Communication in America* (New York: Praeger, 1990).

67. Donald P. Green and Ron Shachar, "Habit Formation and Political Behaviour: Evidence of Consuetude in Voter Turnout," *British Journal of Political Science* 30 (2000): 561–72.

68. See for example, Sears and Chafee, "Uses and Effects of the 1976 Debates: An Overview of Empirical Studies" and Geer, "The Effects of Presidential Debates on the Electorate's Preferences for Candidates."

69. See comments from Allan Lounden in Green, "Presidential Debates Rarely Have Much Effect on Election Outcomes."

70. Ibid.

71. Linda L. Swanson and David L. Swanson, "The Agenda-Setting Function of the First Ford-Carter Debate," *Communication Monographs* 45 (1978): 347–53.

72. Mike Yawn, Kevin Ellsworth, Bob Beatty, and Kim Fridkin Kahn, "How a Presidential Primary Debate Changed Attitudes of Audience Members," *Political Behavior* 20 (1998): 155–81.

73. William L. Benoit, Glenn J. Hansen, and Rebecca M. Verser, "A Meta-analysis of the Effects of Viewing U.S. Presidential Debates," *Communication Monographs* 70 (2003): 335–50.

FOR MORE READING

Benoit, William L. *Political Election Debates: Informing Voters About Policy and Character.* Lanham, MD: Lexington Books, 2014.

Erikson, Robert S. and Christopher Wlezien. *The Timeline of Presidential Elections: How Campaigns Do (And Do Not) Matter.* Chicago: University of Chicago Press, 2012.

Holbrook, Thomas M. *Do Campaigns Matter?* Thousand Oaks, CA: Sage, 1996.

Jamieson, Kathleen Hall. *Presidential Debates: The Challenge of Creating an Informed Electorate.* New York: Oxford University Press, 1990.

Chapter 10

Science or Voodoo? Misconceptions about National Election Polls

I re-word Winston Churchill's famous remarks about democracy and say, "Polls are the worst way of measuring public opinion . . . or of predicting elections—except for all of the others" (Humphrey Taylor, chairman of the Harris Poll).[1]

Public opinion polls are ubiquitous. Rarely does a day pass without a major newspaper featuring the results of some poll. The frequency of polls only increases during an election season, and this is especially true during a presidential election. However, many people do not understand enough about polling to be able to interpret polls accurately. To make matters worse, media outlets occasionally misrepresent the results of polls. Pollsters themselves also miss the mark from time to time, providing forecasts and predictions that fail to materialize. This raises a few questions: Can national election polls be trusted? Are pollsters really able to gauge what Americans believe? One poll conducted in 2000 suggested that only 2 percent of Americans believe that national polls are "always right," while almost 60 percent believe they are right "only some of the time" and 7 percent "hardly ever."[2]

We offer a mixed answer to the question of whether people can trust polls throughout the election cycle. Our objective is less to dispel a particular myth than to give the reader a better understanding of the enterprise of public polling during an election. This understanding is crucial to following news stories throughout the campaign. Our goal is to give readers a set of guidelines on how to read, analyze, and interpret polling results during a campaign.[3] In the end, the answer to the question of whether to trust a particular national opinion poll depends on a variety of factors.

THE BASICS OF PUBLIC POLLING

Election polls have a long history in the United States. Since 1824, news-papers have conducted and reported the results of so-called straws, or straw polls, during presidential elections.[4] Straw polls are informal polls taken to gauge public opinion (which way the wind is blowing the straw). During the nineteenth century, most newspapers were partisan publications. While newspapers purportedly used polls to give readers a sense of which candidate might be more likely to prevail, in actuality they were intended to advance the paper's partisan agenda by giving the public the impression that the paper's favored candidate was in the lead.

The methodology of nineteenth-century polls was hardly scientific. To conduct a poll, a journalist might, for example, ask questions of the passen-gers aboard a particular train or citizens attending a public gathering.[5] For example, in 1876, the following story ran in the *Chicago Tribune*: "An excur-sion train containing some 200 people from Dayton, [Ohio], and neighboring towns, arrived last evening via the Pan Handle Road. . . . A vote was taken, resulting as follows: Hayes 65, Tilden 13, neutral 3, Cooper 2."[6]

Straw polls grew in popularity throughout the nineteenth century and, by the early part of the twentieth century, had become a regular feature in news-paper coverage of presidential elections. However, as popular as they were, they were not very useful in predicting the outcome of presidential elections. This was in part because people who did not sympathize with a given paper's partisan leanings would often refuse to return their questionnaires, leading to wildly biased estimates of the vote totals.

Among the many publications that conducted presidential polls was *Liter-ary Digest*, which at the time was the most widely circulated general reader-ship magazine in the nation. Starting in 1916, *Literary Digest* conducted polls predicting the presidential vote. While the magazine's predicted vote totals were often inaccurate, it correctly predicted the winner in five consecutive elections (1916–1932). However, in 1936, it predicted that the Republican candidate for president, Alf Landon, would receive 57 percent of the vote to Franklin Roosevelt's 43 percent. Of course, Roosevelt won, garnering 62.5 percent.[7]

The ushering in of the modern era of scientific polling began with the *Digest*'s failure in 1936. In addition to the fact that the magazine had incor-rectly predicted Landon's victory, three enterprising individuals with back-grounds in market research correctly predicted the outcome. George Gallup, Elmo Roper, and Archibald Crossley were able to do so by employing more systematic methods of sampling.[8] To understand how Gallup, Roper, and Crossley correctly predicted the winner, and how the *Digest* did not, it is necessary to examine what pollsters do and how they do it.

A poll is an instrument used to measure what a group of people think (or know) about a particular subject or question. Because it is almost impossible to ask all of the people in a particular group (e.g., registered voters) what they think about a particular topic and because such an effort would be too time consuming or costly to be practical, a pollster asks a smaller group of people, or a sample. From this sample, pollsters then estimate what the larger group thinks.

To understand this process better, imagine trying to predict how a large lecture hall with 500 students will vote in a presidential election. One approach would be to ask all 500 students. However, by the time one handed out, collected, and counted all of the ballots, the class would be over. Is it reasonable to believe that one could estimate the likely vote outcome by polling only fifty people? Under the right circumstances, the answer is yes.

The reason for this is that polling is based in part on a branch of mathematics known as probability theory, which attempts to quantify how likely it is that a certain event will occur.[9] For example, probability theory (in particular, the central limit theorem) suggests that if one flips a coin one hundred times, it is likely that heads will land face up about fifty times. But to make a sound prediction one would first need to flip the coin a certain number of times. In other words, a certain number of actual observations are required. Probability theory allows pollsters to infer what Americans think based on the actual answers given by approximately 1,500 people, sometimes less.[10]

Yet understanding and applying theories of probability is only one part of the puzzle. In order to gauge public opinion accurately and predict election outcomes we need to insure that we represent the entirety of the political spectrum in our sample. For example, we know that women are more likely to vote Democratic, and men are more likely to vote Republican. We therefore would want to make sure that women and men are included in the sample in roughly similar proportions to their numbers in the whole class. If our class was evenly divided by gender (250 women, 250 men), we would want to poll approximately twenty-five women and twenty-five men. Furthermore, we know that people who frequently attend church vote differently than those who do not; that the more affluent cast their ballots differently than those who are less economically fortunate; and so on. In short, to have any confidence that the results from our fifty-person sample would correctly predict the vote of all 500 students, we would want to ensure that the fifty students who were polled were broadly representative of the entire class.

How is a representative sample identified by a pollster? There are four main strategies for doing this, all of which rely—in some way—on randomly selecting the individuals who take the poll. In the language of survey research, these are known as "probability samples," a reference to the fact that randomness—or random selection of the cases used to make the prediction—plays a central role in theories of probability.

The first strategy is random sampling. In a simple random sample, there is an equal chance of selecting each person in the larger group, or population. For example, if everyone in our hypothetical class of 500 had a seat number, we could put slips of paper numbered one to five hundred in a basket, shuffle them around, and pick fifty. If conducted fairly (e.g., all sheets of paper are of equal size, folded in half to hide the number, sufficiently shuffled or mixed), the process would provide an equal chance of selection for each student.

A second strategy, a variant of the first, is systematic sampling. Instead of selecting individuals strictly at random, systematic sampling involves moving through a list and selecting names according to a preset strategy. The list itself is assumed to be randomly distributed. For example, in systematic sampling, we could go through our alphabetical class roster and select every tenth name in order to create a fifty-person sample.

Another technique is stratified sampling. Here, the pollster divides the sampling frame, or the entire group, into strata, or smaller groups. Within each stratum (group), the pollster selects a sample using simple random or systematic sampling. This helps to ensure that the sample sufficiently represents all relevant subgroups. For example, if our class has 300 men and 200 women, we would select a sample of thirty men and twenty women.

Multistage cluster sampling follows a similar principle, although here, rather than use subgroup characteristics as the initial basis for sampling, the pollster uses geography instead. For example, a pollster could first select a geographic unit (say, a state), and within that unit, select a smaller unit (a county), and within that unit, choose an even smaller one (a neighborhood) and then select potential respondents—at random—from the smallest unit. This process reduces costs for the polling firm by concentrating efforts in several small areas. In our class example, we might think about selecting every fifth row of students, then randomly selecting respondents from each.

The important point with respect to sampling, regardless of the technique used, is that the respondents must be representative of the population that the pollster or researcher examines. Probability sampling rests on an assumption that if selected randomly, a sample will be representative of the population. Box 10.1 summarizes these four techniques.

This admittedly simplistic explanation of sampling allows us to understand why the *Literary Digest* poll failed to predict Roosevelt's victory correctly in 1936. The magazine sent out over ten million questionnaires, and over 2.3 million people filled out and returned these surveys. This was more than a sufficient number upon which to base a prediction of how the American public would vote. However, automobile registration and telephone number lists produced the list of people the magazine used in mailing the questionnaire.

Box 10.1   Techniques for Selecting a Probability Sample

Random: Individuals are selected from the entire population of interest by chance.

Systematic: Individuals are selected from the entire population of interest according to a set strategy.

Stratified: The population of interest is divided into subgroups, and within each, a certain number of individuals are selected either randomly or systematically.

Multistage Cluster: A number of geographic areas are identified, and within each, individuals are selected either randomly or systematically.

The problem with this was that in 1936, people who owned automobiles or had telephones in their home were more likely to have been Republicans (thus, Landon voters) rather than Democrats (Roosevelt supporters). In addition, subsequent research has shown that Landon voters were more likely to return their questionnaires. Coupled together, this produced a sample that was biased, or not representative of the general population.[11]

In sum, assuming that researchers administer a survey to a sufficiently large and representative sample, and assuming that they fairly word the questions they ask, most polls can be trusted. However, not all polls are created equal. In particular, presidential campaign polls have some common pitfalls worth noting.

PROBLEM OF PSEUDO POLLS

There are many reputable polling firms, as well as countless research institutions and university professors around the country that conduct scientifically grounded polls. In general, the results of these polls are trustworthy, if one uses a certain amount of discretion in interpreting the results. However, anyone can write and administer a poll. As noted earlier, a variety of different sources present us with various poll results every day. Which polls should we trust, or more to the point, which should we *not* trust?

"Pseudo polls" are one general category of polls to disregard altogether, especially in understanding the dynamics of a presidential campaign. Websites (including blogs), local news organizations, talk radio, college newspapers, and others often administer these types of polls. The major problem with pseudo polls is that they typically rely on what some refer to as "convenience" or nonprobability samples. Here, poll administrators simply invite people to participate in the poll and then tabulate the results. The individuals who take the survey are, in other words, self-selected—not randomly selected. Fox

News' "You Decide" (http://nation.foxnews.com/poll) is a good example of these types of polls. While they include a disclaimer stating that the poll results are not representative of the general public (unofficial polls based on user votes), it is unclear whether the average viewer understands what this means.[12]

The problems with polls that rely on self-selected samples are twofold. First, not everyone has a chance to participate. For example, in the case of Internet polls, the sample includes only those who visit the poll's website. Moreover, most of these media cater to a specific type of person (e.g., most talk radio listeners tend to be conservative).[13] Another problem with this sampling technique is that people who are motivated to respond to the poll usually have more extreme views than the general population. The end result is that the samples in pseudo polls are not representative of the population at large, nor are the views expressed in these polls representative of the views of the population at large.[14]

HOW TO DETERMINE LIKELY VOTERS?

A reliable poll of presidential preference should sample only those people who will actually vote. To understand the scope of this problem, consider that there are upwards of 200 million citizens over the age of eighteen in the United States. As chapter 3 notes, roughly 50 to 60% of the voting age population casts a ballot in a typical presidential election.[15]

How should a polling organization construct a sample of people who will vote, or who will be likely to vote? Unfortunately, there is no reliable or accepted way to determine whether an individual will exercise this most basic of political freedoms. Simply asking a person if they are likely to vote will not help identify likely voters. Most people, based on ideas about good citizenship, are reluctant to admit they might not vote. Thus, voter turnout is typically lower than the percentage of people who say they are likely to vote. For example, the Pew Research Center conducted a survey prior to the 1996 election asking respondents about their intention to vote. Of those responding, 69 percent said they were "absolutely certain" they would vote, and another 18 percent replied they were "fairly certain." In actuality, voter turnout in 1996 was 49 percent (of the voting age population).[16]

Most polling firms will use at least one, and typically several, screening questions in their attempt to narrow their sample down so that it only includes likely voters. The first stage of this screening is almost always to ask whether the respondent is a registered voter. From those who respond in the affirmative, the polling firm will ask additional questions in an attempt to gauge how likely the individual is to vote. For example, Gallup has asked whether the respondent is likely to vote, how often they have voted in the past, whether they know where their polling place is, their level of interest in politics, their interest in a particular campaign, and their level of commitment to a particular candidate. Most of the reputable national polling organizations use some combination of questions similar to Gallup's to gauge whether an individual is likely to vote.[17] In 2012, the Pew organization asked nine questions to make this determination.[18]

In a presidential preference poll, especially one conducted close to the election, the sample should consist of only those who are registered and likely to vote. How well the polling firm constructs the sample in this regard can have a direct effect on the results. For example, one Harris Poll from October of 2004 suggested that President Bush was leading Senator John Kerry by two percentage points according to one measure of likely voters. But a second poll, employing a different method of measuring registered and likely voters, had Bush ahead by eight points (51 to 43 percent).[19]

Therefore, it seems prudent to take note of whether the poll bases its results on responses from registered or likely voters. Most major news organizations will include this information somewhere in the story. For example, a *Washington Post* story from early August 2004 reported that John Kerry had "the support of 50 percent of all registered voters." A story from late October 2004 suggested that Bush led Kerry "by 51% to 46% among *likely* voters" (emphasis added).[20]

WHAT ABOUT UNDECIDED VOTERS?

As complicated as it is to ensure that a poll sample includes only those voters most likely to vote, another issue is how to count the people who say they are undecided. In most presidential campaigns, the number of "undecideds" is as high as 15 percent, and although this percentage drops as the campaign nears its end, it can still be as high as 5 percent in the days prior to Election Day. While it would be a simple matter for a news organization to report the percentage of undecideds in addition to the percentage that favor each candidate, most do not, because it makes for less interesting reading if the poll numbers present an uncertain picture. One strategy to deal with undecided voters is to have a follow-up question asking the respondent if he or she "leans" toward, or favors, either candidate.[21] While this reduces the number of undecideds, it paints an inaccurate portrait of voter preferences, given that some of these people might change their minds.[22] This was one of the factors responsible for Gallup mistakenly calling the 1948 election for Thomas Dewey (morning newspapers proclaimed that Dewey won, when in fact, Harry Truman was the victor).[23] Another way to reduce the number of undecideds is to present respondents with a secret ballot, but this requires face-to-face interviewing, a rather costly method.

A more common strategy is to allocate the undecideds to one candidate or the other, based on some formula. For example, one way to allocate them would be to assign them in proportion to the candidate's strength. If 46 percent of respondents have expressed a preference for Candidate A, the pollster might allocate 46 percent of the undecided vote to Candidate A. This strategy, however, poses considerable risks given that the closer Election Day looms, the more likely it is that momentum can shift, disproportionately favoring one candidate over the other. There are other formulas for allocating undecideds as well, including using the respondent's past voting record or partisan identification (if any) as a clue for future voting intentions, whether there is an incumbent in the race (undecideds are generally thought to be anti-incumbent), as well as other, more complex solutions.

Additional ways to address this issue are to continue polling as close to Election Day as is feasible. This reduces the number of undecided voters in the poll. However, this strategy too can result in less than perfect results. In fact, there is a fair degree of error in many of the preelection polls conducted by major polling firms when compared to the actual vote totals. Table 10.1 lists the actual vote margin between the two candidates and the margin taken from the *least* accurate major poll, and the difference between these two figures, from each election cycle from 1980 to 2012.

To be fair, the track record also shows that with the exception of one year, at least one of the major polling firms projected the outcome either exactly or correctly to within one percentage point, and in only one case (the election

Table 10.1   Actual and Projected Margins from Select Election Polls, 1980–2012

Year	Winner, Actual Vote Margin	Margin from Least Accurate Projection	Difference
1980	Reagan +10	Reagan +1 (CBS/*New York Times*)	9
1984	Reagan +18	Reagan +10 (Roper)/ +25 (*USA Today*)	8/7
1988	Bush +8	Bush +12 (Gallup)	4
1992	Clinton +8	Clinton +12 (Gallup/CNN/*USA Today*)	4
1996	Clinton +8	Clinton +18 (CBS/*New York Times*)	10
2000	Bush and Gore (even)	Bush +7 (Hotline)	7
2004	Bush +2.4	Bush +6 (*Newsweek*)	3.6
2008	Obama +7.3	Obama +13 (CBS News)	5.7
2012	Obama +4	Obama +3 (Pew)	1

Source: Data from 1980 through 2000 adapted from Robert S. Erikson and Kent L. Tedin, *American Public Opinion: Its Origins, Content, and Impact*, 7th ed. (New York: Longman, 2005), 44. 2004 data from Robert S. Erikson and Kent L. Tedin, *American Public Opinion: Its Origins, Content, and Impact*, Updated 7th ed. (New York: Longman, 2007), 51. Data for 2008 from "White House 2008: General Election Trial Heats, Presidential Trial Heat Summary," http://www.pollingreport.com/wh08gen.htm, accessed June 1, 2009, and 2012 from "White House 2008: Presidential Trial Heat Summary," *PollingReport.com*, http://www.pollingreport.com/wh12gen.htm, accessed May 20, 2015.

of 2000) did any firm project the winner incorrectly. In 1980, all of the major firms underestimated Ronald Reagan's margin of victory over Jimmy Carter (NBC/AP came within three percentage points of the correct margin). Seven organizations called the election for George W. Bush and two for Al Gore in 2000, while the actual vote was virtually even. (Gore actually polled one-half of a percentage point more than did Bush.) Table 10.1 illustrates the reality that many voters make their decision in the final days of the campaign, after the completion of the last polls. It also highlights the difficulties polling organizations have in dealing with late-deciding voters.

PROBLEM OF TIMING: PHASES OF THE CAMPAIGN

Polls taken and released during certain periods of time during the campaign can be misleading, giving a false impression of a candidate's strength or weakness. Readers of these polls need to interpret them cautiously. This is especially true with respect to polls taken during the preprimary phase of the campaign, immediately after each party convention, and after the debates.

Preprimary polls, or those taken before the Iowa caucuses and New Hampshire primary, have in the past been a fairly good predictor of who will win the party nomination. From 1980 to 2000, all but one candidate (Gary Hart, in 1988) who was leading in the Gallup poll of party identifiers immediately prior to the Iowa caucuses has won their party's nomination.[24] This said, there is considerable fluctuation in these poll numbers before January of the election year. For example, in 2003, several candidates, including Joe Lieberman, Dick Gephardt, Wesley Clark, and the eventual presumed front-runner, Howard Dean, led in these preprimary polls.[25] John Kerry was the eventual winner of the Democratic nomination. In fact, in 2008, neither of the two candidates who led in the final poll before Iowa (Hillary Clinton and Rudy Giuliani) went on to secure their party's nomination.

These "trial heat" polls are not measuring actual preferences as much as they track name recognition or simple familiarity with the name of the individual.[26] In addition, these polls are sensitive to the news cycle. Before Wesley Clark's formal entrance into the race on September 17, 2003, most polls showed other Democratic candidates leading the field. However, in the month following his announcement to enter the race, Clark consistently ranked among the top tier of candidates. One can only assume this was at least partly the result of the media coverage generated by his announcement, because he won only one Democratic primary.[27] Republican Senator Fred Thompson, who also starred in the television series *Law and Order* for five seasons, announced his candidacy in early September of 2007 and polled between 15 and 20 percent throughout the remainder of the year. He did not, however, win a single primary. While polls taken immediately prior to the Iowa caucuses and the New Hampshire primary are a good indicator of who will be the eventual nominee, polls taken much earlier than November or December of the year prior to the election are not very reliable.

In a similar way, polls taken immediately after each candidate's party convention (or a candidate debate) typically do not measure actual candidate strength. While there are exceptions (e.g., 1984, 1996), it is very common for each nominee's numbers to go up 5–10 percent after the convention. Many political observers commonly refer to this as the post convention bump or bounce. Typically, challengers benefit more than incumbents from the post convention bounce because they are less well known to the general public. Still, convention bounces for either candidate can dissipate quickly, as was the case with Al Gore in 2000 and John McCain in 2008. However, they can also be a prelude to a strong fall campaign, as happened for Bill Clinton in 1992.[28] In short, one should treat polls taken immediately after the conventions with caution.

Polls following presidential debates are similarly volatile. This is partly a function of the fact that firms must hastily conduct post-debate polls, using smaller than normal samples (about 600 people). In addition, post-debate polls are sensitive to media coverage of the debate.[29] Often different organizations report somewhat contradictory—or at least differing—results. For example, after the first presidential debate in 2004 (on September 30), one poll had John Kerry winning the debate by a margin of forty-two percentage points (sixty-one to nineteen), another by thirty-two (fifty-eight to twenty-six), and yet another by only sixteen (fifty-three to thirty-seven).[30] All clearly suggested that Kerry won, but by varying margins. And, all reported that Bush's slim lead going into the debate remained largely intact.[31] In other words, post-debate polls might suggest something about how voters viewed the candidates' performances in the debates, but they are a poor indicator of how well a particular candidate is doing in the campaign (see also Chapter 9).[32]

Taken in isolation, few of these polls (preprimary, post convention, post debate) are good indicators of candidate strength. Moreover, as suggested earlier, there is often considerable variation in candidate strength as Election Day approaches. The closer a poll is conducted to Election Day, the more likely it is to be accurate.

•

SAMPLES, DATA, AND REPORTING

As we have stressed throughout this chapter, most polls that major news organizations report are well designed and administered. Yet, sometimes news organizations do not fully explain the results. For example, as previously mentioned, some stories might not indicate whether their sample consisted of registered or likely voters. It is more common to misrepresent what a poll actually means, especially with respect to the margin separating the candidates. This leads to a discussion of the margin of error of polls.

In discussing sampling, it is possible to infer what a population thinks by relying on the responses of a properly constructed probability sample. It is important to remember, nonetheless, that the theory driving this inference is one of probability, not certainty. So, if we flip a coin one hundred times, it is probable that heads will land face up about fifty times. However, common sense suggests that it might be as many as fifty-three times, or as few as forty-seven. Probability theory suggests that if one repeated the coin flip twenty times, heads would come up approximately 50 percent of the time in nineteen cases.[33] The difference between the expected outcome (heads fifty times, or 50 percent) and what repeated tests would actually yield is known as the margin of error.[34]

Most news organizations report the sampling error of a given poll by telling consumers that a poll is accurate to within a certain percentage. This number appears in plus or minus terms (+/−) and is variously referred to as the margin of error, sampling error, or the poll's error margin. For example, one story from 2004 reported that 42 percent of the people who watched the last presidential debate believed Kerry was the winner and that the poll "results have a 4.5 percent error margin."[35] Translated, this meant that as few as 37.5 (42 − 4.5) percent, and as many as 46.5 (42 + 4.5) percent thought Kerry performed better than Bush in the debate.

This is important to understand because headlines and news stories sometimes misrepresent what is actually happening in election polls with respect to sampling error.[36] Although the story qualified the claims, one Harris Poll report from October 2000 claimed that "Bush Leads Gore by Five Points," 48 to 43 percent. But with the survey's margin of error (3 percent) factored in, Bush could have had as little as 45 percent, and Gore as much as 46 percent.[37] CBS News reported in 2000 that Gore won the last presidential debate by five percentage points over Bush (45 to 40 percent), but the margin of error for this poll was 4 percent—almost as much as the difference between the two.[38] Margin of error matters, especially if the two candidates are in a competitive race, which is usually the case in presidential elections.

Another point is that the media often report the poll numbers of various subgroups in preelection presidential polls as well. In these polls, a reliable sample size is sometimes a problem. A national poll based on responses from 1,000 individuals would have a 3 percent margin of error associated with it. If there was a split in the sample according to gender, there would be a subsample of approximately 490 men. The margin of error would be greater for this subsample. If there was a split in the sample for men according to their party identification, the sample would split further into three more categories: one each for Republicans, Democrats, and independents. The sample would continue to grow smaller with further divisions along race, income, or other socioeconomic characteristics. With each division, the sample becomes smaller and therefore associated with a greater margin of error. As such, one should treat group analyses of presidential polling data with caution given that subgroups have higher margins of error associated with them.[39]

APPLYING NATIONAL POLLING RESULTS TO A STATE-BY-STATE CONTEST

This particular problem with preelection presidential polls centers on the fact that most of the preelection polls the national news organizations report are national polls. If done well, the results mirror the outcome one would expect to find in a national vote for the president. However, the United States does not have a national vote for president. The Electoral College allocates votes on a state-by-state basis, dependent (in all but two states) on the winner of the popular vote in that state. Only once in the past one hundred years has the loser of the popular vote been selected president, the election of 2000. Interestingly, most preelection polls during that campaign season had George W. Bush—the eventual loser of the popular vote and winner of the Electoral College vote—ahead.[40]

For those who are only passively interested in following presidential campaigns, tracking national polls will probably suffice. However, if one is truly interested in the dynamics of the campaign, watching state polling results is the only answer. Fortunately, in the age of the World Wide Web, this has become fairly convenient. Several websites collect and present such information in easily understandable formats.[41] This approach is especially important in close races (as it was in 2000 and 2004) when it is known in advance that the outcome might hinge on the results from a few key "battleground" states (states with a fairly large number of Electoral College votes that could realistically swing to either candidate). Watching state polls allows one a more nuanced—and accurate—view of how each candidate is doing and, more importantly, where each candidate is doing well or poorly.

One interesting development within the past few years in this regard has been the emergence of election (presidential and congressional) predictions based on statistical analyses of aggregations of state-level polling results. The individuals doing this type of analysis are few, but their results are remarkably accurate. In 2008 and 2012, for example, several correctly predicted the results in all 50 states and the District of Columbia (and thus the Electoral College), in most cases within a few tenths of a percentage point.[42] The most well known of these analysts is Nate Silver, who began his career in statistical analysis forecasting the performance of baseball players and developed his "538" blog (website) for the 2008 election. Others include Drew Linzer (http://votamatic.org/), Sam Wang (http://election.princeton.edu/), and Simon Jackman (http://www.huffingtonpost.com/simon-jackman).

CONCLUSION

So, is polling an art, a science, or some form of modern voodoo? As we hope our discussion has made clear, polling is a science, but hardly an exact science. Table 11.1 is a good example of this point. One objective of this chapter was to provide the tools to become better consumers of preelection presidential polls. Box 10.2 summarizes the various points made throughout the chapter in short question form. While it is not necessary to study every poll intensively, moving mentally through this checklist is a helpful way to understand what the polls are really telling us.

Box 10.2   Interpreting Preelection Polls: A Checklist

- Who conducted the poll? A reputable firm or university research team?
- Is the poll based on a representative sample of the population?
- Is the poll based on responses from registered or likely voters?
- How has the poll dealt with undecided voters?
- Is the poll focused on too narrow a phase of the campaign, and if so, does the accompanying story account for that?
- Is the sample (or the subsamples) large enough to base inferences on?
- Does the accompanying story or headline properly account for the poll's margin of error?
- In a close presidential race, does the story accompanying the poll account for the fact that certain state races will be more important in determining the Electoral College winner?

NOTES

1. Humphrey Taylor, "Myth and Reality in Reporting Sampling Error: How the Media Confuse and Mislead Readers and Viewers," *Polling Report*, May 4, 1998, www.pollingreport.com/sampling.htm.

2. Figures were obtained from a LexisNexis Academic Reference Search of Polls & Surveys, Roper Center, "Public Opinion Online," June 2, 2000, Question Number 185.

3. In this sense our objective is similar to Herbert Asher's, whose text (Polling and the Public: *What Every Citizen Should Know*, 6th ed. [Washington, DC: CQ Press, 2004]) is not only one of the leading textbooks in the field but also was an invaluable source of material for this chapter.

4. Tom W. Smith, "The First Straw? A Study of the Origins of Election Polls," *Public Opinion Quarterly* 54 (1990): 21–36.

5. See Susan Herbst, "Election Polling in Historical Perspective," in *Presidential Polls and the News Media*, ed. Paul J. Lavrakas, Michael W. Traugott, and Peter V. Miller (Boulder, Colo.: Westview, 1995).

6. From Herbst, "Election Polling in Historical Perspective," 26.

7. Robert S. Erikson and Kent L. Tedin, *American Public Opinion: Its Origins, Content, and Impact*, 7th ed. (New York: Longman, 2005).

8. Peverill Squire, "Why the 1936 Literary Digest Poll Failed," *Public Opinion Quarterly* 52 (1988): 125–33.

9. Olav Kallenberg, *Foundations of Modern Probability*, 2nd ed. (New York: Springer, 2002).

10. Herbert F. Weisberg, Jon A. Krosnik, and Bruce D. Bowen, *An Introduction to Survey Research, Polling, and Data Analysis*, 3rd ed. (Thousand Oaks, Calif.: Sage, 1996), 33.

11. Squire, "Why the 1936 Literary Digest Poll Failed."

12. Asher, *Polling and the Public*, 13.

13. Ibid., 10–11.

14. Ibid., 10–14.

15. U.S. Census Bureau, Current Population Survey, November 2012.

16. Erikson and Tedin, *American Public Opinion*, 45.

17. Asher, Polling and the Public, 151–4; Erikson and Tedin, *American Public Opinion*, 45–6.

18. U.S. Survey Research, "Election Polling." Pew Research Center. Available at http://www.pewresearch.org/methodology/u-s-survey-research/election-polling/

19. "Bush Leads by Eight Points-or Two-Depending on Definition of Likely Voters," PRNewswire, October 20, 2004, www.prnewswire.com/cgi-bin/stories.pl?ACCT=105&STORY=/www/story/10-20-2004/0002289475. See also Robert S. Erikson, Costas Panagopoulos, and Christopher Wlezien, "Likely (and Unlikely) Voters and the Assessment of Campaign Dynamics," *Public Opinion Quarterly* 68 (2004): 588–601, for an in-depth exploration of the methods of measuring likely voters by the Gallup Organization.

20. Richard Morin and Dan Balz, "Convention Gives Kerry Slight Lead over Bush," *Washington Post*, August 3, 2004, A1; Bill Nichols and Susan Page, "Poll: Bush Lead over Kerry among Likely Voters Narrows a Bit," *USA Today*, October 26, 2004, 2A.

21. Erikson and Tedin, *American Public Opinion*, 43.

22. Irving Crespi, *Pre-Election Polling: Sources of Accuracy and Error* (New York: Russell Sage, 1988).

23. Erikson and Tedin, *American Public Opinion*, 43.

24. William G. Mayer, "Forecasting Presidential Nominations, or My Model Worked Just Fine, Thank you," *PS: Political Science & Politics* 36 (2003): 153–7.

25. See the various polls at "White House 2004: Democratic Nomination," *Polling Report*, 2004, www.pollingreport.com/wh04dem.htm.

26. Asher, *Polling and the Public*, 128.

27. "Clark Bows Out after Kerry Wins in South," CNN, February 13, 2004, www.cnn.com/2004/ALLPOLITICS/02/11/elec04.prez.main/index.html.

28. Thomas Holbrook, "Campaign Dynamics and the 2004 Presidential Election," American Political Science Association, www.apsanet.org/content_5167.cfm.

29. Asher, *Polling and the Public*, 145.

30. See, respectively, "Newsweek Poll: First Presidential Debate," PRNewswire, October 2, 2004, www.prnewswire.com/cgi-bin/stories.pl?ACCT=109&STORY=/www/story/10-02-2004/0002263797; "Kerry Wins Debate, but Little Change in Candidate Images," Pew Research Center for the People and the Press, October 4, 2004, people-press.org/reports/display.php3?ReportID=227; "Kerry Holds Edge over Bush Following First Debate," *USA Today*, www.usatoday.com/news/politicselections/nation/polls/2004-09-30-debate-poll.htm.

31. See, for example, "Kerry Wins Debate."

32. Stephen J. Wayne, *The Road to the White House, 2004: The Politics of Presidential Elections* (Belmont, Calif.: Wadsworth, 2004).

33. The range of possibilities includes values between forty and sixty, or specifically, 40.2 and 59.8). This assumes a confidence interval of 95 percent; see Erikson and Tedin, *American Public Opinion*, 27.

34. Asher, *Polling and the Public*, 78–80.

35. Gary Langer, "Poll: Last Presidential Debate Is a Draw: Equal Numbers Call Bush, Kerry the Winner," ABC News, October 13, 2004, abcnews.go.com/Politics/print?id=163784.

36. Some stories do not report the margin of error at all. See, for example, Carla Marinucci's ("Poll Boosts Bush into a Slim Lead," *San Francisco Chronicle*, September 28, 2000, A3) story about Bush's six-point lead. Although not reported, the margin of error must have been at least three points, perhaps more.

37. Humphrey Taylor, "Bush Leads Gore by Five Points," Harris Poll #65, October 28, 2000, www.harrisinteractive.com/harris_poll/index.asp?PID=127.

38. "Gore Edges Bush in CBS News Poll," CBS News, October 17, 2000, www.cbsnews.com/stories/2000/10/18/politics/main242058.shtml.

39. Asher, *Polling and the Public*, 79–80.

40. See the various polls at "White House 2000: Trial Heats," *Polling Report*, www.pollingreport.com/wh2gen1.htm.

41. For just one, see Real Clear Politics, www.realclearpolitics.com.

42. Gwern Branwen, "Was Nate Silver the Most Accurate 2012 Election Pundit?" Center for Applied Rationality, November 9, 2012, http://rationality.org/2012/11/09/was-nate-silver-the-most-accurate-2012-election-pundit/; Simon Jackman, "Pollster Predictive Performance, 51 out of 51," *HuffPost*, November 7, 2012, http://www.huffingtonpost.com/simon-jackman/pollster-predictive-perfo_b_2087862.html.

FOR MORE READING

Asher, Herbert. *Polling and the Public: What Every Citizen Should Know*, 8th ed. Washington, DC: CQ Press, 2012.

Erikson, Robert S. and Tedin, Kent L. *American Public Opinion: Its Origins, Content, and Impact*, 9th ed. New York: Routledge, 2014.

Traugott, Michael W. and Lavrakas, Paul J. *The Voter's Guide to Election Polls*, 4th ed. Lanham, MD: Rowman & Littlefield, 2007.

Part III

ELECTION OUTCOMES AND THEIR AFTERMATH

Chapter 11

May the Best Man Win? The Misconception of Competitive Congressional Elections

> If a group of planners sat down and tried to design a pair of assemblies with the goal of serving members' reelection needs year in and year out, they would be hard pressed to improve on what exists [in the U.S. Congress] (David R. Mayhew).[1]

Democratic theory specifies that in a democracy, citizens elect most of their leaders in free, fair, and regular elections.[2] The notion that these elections should be competitive is almost self-evident. There would be little reason to hold an election if the outcome was a foregone conclusion. Interestingly, and perhaps not surprisingly, most Americans believe that congressional elections are competitive. According to a poll conducted prior to the 2006 midterm elections, more than 71 percent of those who had an opinion on the question anticipated a "close" contest in their district for the U.S. House.[3]

However, a significantly smaller percentage of congressional races actually are competitive. This chapter examines this lack of electoral competitiveness in congressional elections. We begin by showing that congressional elections have become less competitive in recent years, especially elections to the House of Representatives. In particular, we illustrate that incumbents rarely lose in their bids for reelection. As Ronald Reagan once quipped, there was more turnover in the former Soviet Union's presidium than in the U.S. Congress.[4] In addition to winning, incumbents are doing so by greater margins.

In the following section, we examine the advantages incumbents have in their bids for reelection. First, there are various institutional factors associated with the job that give them an advantage. These include an organizational base for their campaign in the form of offices and staffers, a greater ability to communicate easily with voters and potential voters, as well as being in a position to solve problems constituents might be having with the federal bureaucracy. In addition, certain legislative norms in Congress itself help members enhance their reputations. Incumbents also have greater access to interest groups and political action committees (PACs) to help finance their campaigns. This greater ability to raise funds contributes to a "scare-off" effect, which in turn helps depress the entrance of adequately funded quality challengers. Finally, recent trends in congressional redistricting, greater name recognition, and voter loyalty advantages incumbents as well.

In the final section of the chapter, we shift gears, discussing how incumbents can lose. We focus on the fact that the "scare-off" effect does not always work, on how presidential politics affects congressional elections, and on the occasional effect of "national tides" on what are essentially local congressional elections. We conclude that while American elections generally satisfy the conditions for a democracy, the lack of competitiveness in congressional elections poses some problems for a healthy democratic system.

BACKGROUND

For many years, Congress was not considered a career. Until the 1900s, it was quite common for a member of Congress, especially in the House, to serve only one or two terms (senators were not directly elected until after the ratification of the Seventeenth Amendment in 1913). There were a relatively high number of incumbents who did not seek reelection each election cycle. Three general explanations shed light on this.

First, in earlier times, the notion of a "career" in Congress was not desirable to most ambitious professionals. Mediocre salaries, hot and humid summers in Washington, D.C., long stretches of time away from home, and the rather limited responsibilities of the federal government all combined to make the job of a U.S. Congressman less attractive than it is today. Second, even those who wished to stay in Washington for multiple terms were hard pressed to do so. Most congressional elections were highly contested, close races. Third, many members were prevented from running for more than one or two terms. In many states, especially non-Southern states, party organizations had informal term limits that prevented members from seeking the nomination more than one or two times (during this time, political parties controlled the nomination process).[5]

However, as the century progressed, the percentage of House incumbents running for reelection increased, and the percentage of those retiring— voluntarily or otherwise—decreased. Table 11.1 shows that over time, considerably more House incumbents ran for reelection and a much smaller percentage opted to retire. Another way to look at this would be to track the number of first-term members (freshman) in the House or the average number of terms served by House members over time.[6] As Table 11.2 indicates, the percentage of freshman in the House dropped more than thirty percentage points (from 51.3 to 20.4), and the average number of terms that members served more than doubled (from 1.88 to 4.34) in the century after 1850. Together, Tables 11.1 and 11.2 display a pattern of steadily increasing tenure in the House from the mid-1800s forward.

The pattern of increased numbers of incumbents running for and winning elections accelerated in the post–World War II era (see Table 11.3). Since 1946, an average of 91.4 percent of House incumbents sought reelection per election cycle, and the percentage of those seeking reelection dipped below 87 percent only once. This occurred in 1992, in the aftermath of a major check-writing scandal, when only 84.6 percent of House incumbents sought reelection. During this period, very few of those seeking reelection lost in either the primary or general elections. An average of 1.7 percent of incumbents per election cycle did not win their party's primary; and the average number defeated in the general election was just 6.2 percent.

Table 11.1   House Incumbents Running for Reelection and Retirement Rates, by Decade (1850–1910)

Decade	Number Running for Reelection	Percentage Retiring
1850s	60	27.1
1870s	64	22.8
1880s	66	20.0
1890s	73	17.3
1900s	80	11.2

From: Kernell, "Toward Understanding Nineteenth Century Congressional Careers," 684, Table 2, and John B. Gilmour and Paul Rothstein, "A Dynamic Model of Loss, Retirement, and Tenure in the U.S. House of Representatives," *The Journal of Politics* 58 (1996): 54–68, 57, Table 1. Data for the 1860s are not included because Southern states did not hold elections to Congress during the Civil War years.

Table 11.2   Percentage of First-Term Members and Average Tenure, House of Representatives, by Decade (1851–1949)

Decade	Percentage First-term Members	Average Number Terms
1850s	51.3	1.88
1870s	49.1	2.09
1880s	39.0	2.47
1890s	39.7	2.54
1900s	23.8	3.43
1910s	26.2	3.55
1920s	19.6	3.99
1930s	25.6	3.92
1940s	20.4	4.34

From: Nelson W. Polsby, "The Institutionalization of the U.S. House of Representatives," *The American Political Science Review* 62 (1968): 144–68, 9. 146, Tables 1 and 2.

Table 11.3   Reelection Rates for House Incumbents, 1946–2012

Year	Number of Incumbents Seeking Reelection (%)		Sought Reelection, Defeated in Primary (%)		Won Primary, Defeated in General Election (%)		Percentage Running Reelected
1946	398	(91.5)	18	(4.5)	52	(13.7)	82.4
1948	400	(92.0)	15	(3.8)	68	(17.7)	79.3
1950	400	(92.0)	6	(1.5)	32	(8.1)	90.5
1952	389	(89.4)	9	(2.3)	26	(6.8)	91.0
1954	407	(93.6)	6	(1.5)	22	(5.5)	93.1
1956	411	(94.5)	6	(1.5)	16	(4.0)	94.6
1958	396	(91.0)	3	(0.8)	37	(9.4)	89.9
1960	405	(93.1)	5	(1.2)	25	(6.3)	92.6
1962	402	(92.4)	12	(3.0)	22	(5.6)	91.5
1964	397	(91.3)	8	(2.0)	45	(11.6)	86.6
1966	411	(94.5)	8	(1.9)	41	(10.2)	88.1
1968	409	(94.0)	4	(1.0)	9	(2.2)	96.8
1970	401	(92.2)	10	(2.5)	12	(3.1)	94.5
1972	393	(90.3)	11	(2.8)	13	(3.4)	93.6
1974	391	(89.9)	8	(2.0)	40	(10.4)	87.7
1976	384	(88.3)	3	(0.8)	13	(3.4)	95.8
1978	382	(87.8)	5	(1.3)	19	(5.0)	93.7
1980	398	(91.5)	6	(1.5)	31	(7.9)	90.7
1982	393	(90.3)	10	(2.5)	29	(7.6)	90.1
1984	411	(94.5)	3	(0.7)	16	(3.9)	95.4
1986	394	(90.6)	3	(0.8)	6	(1.5)	97.7
1988	409	(94.0)	1	(0.2)	6	(1.5)	98.3
1990	406	(93.3)	1	(0.2)	15	(3.7)	96.0
1992	368	(84.6)	19	(5.2)	24	(6.9)	88.3
1994	387	(89.0)	4	(1.0)	34	(8.9)	90.2
1996	384	(88.3)	2	(0.5)	21	(5.5)	94.0
1998	402	(92.4)	1	(0.2)	6	(1.5)	98.3
2000	403	(92.6)	3	(0.7)	6	(1.5)	97.8
2002	398	(91.5)	8	(2.0)	8	(2.1)	96.2
2004	404	(92.9)	2	(0.5)	7	(1.7)	92.9
2006	403	(92.6)	2	(0.5)	22	(5.5)	94.0
2008	399	(91.7)	4	(1.0)	19	(4.8)	94.2
2010	397	(91.3)	4	(1.0)	54	(13.7)	85.4
2012	391	(89.9)	13	(3.3)	27	(7.1)	89.9

Source: Norman J. Ornstein, Thomas E. Mann, Michael J. Malbin, Andrew Rugg, and Raffaela Wakeman. 2014. *Vital Statistics on Congress* (Washington DC: Brookings Institution).

Most incumbents who survive their primaries win in the general election. Since World War II, the percentage of incumbents winning reelection rarely dips below 90 percent, and that number has not fallen below 85 percent since 1950. Even in 1974, a bad year for Republicans tainted with the scandal of Watergate, a full 77 percent of the Republicans seeking reelection returned to office.[7] In fact, it is often the case that incumbents face no major-party opposition in the general election. In 1998, almost one in four incumbents (94, or 23.4 percent) had no major-party opposition. In 2014, this number fell to a "mere" 73 (16.8 percent). Races like these are clearly uncompetitive.

While the House returns a very high percentage of incumbents, the Senate is slightly more competitive. In the post–World War II era, 81.4 percent of Senate incumbents have sought reelection (see Table 11.4). Approximately one in twenty (4.6 percent) lost their primary bids, and of those who gained

Table 11.4 Reelection Rates for Senate Incumbents, 1946–2012

Year	Number of Races	Sought Reelection (%)		Sought Reelection, Defeated in Primary (%)		Won Primary, Defeated in General Election (%)		Percentage Running Reelected
1946	37	30	(81.1)	6	(20.0)	7	(29.2)	56.7
1948	33	25	(75.8)	2	(8.0)	8	(34.8)	60.0
1950	36	32	(88.9)	5	(15.6)	5	(18.5)	68.8
1952	35	29	(82.9)	1	(3.4)	10	(35.7)	62.1
1954	38	32	(84.2)	2	(6.3)	5	(16.7)	78.1
1956	35	30	(85.7)	0	–	4	(13.3)	86.7
1958	36	27	(75.0)	0	–	10	(37.0)	63.0
1960	35	29	(82.9)	0	–	2	(6.9)	93.1
1962	39	35	(89.7)	1	(2.9)	5	(14.7)	82.9
1964	35	32	(91.4)	0	–	4	(12.5)	87.5
1966	35	32	(91.4)	3	(9.4)	1	(3.4)	87.5
1968	34	27	(79.4)	4	(14.8)	4	(17.4)	70.4
1970	35	31	(88.6)	1	(3.2)	6	(20.0)	77.4
1972	34	27	(79.4)	2	(7.4)	5	(20.0)	74.1
1974	34	27	(79.4)	2	(7.4)	2	(8.0)	85.2
1976	33	25	(75.8)	0	–	9	(36.0)	64.0
1978	35	25	(71.4)	3	(12.0)	7	(31.8)	60.0
1980	34	29	(85.3)	4	(13.8)	9	(36.0)	55.2
1982	33	30	(90.9)	0	–	2	(6.7)	93.3
1984	33	29	(87.9)	0	–	3	(10.3)	89.7
1986	34	28	(82.4)	0	–	7	(25.0)	75.0
1988	33	27	(81.8)	0	–	4	(14.8)	85.2
1990	35	32	(91.4)	0	–	1	(3.1)	96.9
1992	36	28	(77.8)	1	(3.6)	4	(14.8)	82.1
1994	35	26	(74.3)	0	–	2	(7.7)	92.3
1996	34	21	(61.8)	1	(4.8)	1	(5.0)	90.5
1998	34	29	(85.3)	0	–	3	(10.3)	89.7
2000	34	29	(85.3)	0	–	6	(20.7)	79.3
2002	34	27	(79.4)	1	(3.7)	2	(7.7)	88.9
2004	34	26	(76.5)	0	–	1	(3.8)	96.2
2006	34	28	(82.4)	1	(3.6)	6	(22.2)	78.6
2008	35	30	(85.7)	0	–	5	(16.7)	83.3
2010	37	25	(67.6)	3	(12.0)	2	(9.1)	84.0
2012	33	23	(69.7)	1	(4.3)	1	(4.5)	91.3

Source: Norman J. Ornstein, Thomas E. Mann, Michael J. Malbin, Andrew Rugg, and Raffaela Wakeman. 2014. *Vital Statistics on Congress* (Washington DC: Brookings Institution).

their party nomination and stood in the general election, less than one in five (16.9 percent) lost. Taken together, 79.7 percent of incumbent senators seeking reelection were successful. While there is more variation in reelection rates than in House races, the general trend of elections becoming less competitive is similar. For example, in the eleven election cycles from 1982 to 2002, only 8 of 440 Senate incumbents lost in their party's primary.

Congressional incumbents are not only winning, but they are doing so by larger margins. In 1974, political scientist David Mayhew noted that fewer elections in the postwar era could be classified as competitive. Mayhew dubbed this trend "the case of the vanishing marginals," a reference to the fact that close races in the House were becoming rare (Senate races tend to be more competitive, for reasons we will discuss shortly).[8]

As Figure 11.1 shows this trend has become more pronounced over time, especially in the House. The figure represents the percentage of House races in which the winner received more than 60 percent of the vote (traditionally defined as an uncompetitive election).[9] To be fair, it is worth noting that open seat elections to Congress are in fact quite competitive. Still, incumbency reelection rates and their margins of victory are impossible to ignore. Some scholars have attempted to quantify the value of incumbency in an election. Various measures suggest that incumbency in the House was worth between 2.1 to 3.3 percent of the vote from 1946 to 1966 and jumped to between 7 and 8.6 percent from 1968 to 2000. In the Senate, from 1914 to 1960, incumbency

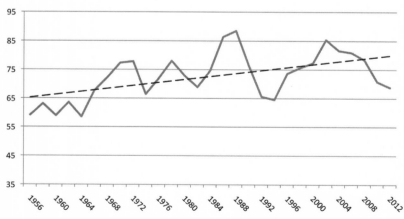

Figure 11.1 Percentage of House Incumbents Reelected with at Least 60% of the Major Party Vote, 1956–2012. *Source*: Norman J. Ornstein, Thomas E. Mann, Michael Malbin, Andrew Rugg and Raffaela Wakeman. April 7, 2014. *Vital Statistics on Congress.* The Brookings Institution. Available at http://www.brookings.edu/~/media/research/files/reports/2013/07/vital%20statistics%20congress%20mann%20ornstein/vital%20statistics%20chapter%202%20%20congressional%20elections.pdf.

was worth a bit more than 2 percent of the vote and jumped to 7 percent from 1962 to 1992.[10]

Why are congressional elections so noncompetitive? There are several contributing factors, most of which revolve around the various advantages incumbents enjoy by virtue of being the current officeholder. This is the subject of the next section.

THE ELECTORAL ADVANTAGES OF INCUMBENCY

Our discussion of the advantages of incumbency is divided into several sections. The first section deals with various institutional factors, or perks, of the office. These advantages include a large staff working for members of Congress as well as office space, computers, and so on. In addition, members of Congress employ various ways to communicate with their constituents at taxpayers' or at little expense. Incumbents also aggressively solve various bureaucratic problems for members of their district in hopes that voters will return those favors on Election Day. Finally, there are certain norms guiding legislative activity itself that favor incumbents, allowing them to build and present their record in a favorable light.

In addition to these institutional advantages, there are other aspects of incumbency that give incumbents an edge over challengers. One is an overwhelming edge in raising campaign funds, which can sometimes scare off quality challengers.[11] Congressional redistricting efforts have also helped incumbents in recent years. Finally, the criteria that people use to make their voting decisions favor incumbents as well. Together, these factors provide the current officeholder with an enormous edge in his or her bid for reelection.

Office and Staff

Institutional advantages are those associated with doing the job of a congressional member. Congressional office comes with various perks, often referred to (e.g., in American government textbooks) as "in kind" advantages, some of which aid in the reelection efforts of members. One advantage is the fact that each member of Congress has a staff that also serves as the nucleus of a permanent campaign organization, and the number of these staffers has increased dramatically in the past century.

The number of employees in the House of Representatives has increased approximately sevenfold since 1930. In 1950, the House employed slightly fewer than 2,000 staffers. By 1990, that number exceeded 7,500. Individually, the average member has fourteen employees (staffers) but is allowed eighteen full-time and four part-time employees.[12] Total staff growth of the

Senate has been slightly less. In 1955, there were approximately 1,000 staff-ers in the Senate and, by 1990, 4,000. However, individually they average thirty-four staffers per senator, from as few as thirteen to as many as seventy-one. There are no limits to the number of staffers a senator may employ.[13] Beyond serving as an unofficial nucleus for their campaign organization, members of Congress use staffers for casework in their home districts, espe-cially if it looks to be a tight race. The percentage of total staff working for House members in their districts nearly doubled from 1972 to 1992 (22 to 42 percent), and for senators the percentage almost tripled during the same period (from 12 to 32 percent).[14]

Members of Congress are also given allowances for "travel, communica-tions, office rental, stationery, computer services, and mail."[15] House mem-bers average about 2.3 offices in their districts, while senators average four offices per district (state).[16] All of this comes at the expense of the taxpayer. While these staffers technically cannot be used for the campaign, the mem-ber's press secretary is especially important helping to generate favorable news about the congressperson at the local level.[17] In addition, staffers help with constituency service, which creates a favorable impression that may translate into votes on Election Day.

Direct Communications

Members of Congress take full advantage of what is known as the "frank-ing" privilege. This is the right of members of Congress to send letters to their constituents informing them about what is happening in Washington, at government expense. The rationale for this is straightforward. The health of a representative democracy depends in part on an informed citizenry, and central to this is knowing what our representative is doing in government. In fact, the precedent for this practice dates back to 1660 in the British House of Commons and was granted by the Continental Congress to members in 1775. Subsequently, the first U.S. Congress passed a law granting its members the privilege in 1789.[18]

One widely circulated account suggests that new members are urged to "use the frank,"[19] and by all accounts, they do so. Members of Congress send mass newsletters to all constituents as well as more narrowly tailored mes-sages to different segments of their electorate. Often recipients are invited in these messages to send their thoughts to their member of Congress. Estimates suggest that from the mid-1960s to 1990, the volume of franked mail has at least tripled and perhaps quadrupled. Importantly, the amount of franked mail is higher during election years.[20] In 1990, Congress enacted new regulations limiting the amount of franked mail to one piece per address per state for a senator and three pieces per address per House district. Other regulations, such as prohibiting personal photographs of or references to the member and integrating franking costs into the members' office expenses were added. However, at minimum, these communications keep the incumbent's name fresh in voters' minds and present a favorable image of him or her.

Bureaucratic Ombudsmanship: Casework in the District

It is not unusual for an ordinary citizen to need assistance from time to time navigating or circumventing the bureaucracy that makes up modern government. Citizens might contact their member of Congress for any number of reasons, which could include, for example, requests or questions about an expired passport only days before a planned trip or a tax problem with the Internal Revenue Service. Here, the member would be acting in a capacity analogous to that of an ombudsman (or ombudsperson), a government-appointed individual who looks after the rights and needs of citizens in disputes with government. Originally a Scandinavian concept, ombudsmen are found in virtually all modern bureaucracies (including some larger corporations). Members of Congress take this type of work—referred to as casework—very seriously.

Each member of Congress receives thousands of such requests each year. While it is impossible for members to handle each request personally, much of the staff work handled in district offices is devoted to resolving citizens' problems and answering requests. This is an extremely effective way to win the loyalty and votes of citizens and others. A favor done for a constituent makes it more likely that he or she will repay the kindness come election time—and perhaps even tell others. This type of interpersonal, word-of-mouth, advertising is invaluable.[21]

Favorable Local Media

Incumbents have certain advantages with various media that make it easier to boost name recognition among their constituents as well as communicate and cultivate a favorable view among supporters and potential supporters. First, all members of Congress have their own websites, which allow interested parties to learn about what they are doing in Washington.[22] The government pays for these websites, and members use them to publicize their achievements, downplay their shortcomings, and invite visitors to send comments and feedback.

Second, both parties in each house of Congress, as well as the chambers themselves, have state-of-the-art audiovisual studios. Members can produce short statements to the press, interviews, and other types of programming. Along with satellite link technology, this allows incumbents to feed the local media, which is always looking for story material, especially on

90- or 120-minute evening newscasts.[23] Some members are regular guests on various local programs; others have their own local programs (e.g., a call-in show). Almost all produce press releases on a fairly regular basis that local news organizations print or air unedited, presenting them as news.

The link with local media outlets is important because studies show that local news organizations are rarely as confrontational as the national press. When these outlets feature members in a thirty-second spot answering a few questions, the questions are rarely difficult and the answers rarely challenged. This is in part because the news organizations in question (typically the electronic media) are in need of material and want to make sure they have access in the future, so they work at not offending the member. In addition, local reporters are often less well prepared for the interview or versed in national politics in general. The result is generally favorable coverage in local media, which is especially helpful for members of the House, who mainly run on local issues.[24]

Legislative Norms

In a representative democracy, an assumption exists that there is a link between what people want and what elected officials work to accomplish. Members of Congress understand that this is what people expect. Therefore, it is not surprising that their legislative activity is geared toward working—or at least appearing to work—for the people in their district. With so many decentralized committees and subcommittees in Congress, new members have almost no trouble seeking out and receiving an assignment on a committee that deals with policy concerns important to their district. For example, if the legislator is from Washington state, he or she might seek assignment on the Merchant Marine and Fisheries Committee; if from the Midwest, on agriculture. Because the details of most policy is worked out in committees, this allows the legislator to go back to the district and claim to be doing something for the district.[25]

Another legislative norm is that a member is not required or expected to vote with his or her party if that vote will damage them electorally. Weak party discipline allows members to protect themselves if the party's position contradicts what constituents expect. Finally, most members cooperate with other members when it comes to distributive legislation. If there is "pork" (government projects that benefit a specific locale) to be spread around, everyone gets a piece to take home to the district. Additionally, a member will support another member's bill with the expectation of reciprocity. This reciprocity is referred to as "logrolling," and allows members at the end to claim credit for passing legislation that is popular back home.

Financial Advantages

Congressional elections cost a great deal of money. One estimate suggested that all congressional elections combined would cost a total of approximately $4 billion in 2014.[26] In the five most expensive House races in 2014, candidates alone raised an average of $12 million. In the Senate, candidates in the five most expensive races raised an average of $43 million.[27] Unlike other incumbent advantages, financial aspects of congressional campaigns are easy to quantify, and a good deal has been written on this subject.[28] Until recently, the United States has had one of the most transparent campaign finance systems in the world.[29] This provided a detailed understanding of the financial advantage incumbents have over their challengers.

Most incumbents start their campaigns with money left over from the previous campaign. This is referred to as their "war chest," and the amount of money accumulated in them can be substantial. For example, in 2002, the average returning House member had $300,000 left in their campaign coffers after the election.[30] Even with this advantage, incumbents continue to raise enormous sums of money. They do this because reelection is never a certainty.[31]

Beyond having a head start in the money race, incumbents can raise money more easily than most challengers. This is especially true when soliciting funds from Washington-based PACs, which are six times more likely to give to an incumbent.[32] One reason for this is that PACs know that incumbents are more likely to win, and they want to ensure future congressional access by backing the winning candidate. Incumbents also have financial backing from congressional party campaign committees, as well as access to money from state party organizations. In addition, individual donors who give large sums of money are more likely to give to incumbents. The point is that most campaign dollars go to incumbents, making it difficult for challengers to raise the necessary resources to be competitive.

During the past two decades, the financial advantages of incumbency have grown tremendously. In 1990, for example, House incumbents had a four to one financial advantage over challengers, while in the Senate the ratio was two to one in 1990. By 2008, that ratio had grown to almost six to one in the House and almost ten to one in the Senate.

Lack of Quality Challengers

Another reason why incumbents enjoy high reelection rates is the lack of quality challengers. A quality challenger is an individual who can mount a viable campaign and possesses a combination of characteristics that can convince voters that he or she is qualified to be their representative. These qualities include, but are not limited to, having previously held public office (either elective or otherwise), being a celebrity (show business, sports, etc.), or being a prominent local business, religious, or community leader. At minimum, a quality challenger usually enjoys some name recognition in the community (or district, state) and has enough ties to support fund-raising efforts to raise the money necessary to challenge a congressional incumbent.[33]

Most challengers in congressional elections are amateurs, or lesser quality candidates. They lack some, or all, of the various characteristics, background, and experience mentioned earlier. Importantly, experienced politicians or prominent leaders—potential quality challengers—have enough political savvy to know that the chances of defeating an incumbent member of Congress are slim. Generally, open-seat races are more likely to attract quality candidates, leaving most incumbents to face off against relative amateurs. As previously noted, fundraising efforts by incumbents further deter quality candidates. Raising early money, as well as being active in the district, goes a long way toward deterring potential challengers. This is the so-called "scare-off" effect,[34] and while it is clear that anything can happen in a campaign, most challengers pose little threat to incumbents.[35]

Congressional Redistricting

House district boundaries in almost every state are redrawn every ten years following the census. This ensures that districts within each state contain approximately equal numbers of people. Few voters know about or pay much

Box 11.1   Example: Partisan Effects of Districting

attention to this process.[36] Redistricting is a very contentious exercise because it almost always gives an advantage to a certain party or group.

To illustrate how districting could advantage one group over others, imagine a state with twelve equal geographic divisions (e.g., counties), with each division containing equal numbers of straight partisan voters. In other words, all voters in each geographic division vote the party line in every election. The top figure in Box 11.1 represents this scenario, as well as which geographic divisions belong to which party (D = Democrat, R = Republican). Each party can claim six of these geographic divisions, meaning that support for each party is evenly split. From this state, four congressional districts, each containing roughly equal numbers of voters and three of these geographic divisions, is drawn. The figures below the "partisan distribution" illustration show three of the ways in which these districts may be drawn. In "Districting Plan #1," Democrats and Republicans will each win in two districts. However, if district lines are drawn slightly differently, as shown in "Districting Plan #2," Republicans win in only one district, while Democrats win in three. "Districting Plan #3" gives the Republicans the advantage.[37]

Drawing district lines to maximize the electoral advantage of a group, party, or faction is known as "gerrymandering." The term, first used in 1812, characterized the salamander-like redistricting plan drawn up by Massachusetts Governor Elbridge Gerry. Partisan gerrymandering, or redistricting that favors a specific party, enjoys a long history in the United States. While not an exact science, since the 1990s gerrymandering has evolved into a practice of incumbent-based, or "sweetheart," gerrymandering. This is a true bipartisan effort where district lines are drawn to ensure that there is a high concentration of each party's supporters in "their" respective districts.[38] Thus, the status quo (incumbents of each party) is protected. While some recent research suggests that the effect is minimal, many claim that incumbent-based districts lead to a decline in the number of competitive elections, at least in the House, as more districts are "packed" on a partisan basis.[39]

A "Sorting" of the Electorate

In addition to partisan congressional redistricting plans, incumbents are also helped by the fact that congressional districts are more likely to be comprised of politically like-minded individuals. In other words, congressional districts are less politically diverse. This makes it more likely that incumbents, already advantaged by partisan districting plans, will win.

Several works have noted that geographic divisions in the United States capture significant political differences within the electorate.[40] Perhaps the most extensive work on the politics of geography (or the "politics of place") comes from Bill Bishop's *The Big Sort*. Bishop's work shows that most counties in the United States have become increasingly partisan over the past few decades. According to Bishop, as Americans have clustered into like-minded communities that share the same political and cultural values, divisions across different communities have grown.[41] For example, in the nationally competitive presidential election of 1976, approximately 27 percent of the public resided in a county where either Republican Gerald Ford or Democrat Jimmy Carter won by a landslide (more than 20 percentage points). In the elections of 2004 and 2008, that percentage increased to 48 percent.

Even at the state level, landslide results have become more common. In 1976, there was an average winning margin of 10 percentage points in the 50 states and the District of Columbia. This increased to 15 percentage points in 2000, 16 percentage points in 2004, and then to 17 percentage points in 2008. Likewise, there were only 14 states where the presidential contest was decided by 10 points or less in 2008 compared to 31 states in 1976. Political scientist Alan Abramowitz has concluded that, "the divide between the red states and blue states is deeper than at any time in the past 60 years."[42] This divide is evident within states as well. Republicans consistently capture better than 20 percent more of the vote for president than Democrats in rural areas than in urban areas (see Figure 11.2).

In fact, divisions between rural and urban voting patterns are increasing. The voting patterns of rural and urban residents differed only slightly in 1976. However, by 2004, George W. Bush dominated in rural America, winning roughly three of every five votes there. Obama performed slightly better than

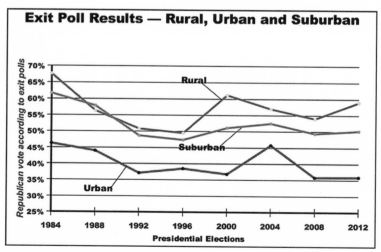

Figure 11.2   Republican Vote Share for President in Rural, Suburban, and Urban Counties, 1984–2012. *Source*: Bill Biship and Julie Ardery, "Exit Polls: Romney Improves in Rural," *Daily Yonder*, November 7, 2012, available at http://www.dailyyonder.com/exit-polls-romney-improves-rural/2012/11/07/4912.

Kerry in rural counties in 2008, but he also increased the Democrats' winning margin in urban counties. As Bishop's latest research demonstrates, "Republican and Democratic counties were entirely different kinds of places. The average population of an Obama landslide county was 278,601. The average McCain landslide county had 37,475 people." These aggregate patterns suggest that communities are growing more politically polarized, which in the end, typically advantages the partisan incumbent who represents the district.

Voting Behavior

To round out our discussion, we should also note something about voting behavior, or how people vote. A few aspects of voting in congressional elections are important with respect to incumbent advantages. First, the electorate usually knows the incumbent better than the challenger. Second, with more campaign funding, incumbents can advertise more, beyond the free advertising they receive from franking, local media, and so on.

In House elections from 1980 to 2002, on average, respondents were almost twice as likely to recognize the incumbent's name as opposed to the challenger's name (92 to 53 percent) and better than twice as likely to be able to recall—unprompted—the incumbent's name rather than the challenger's name (46 to 17 percent). For Senate candidates, the percentages are more even, but incumbent names are recognized and recalled more than those of their challengers (97 to 77 percent recognition, 58 to 35 percent recall). While people do not always cast their votes for the better-known candidate, the converse of this is probably a fair assumption: people are less likely to vote for an unknown candidate.[43] This is especially true in midterm elections where interest is lower than in presidential election years. For example, turnout in midterm elections has decreased over the past half century.[44] Generally, lower turnout advantages incumbents.

Another factor that favors incumbents is the party loyalty of voters. Ticket splitting, or casting one's vote for the presidential candidate of one party while voting for the congressional candidate of the other party, increased consistently throughout the middle part of the past century. This trend seems to have reversed itself. In 1972, 192 districts split their votes in this way. In 2000, only 86 did so. According to one account, "In 2012 only around 11 percent of districts voted for one party for the House and the other party for president. Just fifteen House Republicans won in districts that were carried by President Obama."[45] In short, voters, who are packed into increasingly partisan-leaning districts are voting to support their party. But since recent redistricting efforts have generally protected incumbents, "their party" is more likely to be the party of the incumbent.

Finally, it should be noted that members of Congress pay special attention throughout their careers, and especially during the campaign, to the way in which they present themselves. Here, the landmark study of Richard Fenno is informative.[46] Fenno followed and observed a number of House members, concluding that they self-consciously adopted a style or persona that was compatible with the culture of their district. He labeled this their "home style." For example, a House member from rural Georgia would be hard pressed to win an election if he traveled the district in a three-piece Brooks Brothers suit. In a district like this, a candidate would likely present himself as a common member of the local community, hoping to establish a connection with the majority of voters. This example is a bit exaggerated, but according to Fenno's work, not by much. And it seems to pay off.

CONCLUSION: CAN INCUMBENTS LOSE?

Challengers clearly face uphill battles. However, there are some factors that make it more likely that a challenger can be competitive. First, the scare-off effect does not always work.[47] Incumbents sometimes show signs of weakness or are weakened by circumstance. This can be the result of any number of factors including unfavorable redistricting, a small war chest, press criticism, or scandal. All of these factors can make incumbents look vulnerable, attracting quality challengers to the fray. Or, more simply, any of these factors can actually make an incumbent more vulnerable, giving challengers a better chance to win.

Second, presidential politics sometimes affects congressional elections. The two most obvious ways in which this occurs are either the "coattail" effects of a popular presidential candidate or the historic tendency for a president's party to lose seats in midterm elections. In the first case, an extremely popular presidential candidate can increase the popularity—and thus the chances for victory—of the congressional candidates in his party. This happened, for example, in 1980, when Ronald Reagan's popularity helped the Republicans win control of the Senate for the first time since 1954. Barack Obama's popularity helped many Democratic candidates in 2008. Alternatively, it is also historically the case that the president's party loses seats in the midterm elections (see Table 11.5). Some midterm elections bring greater losses than others, but in most, a fairly significant number of the president's party loses. Incumbents inevitably suffer some of these losses. In 2006, Republicans lost their majorities in both the U.S. House and Senate, in part because of their association with President George W. Bush whose popularity gradually and steadily dropped following his reelection in 2004. Democrats, with Barack Obama in the White House, lost 63 seats in the House and six in the Senate in 2010, followed by further losses in 2014.

A final factor is the occasional effect of what scholars refer to as "national tides" on congressional elections. Local elections generally favor incumbents.

Table 11.5   Midterm Losses for Presidential Party

Year	President (Party)	House	Senate*
1946	Franklin Roosevelt and Harry Truman (Dem.)	45	12
1950	Harry Truman (Dem.)	29	6
1954	Dwight Eisenhower (Rep.)	18	1
1958	Dwight Eisenhower (Rep.)	48	13
1962	John Kennedy (Dem.)	4	(3)
1966	Lyndon Johnson (Dem.)	47	4
1970	Richard Nixon (Rep.)	12	(2)
1974	Richard Nixon and Gerald Ford (Rep.)	48	5
1978	Jimmy Carter (Dem.)	15	3
1982	Ronald Reagan (Rep.)	26	(1)
1986	Ronald Reagan (Rep.)	5	8
1990	Gorge H. W. Bush (Rep.)	8	1
1994	Bill Clinton (Dem.)	52	8
2006	George W. Bush (Rep.)	30	6
2010	Barack Obama (Dem.)	63	6
2014	Barack Obama (Dem.)	13	9

*Numbers in parentheses were gains for the presidential party.
From: Gerhard Peters, "Seats in Congress Gained/Lost by the President's Party in Mid-Term Elections," *The American Presidency Project*, ed. John T. Woolley and Gerhard Peters. Santa Barbara, CA: University of California. 1999–2015. Available from the World Wide Web: http://www.presidency.ucsb.edu/data/mid-term_elections.php.

Congressional elections are primarily local affairs, more so in the House than in the Senate. However, national political factors sometimes influence congressional elections, favoring one party over the other. This was the case, for example, in 1974, when an anti-Watergate sentiment swept the country, and the Democrats made large gains. In 1980, anti-Carter sentiment and a national recession helped produce a significant number of victories for Republicans. Anti-incumbent and anti-congressional feelings in 1992 (surrounding various congressional scandals and the Clarence Thomas hearings) helped 110 newcomers win election to Congress. Republicans won both houses of Congress for the first time in more than four decades in 1994, partly as the result of an anti-Congress and anti-Clinton mood prevailing in the country. In 1998, anti-impeachment sentiment helped the Democrats reverse historical trends and gain seats, and in 2002, national security concerns helped Republicans do the same. In all of these cases, a prevailing mood in the country overcame local concerns to help oust a significant number of incumbents.

In short, incumbents rarely lose, although challengers can sometimes capitalize on national conditions that might be in their favor (as in 1994 and 2006). The word "campaign" was originally used to refer to military operations and adopted for political use later. To use this metaphor, challengers face an overwhelming disadvantage given that their opponents have been gearing up for battle for months, are already on the field, and have an arsenal in place.

Certainly, we are not the first observers to note that congressional elections have become less competitive over the course of the last century.[48] However, many Americans do not realize or appreciate how uncompetitive congressional elections have become. While the high rate of incumbent victories might, to some degree, equate to voter satisfaction, it more likely reflects the numerous advantages that incumbents have. This has undoubtedly increased the number of uncompetitive congressional contests, which, as noted earlier, has democratic consequences.

NOTES

1. David R. Mayhew, *Congress: The Electoral Connection* (New Haven, Conn.: Yale University Press, 1974), 81–2.

2. Joseph A. Schumpeter, *Capitalism, Socialism and Democracy* (New York: Harper, 1942); Robert A. Dahl, *A Preface to Democratic Theory* (Chicago: University of Chicago Press, 1956).

3. Figures were obtained from a LexisNexis Academic Reference Search of Polls and Surveys, Roper Center, "Public Opinion Online," October 27, 2006, Question Number 263.

4. James C. Miller III, "Incumbents Advantage," Citizens for a Sound Economy Foundation, economics.gmu.edu/working/WPE_98/98_05.pdf.

5. Samuel Kernell, "Toward Understanding 19th Century Congressional Careers: Ambition, Competition, and Rotation," *American Journal of Political Science* 21 (1977): 669–93.

6. David Brady, Kara Buckley, and Douglas Rivers, "The Roots of Careerism in the U. S. House of Representatives," *Legislative Studies Quarterly* 24 (1999): 489–510.

7. Gary C. Jacobson, *The Politics of Congressional Elections*, 6th ed. (New York: Longman, 2004), 25.

8. David R. Mayhew, "Congressional Elections: The Case of the Vanishing Marginals," *Polity* 6 (1974): 295–317.

9. See also Jacobson, *Politics of Congressional Elections*, 26–31.

10. Jacobson, *Politics of Congressional Elections*, 31.

11. Janet M. Box-Steffensmeier, "A Dynamic Analysis of the Role of War Chests in Campaign Strategy," *American Journal of Political Science* 40 (1996): 352–71.

12. Roger H. Davidson and Walter J. Oleszek, *Congress and Its Members*, 9th ed. (Washington, DC: CQ Press, 2003), 143–4.

13. Jacobson, *Politics of Congressional Elections*, 33.

14. Ibid., 35.

15. Davidson and Oleszek, *Congress and Its Members*, 143.

16. Ibid., 145.

17. Stephen Hess, *Live from Capitol Hill: Studies of Congress and the Media* (Washington, DC: Brookings Institution, 1991); Timothy E. Cook, *Making Laws and Making News: Media Strategies in the U.S. House of Representatives* (Washington, DC: Brookings Institution, 1990).

18. "In addition to senators and representatives, the president, cabinet secretaries, and certain executive branch officials [are also] granted the frank." See "January 22, 1873: Senate Ends Franked Mail Privilege," *U.S. Senate, Historical Minutes*, 1851–1877, www.senate.gov/artandhistory/history/minute/Senate_Ends_Franked_Mail_Priviledge.htm.

19. Morris P. Fiorina, "The Case of the Vanishing Marginals: The Bureaucracy Did It," *American Political Science Review* 71 (1977): 177.

20. Davidson and Oleszek, *Congress and Its Members*, 145.

21. Ibid., 141–3; Morris P. Fiorina, *Congress: Keystone of the Washington Establishment* (New Haven, Conn.: Yale University Press, 1977).

22. For Senate members, see http://www.senate.gov/senators/contact/; for members of the House, see http://www.house.gov/representatives/.

23. Michael J. Robinson, "Three Faces of Congressional Media," in *The New Congress*, ed. Thomas E. Mann and Norman J. Ornstein (Washington, DC: American Enterprise Institute, 1981).

24. Davidson and Oleszek, *Congress and Its Members*, 147–9.

25. For the classic treatment of this, and other legislative norms geared toward the goal of reelection, see Mayhew, Congress.

26. "Election to Cost Nearly $4 Billion, CRP Projects, Topping Previous Midterms," Center for Responsive Politics, October 22, 2014, http://www.opensecrets.org/news/2014/10/election-to-cost-nearly-4-billion-crp-projects-topping-previous-midterms/.

27. "Most Expensive Races," Center for Responsive Politics, https://www.opensecrets.org/overview/topraces.php.

28. See, for example, any of the quadrennial "Financing the [Year] Election" books, the first of which was by Herbert E. Alexander, *Financing the 1960 Election* (Princeton, NJ: Citizens Research Foundation, 1962), the latest of which is David B. Magleby, Anthony Corrado, and Kelly D. Patterson, eds., *Financing the 2004 Election* (Washington DC: Brookings Institution, 2006). See also Peter L. Francia, John C. Green, Paul S. Herrnson, Lynda W. Powell, and Clyde Wilcox, *The Financiers of Congressional Elections: Investors, Ideologues, and Intimates* (New York: Columbia University, 2003).

29. Herbert E. Alexander, *Financing Politics: Money, Elections, and Political Reform*, 4th ed. (Washington, DC: CQ Press, 1992).

30. Davidson and Oleszek, *Congress and Its Members*, 69.

31. Anthony King, *Running Scared: Why American's Politicians Campaign Too Much and Govern Too Little* (New York: Martin Kessler, 1997).

32. Davidson and Oleszek, *Congress and Its Members*, 74.

33. Paul S. Herrnson, *Congressional Elections: Campaigning at Home and in Washington*, 4th ed. (Washington, DC: CQ Press, 2003), 40–8; Davidson, Oleszek, and Lee, *Congress and Its Members*, 62–4.

34. Gary W. Cox and Jonathan N. Katz, "Why Did the Incumbency Advantage in U.S. House Elections Grow?" *American Journal of Political Science* 40 (1996): 478–97.

35. Herrnson, *Congressional Elections*, 41.

36. Figures were obtained from a LexisNexis Academic Reference Search of Polls and Surveys, Roper Center, "Public Opinion Online," October 27, 2006, Question Number 269.

37. This example was taken from Michael D. Robbins, "Gerrymander and the Need for Redistricting Reform," October 25, 2006, www.fraudfactor.com/ffgerry-mander.html.

38. For a fairly comprehensive look at how different states deal with redistricting, see the "Voting and Democracy Research Center" ("Redistricting") section at the FairVote website, at www.fairvote.org.

39. David Lublin, *The Paradox of Representation: Racial Gerrymandering and Minority Interests in Congress* (Princeton, NJ: Princeton University Press, 1997). See also Davidson, Oleszek, and Lee, Congress and Its Members, 47–50.

40. Juliet F. Gainsborough, *Fenced Off: The Suburbanization of American Politics* (Washington, DC: Georgetown University, 2001); see also Peter L. Francia and Jody C Baumgartner, "Victim or Victor of the 'Culture War'? How Cultural Issues Affect Support for George W. Bush in Rural America," *American Review of Politics* 26 (Fall/Winter 2005–2006): 349–67; and Seth C. McKee, "Rural Voters and the Polarization of American Presidential Elections," *PS: Political Science & Politics* 41 (2008): 101–8.

41. Bishop, *The Big Sort.*

42. Quoted in Bishop, "No We Didn't."

43. Jacobson, *Politics of Congressional Elections*, 122–7.

44. Statistics from the U.S. Election Assistance Commission, www.eac.gov/election_resources.asp.

45. Roger H. Davidson and Walter J. Oleszek, *Congress and Its Members*, 14th ed. (Washington, DC: CQ Press, 2014), 86.

46. Richard F. Fenno Jr., *Home Style: House Members in Their Districts* (New York: Longman, 2003).

47. Jay Goodliffe, "The Effect of War Chests on Challenger Entry in U.S. House Elections," *American Journal of Political Science* 45 (2001): 830–44.

48. More recently, see James E. Campbell and Steve J. Jurek, "The Decline of Competition and Change in Congressional Elections," in *The United States Congress: A Century of Change*, ed. Sunil Ahuja and Robert Dewhirst (Columbus: Ohio State University, 2003).

FOR MORE READING

Fenno, Richard F., Jr. *Home Style: House Members in Their Districts.* New York: Longman, 2003.

Herrnson, Paul S. *Congressional Elections: Campaigning at Home and in Washington.* 6th ed. Washington, DC: CQ Press, 2012.

Jacobson, Gary C. *The Politics of Congressional Elections.* 8th ed. New York: Pearson, 2012.

Mayhew, David R. *Congress: The Electoral Connection.* New Haven, Conn.: Yale University, 1974.

Chapter 12

"The American People Have Spoken" . . . Or Have They? The Myth of the Presidential Mandate

In the late hours of November 6, 2012, the nation's major news networks announced that President Barack Obama had defeated his Republican opponent, Mitt Romney, to win a second term in office. Almost immediately afterward, journalists and pundits from around the nation began to weigh in on a familiar question: Did the results of the election reflect a policy mandate from the American people? Joan Walsh of *Salon* was one of the first to ask and answer that question, declaring, "President Obama's reelection represents a victory for the Democratic ideal of activist government and a *mandate* for more of it" [italics added].[1] David Weigel of *Slate* followed just a few hours later with an article bearing the headline, "Yes, There Is a Mandate for Higher Taxes."[2]

In 2004, conservative writers and politicians were no less willing to make similar claims about Republican George W. Bush's reelection victory over Democrat John Kerry. Vice President Dick Cheney boldly asserted, "President Bush ran forthrightly on a clear agenda for this nation's future and the nation responded by giving him a *mandate*" [italics added].[3]

The Wall Street Journal echoed a similar opinion, writing that President Bush had won, "by any measure . . . a decisive mandate." The editorial added, "on Social Security private accounts, tort and tax reform, and creating a larger private health-care marketplace, among the other things he campaigned on . . . center-right voters . . . are expecting progress on their priorities."[4]

Presidential elections are not the only ones about which we hear politicians and others claiming to have won a mandate. In midterm elections, a decisive victory for one party or the other also gives rise to talk of a mandate. Republican congressional leaders made such claims following their sweeping midterm election wins in 1994, 2010, and 2014, while Democratic congressional leaders made similar claims following their landslide victory in 2006.

Yet despite the frequency of these claims, the overwhelming consensus among political scientists is that elections, even ones that produce a landslide winner, rarely if ever reflect a strong and uniform desire from the American public for sweeping policy change. Instead, research shows rather clearly that most people base their voting calculation on a variety of different factors. Issues and policies are just one of many considerations. Several other complications, discussed later in this chapter, also exist that make it exceptionally difficult to connect election outcomes to voters' policy preferences.

In fact, there is ample anecdotal evidence to illustrate how the frequent misinterpretation of a "mandate" has led to failed policy proposals, from Bill Clinton's efforts to reform the health-care system to George W. Bush's proposal to amend the Social Security Act. Numerous other examples exist, all of which reinforce the larger point of this chapter: mandates are almost always illusionary. In this chapter, we review the prevalence of the mandate claim in more detail and then define in a more concrete fashion what a mandate entails. We then discuss why genuine mandates are much less common than the claims themselves. Finally, we conclude the chapter with an explanation for why politicians and others so often claim to have won a mandate in spite of evidence that shows elections so rarely produce them.

THE PREVALENCE OF THE MANDATE CLAIM

The origins of the mandate claim have a long history, dating back as far as the presidency of Andrew Jackson.[5] Before Jackson, mandate claims from victorious presidential candidates were virtually nonexistent because they were inconsistent with early conceptions of presidential power and influence. The prevailing thought in the late-eighteenth and early nineteenth centuries was that the executive branch was secondary to Congress when it came to domestic policymaking.[6]

But Jackson, who served as the nation's chief executive from 1829 to 1837, argued that because the President of the United States was the only public figure to run in a nationwide election, a victory in this contest carried special meaning. The winning presidential candidate had won not only the right to serve as President of the United States, but could also rightfully claim to be the one true representative of the people nationwide. Members of Congress, after all, represented only the local interests of their constituents. The policies that winning presidential candidates promised during the election therefore best reflected the general will, allowing the President to command a dominant role in policymaking. Such an interpretation allowed Jackson to justify the actions he undertook as president to eliminate the Second Bank of the United States. These actions included the firing of Treasury Secretary William

Duane, who had refused to carry out Jackson's order to remove deposits from the central bank and to transfer them to state banks. In Jackson's own words, "the President is the direct representative of the American people, but the Secretaries are not."[7]

In the years following Jackson's presidency, several other presidents made similar claims. President James Polk remarked that the president represented "the whole people of the United States."[8] Woodrow Wilson not only agreed, but argued further that the president, as the only representative of the whole nation, held a special place in the government that entitled the chief executive to take a dominant role over Congress in policymaking.[9] Likewise, Franklin Roosevelt, following his victory over Herbert Hoover in 1932, claimed his election to the presidency represented a "mandate for direct, vigorous action."[10]

Two decades after Roosevelt's assertion, President Dwight Eisenhower referenced the "summons to governmental responsibility issued by the American people" following his victory to the White House.[11] In 1980, Vice President-elect George H. W. Bush triumphantly announced that President-elect Ronald Reagan and he had won a "mandate for change."[12] Reporting on Reagan's inauguration in 1981, Hedrick Smith of *The New York Times* observed, "some Republicans believe an irresistible conservative tide has swept the nation . . . they say, the mood of the country and Congress has shifted irreversibly to the right."[13]

Presidential mandate claims have been just as frequent in recent years. One study that systematically examined President George W. Bush's communications in early 2005 reported that nearly one-quarter of his public statements included mandate claims.[14] In 2012, President Obama also could not resist the temptation to claim a mandate after his reelection. In the days following his victory, the president remarked that his win represented a mandate to increase taxes on the wealthiest Americans to help reduce the federal deficit, claiming this was "a central question of the election."[15] Obama then added that it was time for Congress to get behind his plan because it "reflect[ed] the will of the American people."[16]

Not surprisingly, presidents who are landslide winners make common use of mandate rhetoric. Perhaps more interesting, however, is that presidents who win narrow victories use mandate rhetoric almost as frequently. For instance, the frequency of mandate rhetoric by Franklin Roosevelt following his decisive win over Alf Landon in 1936 was roughly the same as that used by Jimmy Carter following his razor-thin victory over Gerald Ford in 1976.[17]

Numerous examples also exist of congressional members and their supporters claiming a mandate after a convincing victory in the midterm elections as well. The 1994 congressional elections shifted control of both the U.S. House and U.S. Senate from the Democratic Party to the Republican

Party for the first time in four decades. Afterwards, House Speaker Newt Gingrich quickly declared a "mandate" for conservative principles and for the Republican Party's "Contract With America," which outlined a series of policies that Republican candidates promised to support if elected.[18] Like Gingrich, some reporters also saw the election as signifying a major change in policy direction. Robert Samuelson of *The Washington Post* observed, "In the mid-1960s, Congress enacted a major tax cut, approved the Civil Rights Act of 1964, and created Medicare and Medicaid. Government was to be society's problem solver. The new Congress is best seen as ending this era."[19]

A little more than a decade later in 2006, the Republicans lost their House majority in a landslide to Democrats. Incoming speaker Nancy Pelosi sounded the familiar mandate theme. In a victory speech to supporters she commented, "tonight is a great victory for the American people. Today the American people voted for change, and they voted for Democrats to take our country in a new direction."[20] Just four years later, Republicans reversed the tide and regained control of the U.S. House in an election that saw the party gain a remarkable net of 63 seats. The incoming Republican leadership, led by John Boehner and Eric Cantor, declared in their victory celebration that Republicans had won a "mandate" to cut the size of government.[21]

In 2014, congressional Republicans expanded their majority in the U.S. House and took control of the U.S. Senate for the first time in eight years. Conservative media commentators wasted no time in declaring that the election represented a public repudiation of President Obama's policies. Andrew McCarthy of the *National Review* wrote, "November was all about Obama's liberty-strangling, crony-coddling, financially reckless agenda. Voters emphatically defeated these policies. The American people want them stopped. That is what they sent Republicans to Washington to do. That is the mandate from the midterms."[22] Not to be outdone, radio host Rush Limbaugh remarked that the Republicans' 2014 success marked, "one of the most important, biggest mandates [to stop a president's policies] I can recall a party ever having."[23]

All of these examples serve to illustrate the fact that mandate claims have been ubiquitous in election after election for nearly two centuries. But what exactly is a mandate? We turn to that question next.

DEFINING A MANDATE

While the use of the term "mandate" has a long history, not everyone agrees on its meaning. To President Kennedy, a mandate required no more than a simple victory on Election Day. Kennedy's speechwriter, Theodore Sorenson, recounted that the former president saw his own narrow victory over

Richard Nixon in 1960 as a mandate. According to Sorenson, Kennedy explained that every election "has a winner and a loser" and that "a margin of only one vote would still be a mandate."[24]

Yet Kennedy's definition would defy the conventional understanding of the word's meaning. Most political scientists and political pundits usually understand a mandate as requiring a relatively large electoral victory by a presidential candidate and even his party in Congress.[25] In 2012, for instance, Barack Obama's reelection failed to sweep his party back into control of the U.S. House of Representatives. House Speaker John Boehner, a Republican, made clear that this tempered any claims of a mandate by the president. Commenting a few days before Election Night, Boehner commented to a reporter, "Listen, our majority is going to get reelected. We'll have as much of a mandate as he [President Obama] will."[26]

Some argue further that a mandate requires more than simply a large electoral victory for the entire party, but an *unexpectedly* large electoral victory.[27] By exceeding expectations, the winning candidate and party can claim that the public has "sent a message." To the winners, this message has inescapable policy implications, as campaign promises ultimately become a central part of the legislative agenda for governing.

Another common element in defining a mandate is that the winning candidates and their party must provide a clear and unified set of policy proposals.[28] In a midterm election, a mandate requires a "nationalized" election in which congressional candidates do not run on their own individualized set of local issues, but instead make the national party's legislative agenda central to their campaigns. The Republicans' "Contract with America" in 1994 was a good example of this. For presidential candidates, a policy mandate requires that they offer specific legislative proposals rather than campaigning on more general principles for governing. When this occurs, the victors can claim that the election results reflect, at least in some measure, popular support for their policy proposals. As one team of political scientists concluded, "no election can be a mandate for policy change without a clear policy message."[29] In fact, the policy message in question must also be unique, and pledge a new and different policy direction, such as Ronald Reagan's pledge in 1980 to increase defense spending significantly and to reduce the size of the federal government.

In addition to candidates offering a clear and unified set of policy proposals during the election, a mandate further requires that voters possess a minimum of knowledge in certain areas.[30] Most notably, voters must have enough knowledge about the major political issues central to the election to be able to form opinions about the policies that the candidates and parties propose. Voters must also possess accurate knowledge of where the candidates and the parties stand on those issues. If voters are largely ignorant of the major issues concerning public policy or if they struggle to connect candidates and parties to their respective policy proposals, election outcomes become a very poor instrument to gauge public support for the policy initiatives of the winning candidates and their party.

Not only must the public be familiar with the issues and the candidates' and parties' positions on these issues, they must also cast their vote on the basis of these issues and policies.[31] An electorate focused on the personal character-istics of the candidates, such as the high marks in honesty that Jimmy Carter received from the public in the 1976 presidential election[32] (which came two years after Richard Nixon's resignation for the Watergate scandal), would fail to qualify as an election that reflected a policy mandate. Even when issues are the central concern of voters, candidates must do more than simply offer policy proposals. Candidates must offer policy proposals that a large segment of the public desires for a mandate to exist.[33] If voter turnout is low, this can complicate claims of a mandate because it becomes more difficult to know if the policy preferences of the voters are consistent with the policy preferences of nonvoters. This matter is of particular relevance in midterm elections when voter turnout is considerably lower than in presidential elections. The opin-ions of nonvoters in midterm elections, who may later become voters in the following presidential election two years later, can quickly become relevant and problematic to the victorious party if their policy proposals are unpopular with this segment of the electorate.

Finally, a policy mandate requires that public opinion be stable on the issues and the policies that candidates and parties campaign on during the election.[34] If public opinion is fleeting, voters' support at election time for a set of policy proposals can quickly dissipate when the time comes for the winning candidates and party to govern. The absence of stable opinion thereby complicates any claims by the president or the party of the congres-sional majority of a policy mandate.

A number of conditions therefore must be met in order for a president or the majority party in Congress to make credible claims of a mandate for the adoption of sweeping policy changes. To summarize, these conditions would include the following:

- A large electoral victory, especially if unexpectedly large;
- The winners (candidates and/or party) have provided a clear and unified set of policy proposals;
- Voters possess enough knowledge about the political issues central to the election, and also know where the candidates and the parties stand on those issues;
- Voters must cast their vote on the basis of these issues;
- Public opinion on the issue(s) must be somewhat stable;
- Voter turnout in the election must be relatively high.

Taken together, this set of conditions is a fairly high hurdle to clear before a legitimate mandate can be claimed.

WHY MANDATE CLAIMS ARE USUALLY WRONG

Despite frequent claims of a mandate by politicians, pundits, and political commentators, few elections ever genuinely produce them. The fact is that election results are only rarely expressions of voter preferences on issues and public policies. Many voters do *not* begin their decision-making process by examining the issues first and then aligning themselves with the candidate who shares their positions on those issues. Instead, scholarship suggests that the process of deciding for whom to vote works quite differently.[35]

Most voters look first to the most basic of cues, a candidate's party affiliation.[36] From there, voters consider a range of other criteria that include retrospective evaluations of the performance of the party in power to the legislative record of the candidates to the personal attributes of those running for office.[37] The issue positions of the candidates are a consideration for some voters, but research on voting behavior shows that the casual direction in this case may run in reverse. In other words, rather than a voter considering their issue positions and then lining this information up with the candidate who most shares their views on the issues, voters more commonly select the candidate and then simply adopt the issue positions of their preferred candidate.[38]

The lack of a firm connection to issues for many voters in most elections severely complicates interpretations of what policies the public wants after an election, even when there is a landslide winner. This is made all the more difficult in a country such as the United States, which has a large and heterogeneous population. In 1984, for example, Ronald Reagan soundly defeated his Democratic opponent, Walter Mondale, by an 18-point margin in the popular vote, 59 to 41 percent. However, exit polls showed voters were more likely to agree with Mondale on a host of major issues ranging from defense spending to environmental protection to civil rights.[39] Quite obviously, these issues were not paramount to many voters in their voting decision.

In addition, presidential candidates often express positions on a wide range of policies. In the case of an issue-oriented voter, agreement on one or even many issues with a candidate does not necessarily translate into support for all of the candidate's issue positions. A voter, for instance, who is strongly pro-choice on abortion, may decide to vote for Barack Obama, who is similarly pro-choice, based on that issue alone. Yet, that same voter might also disagree sharply with Obama's position on how to reform the health-care system. A vote for a presidential candidate may therefore translate into public support on some issues, but not on others.

In midterm elections, the process is even more difficult to disentangle. Congressional candidates in the same party often do not run on the same set of issues or agree on the policies of how best to address those issues. This is especially common in a so-called "candidate-centered" system like the one in the United States, in which candidates rather than political parties take on the dominant responsibilities associated with waging a campaign for public office.[40] For example, given local preferences, a Southern Democrat might oppose gun control policies, whereas a Northeastern Democrat may support gun control policies given their popularity in the candidate's home state or district. Even in the rare circumstances, such as the 1994 election, when congressional Republicans lined up nationally behind their Contract with America, polls still showed only limited public knowledge of many of the policies outlined in it.[41] Given these difficulties, election outcomes correctly have been called a very "blunt instrument" for which to measure public support on issues and policies.[42]

Of course, the availability of exit poll data offers some improved ability to understand whether an issue or set of issues dominated a particular election. Yet even exit poll results must be read and interpreted carefully to determine whether a mandate exists, and if so, for what policies. A 2012 exit poll showed, for example, that economic issues were the top priority of voters (59 percent) and that 70 percent of Obama voters agreed with the president's position that income tax rates should be increased on those earning $250,000 a year or more. A superficial analysis of those figures might suggest to some that Obama won a mandate for higher taxes on the wealthy. But a deeper analysis raises questions about that conclusion. For starters, three in ten Obama supporters disagreed with the president on his position. When combined with those who supported Obama's opponent, Mitt Romney, and who also disagreed with a policy for higher taxes on the wealthy, overall support for Obama's tax plan comes in at 47 percent compared to the 48 percent who opposed it (with the remainder undecided). This is hardly a result that appears to reflect a strong public consensus.

Indeed, more often than not on the issues of most importance and controversy, exit polls fail to show any clear public consensus on matters of public policy. One reason for this is that recent presidential elections have been rather competitive. Since 2000, the largest difference in the popular vote in a presidential election was a seven-point advantage for Barack Obama over John McCain in 2008. Prior to 2000, the winning presidential candidate registered an advantage of more than seven points in five of six elections from 1980 to 1996. With such a divided electorate in recent elections, interpreting and claiming a genuine mandate is a daunting task.

Taken together, a mandate claim in an election is usually just that—a claim. The many conditions necessary for a genuine mandate rarely, if ever, occur. Even during landslide elections, public opinion almost never unifies around a single issue or set of issues. This raises a final question: If elections so rarely produce mandates, then why are mandate claims so common?

REASONS FOR CLAIMING A MANDATE

The main reason for the prevalence of mandate claims is that they can serve as a potentially useful part of a larger legislative strategy for the president and congressional leaders. Both rightfully understand that a successful legislative strategy involves shaping press coverage and public opinion. Creating the perception and promoting the idea of an electoral mandate can have obvious benefits.

For starters, the perception of a mandate affords the winning president or majority party in Congress with enhanced credibility for their legislative proposals. If the policies of the president or the majority party in Congress are consistent with the wishes of the American people, as mandates presume, then those who oppose the policies are not merely offering respectful dissent, but are acting contrary to the public will. If that perception takes hold, opposition itself becomes more challenging because the losing side does not want to be tagged as being "out of touch" with the American people. Moreover, in the immediate aftermath of the election, the party on the losing side must reflect on why its candidates fared poorly in the election. In this environment, the perception of a mandate takes on added significance as the minority party must be concerned with the risk of losing even more electoral support in the next election for opposing policies that have genuine popular backing. Because reelection concerns are always at the forefront of the strategic calculus of any elected official, the perception of a mandate can dampen opposition, empowering the winners of the election to exploit these circumstances by gaining a window of opportunity to enact their policies more easily.[43]

Mandate claims further shape the political dialogue. In the election of 1980, Ronald Reagan's convincing victory over Jimmy Carter failed to show in exit polls that there was a genuine change in the public's policy attitudes.[44] Nonetheless, widespread claims of a Reagan mandate (with some even calling Reagan's victory a "revolution") appears to have influenced the national policy discussion, shifting it from the question of how much the federal government would *spend* on social programs to how much the federal government would *cut* on social programs.[45] Nearly a half-century earlier, Franklin Roosevelt's victory over Herbert Hoover in 1932, and the resulting widespread belief that he had won a mandate, shifted national political discussion away from whether the federal government should act to combat the Great Depression to how much involvement the federal government should have in that regard.[46] Such a shift in the political dialogue presents obvious advantages for the president or majority party in Congress. Indeed, in the case of Roosevelt's first term in office, the belief in a Roosevelt mandate seems to have registered with legislators. In 1933, Congress passed all fifteen of Roosevelt major legislative proposals, with several Republicans even crossing party lines in support.[47]

Mandate claims can also be a function of the imperfect and incomplete information that often comes out of an election campaign.[48] The outcome itself, as previously noted, can have a multitude of potential causes. This leaves the winning presidential candidate and the majority party in Congress with the task of trying to figure out what those causes were and if those causes carried with them popular support for policies promised on the campaign trail. An obvious way to begin to discern this is for the winning side to claim a mandate and then, much like a trial balloon, gauge public response afterward. The public's reaction to any mandate claims, whether favorable or unfavorable, provides helpful information to the president and majority party in Congress about how to pursue a legislative strategy going forward. A favorable reaction, for instance, might indicate a larger ideological change in the electorate, conducive to an aggressive legislative strategy, whereas a negative reaction might indicate that the election outcome was due to idiosyncratic factors. In this case, a more cautious legislative strategy would make sense. In short, mandate claims can help a president and congressional leaders acquire needed information in an environment often dominated by uncertainty concerning the message the public has sent following an election.

Finally, claims of a mandate from presidents may reflect a need for those holding the office to assert their authority.[49] In a political period dominated by partisan polarization in Congress, the prestige and respect for the office of the president has declined in recent years.[50] With less informal power than in the past, recent presidents, dealing with a polarized Congress, have been more inclined to use mandate rhetoric as a means to compensate for these changes in the institutional environment. This development and the other aforementioned explanations all provide valuable incentives for elected officials to claim a mandate, even when a legitimate one may not exist.

CONCLUSION

Two seemingly paradoxical occurrences are a common part of the modern post-election environment: (1) the leaders and supporters of the winning party will claim an electoral mandate, even though (2) the conditions necessary for a legitimate mandate are rarely present. As this chapter discussed, the persistent claims of electoral mandates are the product of numerous incentives that exist for the president and congressional leaders to make such claims. The persistence of such rhetoric, however vacuous, can nonetheless often have significant consequences when presidents and congressional leaders begin to believe their own mandate claims.

Presidents, in particular, have a long history of so-called "over-reach."[51] Indeed, all three of our most recent presidents can attest to this. Bill Clinton witnessed the loss of the Democratic Party's majority status in the U.S. House and U.S. Senate by the Newt Gingrich-led Republicans in the 1994 election after public backlash to Clinton's efforts to reform the health-care system. Early in his second term as president, George W. Bush, believing he had a mandate, pushed to reform Social Security through a partial privatization plan. Even with Republican majorities in the House and Senate, those efforts quickly fell flat as public opinion polls showed little support for Bush's initiative. President Obama also interpreted his 2008 victory as a mandate to bring about "fundamental change,"[52] which like the previous Democratic president, Bill Clinton, included a major proposal to reform the nation's health-care system. While Obama, unlike Clinton, was able to see his health-care reform legislation become law, public opinion polls showed the new law was unpopular with the public,[53] despite Obama's comfortable election victory in 2008. What ultimately became known as "Obamacare," may have contributed to the Democratic Party's historic losses in the 2010 election.[54]

Beyond these anecdotes, political scientists largely agree that mandate claims typically have little merit. While the claims are likely to continue, political scientist Robert Dahl has urged us all to ignore them. Writing several decades ago, Dahl offered a fitting conclusion, "Perhaps the most we can hope for is that commentators on public affairs in the media and in academic pursuits will dismiss claims to a mandate with the scorn they usually deserve."[55] This chapter echoes Dahl's sentiment that "no elected leader, including the president, is uniquely privileged to say what an election means."[56]

The good news is that mandates, whether real or not, are unnecessary for a democracy to function. Elections do not have to "mean" anything. The simple fact that a transition of power has occurred with ballots rather than bullets (i.e., nonviolently) should be cause enough for celebration.

NOTES

1. Joan Walsh, "The Obama Mandate," Salon, November 6, 2012, http://www.salon.com/2012/11/07/the_obama_mandate.

2. David Weigel, "Yes, There Is a Mandate for Higher Taxes," Slate, November 7, 2012, http://www.slate.com/blogs/weigel/2012/11/07/yes_there_is_a_mandate_for_higher_taxes.html.

3. Quoted in Richard W. Stevenson, "After a Tense Night, Bush Spends the Day Basking in Victory," *The New York Times*, November 4, 2004, http://www.nytimes.com/2004/11/04/politics/campaign/04bush.html.

4. "The Bush Mandate," *The Wall Street Journal*, November 4, 2004, http://www.wsj.com/articles/SB109953513161964526.

5. See Jon Meacham, *American Lion: Andrew Jackson in the White House* (New York: Random House, 2008), 141.

6. See Sidney M. Milkis and Michael Nelson, *The American Presidency: Origins and Development, 1776–2014* (Washington, DC: CQ Press, 2015).

7. Quoted in Leonard D. White, *The Jacksonians: A Study in Administrative History* (New York: Macmilla, 1954), 23. For further information, see Daniel Feller, "The Bank War," in *The American Congress: The Building of Democracy*, ed. Julian E. Zelizer (New York: Houghton Mifflin, 2004).

8. Quoted in Robert Dahl, "Myth of the Presidential Mandate," *Political Science Quarterly* 105 (1990): 355–73.

9. Sidney M. Milkis and Emily J. Charnock, "History of the Presidency," in *Guide to the Presidency and the Executive Branch*, 5th ed., ed. Michael Nelson (Washington, DC: CQ Press, 2013), 128.

10. Quoted in Julia R. Azari, "Institutional Change and the Presidential Mandate," *Social Science History* 37 (2013): 483–514.

11. Quoted in Julia R. Azari, *Delivering the People's Message: The Changing Politics of the Presidential Mandate* (Ithaca, NY: Cornell University Press, 2014), 55.

12. Quoted in Dahl, "Myth of the Presidential Mandate," 355.

13. Hedrick Smith, "Reformer Who Would Reverse the New Deal's Legacy," *The New York Times*, January 21, 1981, http://www.nytimes.com/1981/01/21/us/reformer-who-would-reverse-the-new-deal-s-legacy.html.

14. Azari, *Delivering the People's Message*, 23.

15. Quoted in Steven T. Dennis, "Barack Obama Claims Mandate on Taxing the Rich," *Roll Call*, November 9, 2012, http://www.rollcall.com/news/barack_obama_claims_mandate_on_taxing_the_rich-218921-1.html.

16. Quoted in Dennis, "Barack Obama Claims Mandate on Taxing the Rich."

17. Azari, "Institutional Change and the Presidential Mandate" and Azari, *Delivering the People's Message*.

18. Catherine S. Manegold, "The 1994 Election: The G.O.P. Leader; Gingrich Now a Giant, Claims Victor's Spoils," *The New York Times*, November 12, 1994, http://www.nytimes.com/1994/11/12/us/the-1994-election-the-gop-leader-gingrich-now-a-giant-claims-victor-s-spoils.html.

19. Robert J. Samuelson, "The Public Trust: Handle with Care," *The Washington Post*, January 4, 1995, A15.

20. Quoted in William Branigin, "Democrats Take Majority in House; Pelosi Poised to Become Speaker," *The Washington Post*, November 8, 2006, http://www.washingtonpost.com/wp-dyn/content/article/2006/11/07/AR2006110700473.html.

21. "Republicans Capture House in Historic Wave, Claim 'Mandate' to Shrink Government," Fox News, November 3, 2010, http://www.foxnews.com/politics/2010/11/03/republicans-capture-house-historic-wave-make-gains-senate.

22. Andrew C. McCarthy, "The Republican Congress Has a Mandate," *National Review*, January 15, 2015, http://www.nationalreview.com/article/396403/republican-congress-has-mandate-andrew-c-mccarthy.

23. Rush Limbaugh, "The Republicans Have a Huge Mandate—Whether They Know It or Not," The Rush Limbaugh Show, November 3, 2014, http://www.rush-limbaugh.com/daily/2014/11/03/the_republicans_have_a_huge_mandate_whether_they_know_it_or_not.

24. Quoted in Dahl, "Myth of the Presidential Mandate," 364.

25. See for example, Lawrence J. Grossback, David A. M. Peterson, and James A. Stimson. *Mandate Politics* (New York: Cambridge University Press, 2006), and Patricia Heidotting Conley, *Presidential Mandates: How Elections Set the National Agenda* (Chicago: University of Chicago Press, 2001).

26. Quoted in Jake Sherman, "John Boehner: No Tax Hike on Top Earners," Politico, November 5, 2012, http://www.politico.com/news/stories/1112/83363.html.

27. Grossback, Peterson, and Stimson, *Mandate Politics*.

28. See for example, Azari, *Delivering the People's Message* and Grossback, Peterson, and Stimson, *Mandate Politics*.

29. Amy E. Gangl, Lawrence J. Grossback, David A. M. Peterson, and James A. Stimson, "Mandate Elections and Policy Change in Congress," paper presented at the annual meeting of the Midwest Political Science Association, April 1998, Chicago, http://www.polmeth.wustl.edu/media/Paper/gangl98.pdf.

30. George C. Edwards III and Stephen J. Wayne, *Presidential Leadership: Politics and Policy Making*, 9th ed. (Stamford, CT: Cengage Learning, 2014), 104–5.

31. Stanley Kelley, Jr., *Interpreting Elections* (Princeton, NJ: Princeton University Press, 1983).

32. Samuel L. Popkin, *The Reasoning Voter: Communication and Persuasion in Presidential Campaigns* (Chicago: University of Chicago Press, 1991), 155.

33. Edwards and Wayne, *Presidential Leadership*.

34. Kelley, Jr., *Interpreting Elections*, 126–8.

35. For an informative summary on this point, see John Sides, "The 2012 Election Was Not a Mandate," The Monkey Cage, November 7, 2012, http://themonkeycage.org/2012/11/07/the-2012-election-was-not-a-mandate.

36. Larry M. Bartels, "Partisanship and Voting Behavior, 1952–1996," *American Journal of Political Science* 44 (2000): 35–50, and Michael S. Lewis-Beck, William G. Jacoby, Helmut Norpoth, Herbert F. Weisberg, *The American Voter Revisited* (Ann Arbor, MI: University of Michigan Press, 2008).

37. Morris P. Fiorina, *Retrospective Voting in American National Elections* (New Haven, CT: Yale University Press, 1981); Karen M. Kaufmann, "Disaggregating and Reexamining Issue Ownership and Vote Choice," *Polity* 36 (2004): 283–99; and Danny Hayes, "Candidate Qualities Through a Partisan Lens: A Theory of Trait Ownership," *American Journal of Political Science* 49 (2005): 908–23.

38. Gabriel S. Lenz, "Learning and Opinion Change, Not Priming: Reconsidering the Priming Hypothesis," *American Journal of Political Science* 53 (2009): 821–37.

39. George C. Edwards III, *At the Margins: Presidential Leadership of Congress* (New Haven, CT: Yale University Press, 1989), 149.

40. Paul S. Herrnson, *Congressional Elections: Campaigning at Home and In Washington*, 6th ed. (Washington, DC: CQ Press, 2013).

41. George F. Bishop, *The Illusion of Public Opinion: Fact and Artifact in American Public Opinion Polls* (Lanham, MD: Rowman & Littlefield, 2005), 145–6.

42. See the section "Do Elections Matter?" in Steven K. Medvic, *Campaigns and Elections: Players and Processes* (New York: Routledge, 2014).

43. Grossback, Peterson, and Stimson, *Mandate Politics*.

44. Thomas Ferguson and Joel Rogers, "The Myth of America's Turn to the Right," *The Atlantic*, May 1986, http://www.theatlantic.com/past/docs/issues/95dec/conbook/fergrt.htm.

45. Gil Troy, *Morning in America: How Ronald Reagan Invented the 1980s* (Princeton, NJ: Princeton University Press, 2005).

46. William E. Leuchtenburg, *The FDR Years: On Roosevelt and His Legacy* (New York: Columbia University Press, 1995).

47. Jeffrey W. Coker, *Franklin D. Roosevelt: A Biography* (Westport, CT: Greenwood Press, 2005) chapter 8.

48. Dahl, "Myth of the Presidential Mandate.

49. Ibid.

50. Jon R. Bond and Richard Fleisher, eds., *Polarized Politics: Congress and the President in a Partisan Era* (Washington, DC: CQ Press, 2000).

51. Edwards and Wayne, *Presidential Leadership*, 349–50.

52. George C. Edwards III, *Overreach: Leadership in the Obama Presidency* (Princeton, NJ: Princeton University Press, 2012).

53. "USA Today/Pew Poll: Health Care Law Faces Difficult Future," *USA Today*, September 23, 2013, http://www.usatoday.com/story/news/politics/2013/09/16/usa-today-pew-poll-health-care-law-opposition/2817169.

54. Chris Cillizza, "What Effect Did Health-Care Reform Have on the Election?" *The Washington Post*, November 7, 2010, http://www.washingtonpost.com/wp-dyn/content/article/2010/11/07/AR2010110705311.html.

55. Dahl, "Myth of the Presidential Mandate," 365.

56. Ibid., 366.

FOR MORE READING

Azari, Julia R. *Delivering the People's Message: The Changing Politics of the Presidential Mandate*. Ithaca, NY: Cornell University Press, 2014.

Conley, Patricia Heidotting. *Presidential Mandates: How Elections Shape the National Agenda*. Chicago: University of Chicago Press, 2001.

Grossback, Lawrence J., David A.M. Peterson, and James A. Stimson. 2006. *Mandate Politics*. New York: Cambridge University Press.

Index

About the Authors

Dr. Jody C Baumgartner is a professor of political science at East Carolina University. He received his Ph.D. in political science from Miami University in 1998, specializing in the study of campaigns and elections. He has several books to his credit, including *Modern Presidential Electioneering: An Organizational and Comparative Approach* (Praeger, 2000); *Checking Executive Power* (Praeger, 2003), co-edited with Naoko Kada; *The American Vice Presidency Reconsidered* (Praeger, 2006); and, *Laughing Matters: Humor and American Politics in the Media Age* (Routeledge, 2007), co-edited with Jonathan Morris. He has also written or collaborated on three dozen articles and book chapters on political humor, the vice presidency, and other subjects.

Dr. Peter L. Francia is a professor of political science and co-director of leadership studies at East Carolina University. He is the author of numerous academic publications on various topics related to American elections. His books include *The Financiers of Congressional Elections*: *Investors, Ideologues, and Intimates*, co-authored with John C. Green, Paul S. Herrnson, Lynda W. Powell, and Clyde Wilcox (Columbia University Press, 2003); *The Future of Organized Labor in American Politics* (Columbia University Press, 2006); and the volume, *Guide to Interest Groups and Lobbying in the United States* (CQ Press, 2012), co-edited with Burdett A. Loomis and Dara Z. Strolovitch. Dr. Francia's insights on American politics have been included in the press accounts of national media outlets including CNN, National Public Radio, and the *Wall Street Journal*.